Palgrave Macmillan Studies in Banking and Financial Institutions

Series Editor: **Professor Philip Molyneux**

The Palgrave Macmillan Studies in Banking and Financial Institutions are international in orientation and include studies of banking within particular countries or regions, and studies of particular themes such as Corporate Banking, Risk Management, Mergers and Acquisitions, etc. The books' focus is on research and practice, and they include up-to-date and innovative studies on contemporary topics in banking that will have global impact and influence.

Titles include:

Yener Altunbaş, Blaise Gadanecz and Alper Kara
SYNDICATED LOANS
A Hybrid of Relationship Lending and Publicly Traded Debt

Yener Altunbaş, Alper Kara and Öslem Olgu
TURKISH BANKING
Banking under Political Instability and Chronic High Inflation

Elena Beccalli
IT AND EUROPEAN BANK PERFORMANCE

Paola Bongini, Stefano Chiarlone and Giovanni Ferri *(editors)*
EMERGING BANKING SYSTEMS

Vittorio Boscia, Alessandro Carretta and Paola Schwizer
COOPERATIVE BANKING: INNOVATIONS AND DEVELOPMENTS

COOPERATIVE BANKING IN EUROPE: CASE STUDIES

Roberto Bottiglia, Elisabetta Gualandri and Gian Nereo Mazzocco *(editors)*
CONSOLIDATION IN THE EUROPEAN FINANCIAL INDUSTRY

Alessandro Carretta, Franco Fiordelisi and Gianluca Mattarocci *(editors)*
NEW DRIVERS OF PERFORMANCE IN A CHANGING FINANCIAL WORLD

Dimitris N. Chorafas
CAPITALISM WITHOUT CAPITAL

Dimitris N. Chorafas
FINANCIAL BOOM AND GLOOM
The Credit and Banking Crisis of 2007–2009 and Beyond

Violaine Cousin
BANKING IN CHINA

Vincenzo D'Apice and Giovanni Ferri
FINANCIAL INSTABILITY
Toolkit for Interpreting Boom and Bust Cycles

Peter Falush and Robert L. Carter OBE
THE BRITISH INSURANCE INDUSTRY SINCE 1900
The Era of Transformation

Franco Fiordelisi
MERGERS AND ACQUISITIONS IN EUROPEAN BANKING

Franco Fiordelisi and Philip Molyneux
SHAREHOLDER VALUE IN BANKING

Hans Genberg and Cho-Hoi Hui
THE BANKING CENTRE IN HONG KONG
Competition, Efficiency, Performance and Risk

Carlo Gola and Alessandro Roselli
THE UK BANKING SYSTEM AND ITS REGULATORY AND SUPERVISORY FRAMEWORK

Elisabetta Gualandri and Valeria Venturelli *(editors)*
BRIDGING THE EQUITY GAP FOR INNOVATIVE SMEs

Kim Hawtrey
AFFORDABLE HOUSING FINANCE

Otto Hieronymi *(editor)*
GLOBALIZATION AND THE REFORM OF THE INTERNATIONAL BANKING AND MONETARY SYSTEM

Munawar Iqbal and Philip Molyneux
THIRTY YEARS OF ISLAMIC BANKING
History, Performance and Prospects

Sven Janssen
BRITISH AND GERMAN BANKING STRATEGIES

Kimio Kase and Tanguy Jacopin
CEOs AS LEADERS AND STRATEGY DESIGNERS
Explaining the Success of Spanish Banks

Alexandros-Andreas Kyrtsis *(editor)*
FINANCIAL MARKETS AND ORGANIZATIONAL TECHNOLOGIES
System Architectures, Practices and Risks in the Era of Deregulation

M. Mansoor Khan and M. Ishaq Bhatti
DEVELOPMENTS IN ISLAMIC BANKING
The Case of Pakistan

Mario La Torre and Gianfranco A. Vento
MICROFINANCE

Philip Molyneux and Eleuterio Vallelado *(editors)*
FRONTIERS OF BANKS IN A GLOBAL WORLD

Anastasia Nesvetailova
FRAGILE FINANCE
Debt, Speculation and Crisis in the Age of Global Credit

Anders Ögren *(editor)*
THE SWEDISH FINANCIAL REVOLUTION

Dominique Rambure and Alec Nacamuli
PAYMENT SYSTEMS
From the Salt Mines to the Board Room

Catherine Schenk *(editor)*
HONG KONG SAR's MONETARY AND EXCHANGE RATE CHALLENGES
Historical Perspectives

Noël K. Tshiani
BUILDING CREDIBLE CENTRAL BANKS
Policy Lessons for Emerging Economies

The full list of titles available is on the website:
www.palgrave.com/finance/sbfi.asp

Palgrave Macmillan Studies in Banking and Financial Institutions
Series Standing Order ISBN 978–1–4039–4872–4

You can receive future titles in this series as they are published by placing a standing order. Please contact your bookseller or, in case of difficulty, write to us at the address below with your name and address, the title of the series and the ISBN quoted above. Customer Services Department, Macmillan Distribution Ltd, Houndmills, Basingstoke, Hampshire RG21 6XS, England

---

Financial Markets and Organizational Technologies

System Architectures, Practices and Risks in the Era of Deregulation

Edited by

Alexandros-Andreas Kyrtsis
University of Athens, Greece

palgrave
macmillan

First published 2010 by
PALGRAVE MACMILLAN

Palgrave Macmillan in the UK is an imprint of Macmillan Publishers Limited, registered in England, company number 785998, of Houndmills, Basingstoke, Hampshire RG21 6XS.

Palgrave Macmillan in the US is a division of St Martin's Press LLC, 175 Fifth Avenue, New York, NY 10010.

Palgrave Macmillan is the global academic imprint of the above companies and has companies and representatives throughout the world.

Palgrave® and Macmillan® are registered trademarks in the United States, the United Kingdom, Europe and other countries.

ISBN 978–0–230–23405–5 hardback

This book is printed on paper suitable for recycling and made from fully managed and sustained forest sources. Logging, pulping and manufacturing processes are expected to conform to the environmental regulations of the country of origin.

A catalogue record for this book is available from the British Library.

A catalog record for this book is available from the Library of Congress.

10 9 8 7 6 5 4 3 2 1
19 18 17 16 15 14 13 12 11 10

Printed and bound in Great Britain by

CPI Antony Rowe, Chippenham and Eastbourne

Contents

List of Figures and Tables

Figures

Tables

Preface

From the perspective of historians and sociologists of technology, it is still puzzling that we have no clear ideas about the impact of banking and financial operations on the evolution of information and communications technologies. But also in the reverse – and much more frequently discussed – causal direction, our knowledge rests on rather fragmentary and often insecure evidence. We do not know as much as we think about the significance of ICTs for increased efficiency, for raising productivity and for coping with asymmetric information. There are also topics that remain outside of our cognitive horizon. No doubt, academic knowledge is in many cases lagging behind the immense accumulated experience among managers in the industry. For instance we do not make use of conclusive theoretical compasses that could guide the investigation of the ways ICTs contribute to the shaping of organizational practices and operational risks in finance. And there is not much academic discussion about how approaches to information system development in complex banks have emerged from the specifics of the rapid changes in business models and in product and services management, as well as from changes in trading, marketing and sales operations. From the business planner's and the risk officer's perspective the quest for systematic insights in these directions can have far-reaching practical implications. Codifying tacit, local or highly dispersed knowledge through explicit discourses can significantly contribute to the awareness of the complex techno-organizational landscape of finance at the beginning of the twenty-first century. Creating the ground for better-informed and less abstract dialogues on opportunities and risks among knowledgeable researchers can enrich conceptual inspirations. But most importantly, knowledge on the relevant causal relationships can help us weigh the priorities and the content of both managerial and regulatory action, especially in periods of crises with systemic consequences.

Both the macro- and the micro-historical analysis of the development of information systems of financial organizations can be of great significance in this respect. Understanding the historical context and its institutional intricacies implies also a better understanding of the range and limitations of potential practices. The argument, which will be discussed in the following pages, is that the evolution of the business of banking, after financial deregulation accelerated in the 1970s, altered the conditions for the adoption, use and reconfiguration of technologies in the organizational contexts of doing business in banking and finance. The changing terms of co-evolution between finance and ICTs have influenced system architectures, practices and risks in ways that cannot be ignored by researchers and practitioners. IT specialists of this deregulated industry are driven to search increasingly for configurations of organizational solution technologies, instead of just looking for hardware–software configurations. This is due, among other things, to the fact that requirements for the mobilization of organizational and network resources make pulling information more significant than just pushing data around. But beyond technological and organizational considerations, it is the business and the institutional environment that matters most. What actually emerged in terms of organizational and technological patterns of action after the abolishment of the Bretton Woods system, couldn't have been possible without radical economic and institutional shifts. The evolution of the culture of risk management and regulatory practices has also immensely influenced the course of developments. Understanding the history of the techno-organizational configurations in banking and finance is impossible without understanding the history of financial deregulation.

The authors of the chapters elaborate on these ideas, each from a different perspective, and cover a wide range of issues. The hope is that this volume will be a valuable companion for everyone who is interested in the interconnection between the difficulty of overcoming the financial risks we are facing and the global webs of uncontrollable organizational and technological complexity.

This book is the outcome of a one-day conference held at the premises of the Historical Archives of the National Bank of Greece in Athens on 29 November 2008. The event was made possible through the generous support of the National Bank of Greece and the assistance offered by the staff of its Historical Archives. The editor of this volume owes a great debt of gratitude to the former Chairman of the Bank, Takis Arapoglou, and to the Head of the Archives Gerasimos Notaras. Many thanks go also to the only non-academic participant of this conference, Hermann-Josef Lamberti, member of the Group Executive Committee of the Deutsche Bank, who delivered the opening address in which he shared the business perspective of one of the most prominent practitioners in the field.

Alexandros-Andreas Kyrtsis

Notes on Contributors

Bernardo Bátiz-Lazo is Senior Lecturer in Business and Accounting History in the Business School at Leicester University. He combines a full time academic appointment with consulting and executive training in Europe and Asia. He is a member of the council of the Association of Business Historians and a member of the Editorial Boards of *Business History, Journal of Management History, International Journal of Bank Marketing,* and *Cuadernos de Gestión.*

Stefano Battilossi is an Associate Professor at the Department of Economic History and Institutions, Universidad Carlos III Madrid. He specializes in monetary history, as well as in the history of banking and finance in the nineteenth and twentieth centuries. He has been a research fellow at the Business History Unit, LSE, and at the Department of History and Civilization, European University Institute, Florence. He is the co-editor (with Jaime Reis) of *State and Financial Systems in Europe and the USA: Historical Perspectives on Regulation and Supervision in the Nineteenth and Twentieth Centuries* (2010).

David Gugerli is a Professor of History of Technology at the Federal Institute of Technology (ETH) in Zurich. He was a guest researcher at the Maison des Sciences de l'Homme in Paris, visiting professor at the Colegio de México in Mexico City, visiting scholar at Stanford University in Palo Alto, visiting fellow at the International Research Center for Cultural Sciences in Vienna, and a fellow at the Institute for Advanced Study in Berlin. His latest book is a socio-historical study of search engines and databases (*Suchmaschinen: Die Welt als Datenbank*, 2009).

Alexandros-Andreas Kyrtsis, the editor of this volume, is a Professor of Sociology at the University of Athens, in the Department of Political Science and Public Administration. He has been an academic visitor at MIT, LSE, the University of Edinburgh, and at the Institute of Advanced Studies on Science, Technology and Society in Graz. He has also been an adviser to Greek banks, to the Hellenic Bankers Association, and to IT companies with projects in the financial sector. His latest book, in Greek, is on the evolution of the information systems of the National Bank of Greece and the role of IT and operations managers in the period 1950–2000.

Donald MacKenzie holds a personal chair in Sociology at the University of Edinburgh where he has been working since the 1970s in the field of Science and Technology Studies. His current research, which involves developing a 'material sociology of markets', focuses on financial markets, especially on credit-derivatives, and on new markets for permits for greenhouse-gas emissions. He has also done research in the fields of the sociology and history of computing, of statistics, and of nuclear weapons. His latest books are *Material Markets: How Economic Agents are Constructed* (2009) and *An Engine, Not a Camera: How Financial Models Shape Markets* (2006).

Jocelyn Pixley is a Professorial Research Fellow at the Global Policy Institute, London Metropolitan University and Senior Research Fellow at Macquarie University, Sydney. Before holding these positions she was teaching sociology at the University of New South Wales. Her overall research is on transformations in social integration in the world's developed regions and on the sociological analysis of financial decision making. She is the author of *Citizenship and Employment: Investigating Post-Industrial Options* (1993) and *Emotions in Finance: Distrust and Uncertainty on Global Markets* (2004).

Claudia Reese is a Historian specializing in the study of the evolution of markets. She has been a collaborator of the Museum of Contemporary German History in Bonn. She has also had research appointments at Columbia University and at the University of Leicester's School of Management, and teaching appointments at Leicester and at the School of History, University of Nottingham.

Susan V. Scott is a Senior Lecturer in the Information Systems and Innovation Group at the Department of Management, London School of Economics and Political Science. Her research focuses on technology, work and organization from a management studies perspective. More specifically, she has developed a major body of research examining the role of information systems in the transformation of work practices within the financial services sector. Among her latest publications is 'Sociomateriality: Challenging the separation of technology, work and organization', *Academy of Management Annals*, 2(1), 2008: 433–74 (with W. J. Orlikowski).

1
Introduction: Financial Deregulation and Technological Change

Alexandros-Andreas Kyrtsis

The techno-organizational ground

The derivatives revolution, and the exponential growth of the trading of complex financial instruments in exchanges and over-the-counter in the 1990s, have significantly altered the technological image of finance. Financial engineering, trading technologies and telecommunication backbones of electronic financial networks are now defining many people's perception of the use of information technologies in banks and in the wider financial sector (Bodie 1999). The former Chairman of the Federal Reserve, Alan Greenspan, one of the main figures of the modern capitalist era of rapid globalization and securitization, adopts a similar view. In his words, 'information technology has made possible the creation, valuation, and exchange of complex financial products on a global basis heretofore envisioned only in our textbooks. [...] Derivatives are obviously the most evident of the many products that technology has inspired. [...] Calculation capabilities has permitted [...] new ways to unbundle risk' (Greenspan 2000: 109). Yet this focus on 'building systems that model, value, and process financial products such as bonds, stocks, contracts, and money', as we can read in a textbook on financial technologies (Freedman 2006: 1), produces a one-sided perspective. Operational complexities, originating in the evolution of banking institutions offering utilities to a wide range of enterprises and households since the late nineteenth century, have shaped the technological landscape in the long term, and in a much stronger sense. The processing of private clients' transactions with pen and paper and then by mechanical means, which paved the way for unit record and then online systems, created a long evolutionary process that culminated in the computerization of financial intermediation (Horvitz and White

2000; Bátiz-Lazo and Wood 2002). Accounting as the technical basis of asset-liability management and customers' accounts management was a mover accelerating the introduction of digital computers in banks and insurance companies from the early 1960s. Electronic trading platforms for investors came later, when the liberalization of money markets started changing banking, creating the basis for the development of the trading rooms of today. Automated electronic trading, based on computer algorithms using real-time market data, was also made available through the adoption of sophisticated computational techniques and information and communication technologies.

But these processes had to do only with a surface behind which a plethora of technology-backed support mechanisms had to be developed. For instance, every trading act requires processing chains of back-office operations, which are often complex (Millo et al. 2005). The markets for financial products and services have created extremely rich fields of adoption and configuration of technologies. Many of these are visible but there are others which are hidden not only from the public eye but also from bankers accustomed to macro-managing their organizations, who typically have in mind predominantly accounting or risk models.[1] The multifaceted character of the development of the technological landscape at the beginning of the twenty-first century is thus primarily the result of the informational and operational requirements set by a great variety of financial products and services. This is also the result of the growing dependence upon many of the products and services addressed to the wider public, not only upon those addressed to institutional investors. Mutual funds, or other instruments of portfolio management – marketed, bundled with other products and services and sold through retail networks – are an example of this. But beyond trading from customers' accounts, and beyond the securitization of risks from lending activities that led to business practices relying on the originate-to-distribute model, proprietary trading, that is, trading from the bank's own accounts, became a central aspect of bank management. Both the utility banking side and the proprietary trading side have created their dynamically evolving techno-organizational platforms. We can also observe a complex interaction between these two sides with an impact on techno-organizational platforms, as in the case of financial services that are related to the hedging of enterprises' and households' investment risks with securities (Shiller 2008).

These shifts couldn't have been set off without far-reaching economic, institutional and legal changes leading to the liberalization and globalization of financial markets. The regulatory framework created by the Bretton Woods system hindered the emergence of a wide range of business models and techno-organizational practices (Battilossi and Cassis 2002; Stiglitz 2003; Abdelal 2006; Harvey 2005; Hendrickson 2001; Gart 1994; Ingham and Thompson 1993; Swary and Topf 1992). Banks had to comply with tight regulatory measures that defined the margin of interest rates and the character of products and services. Money markets were subject to restricted fluctuations among currencies; and at the national level many methods of hedging financial risks, which are very common today, were banned by gambling laws. As Stefano Battilossi sets out in Chapter 2, the formal abolishment of the Bretton Woods system in the early 1970s as a consequence of its watering down by the Eurocurrency markets has led to a radical change in the business of banking and its financial technologies. Battilossi proposes to regard financial technologies as bodies of knowledge that specify the process by which the operational aspects of action are shaped, and economic value is created in financial intermediation. According to his analytics, these encompass product, process and organizational technologies as clearly distinct elements. But the most crucial aspect of this view is Battilossi's refutation of technological determinism. The point he makes is that the techno-organizational processes one can observe after the turn of the early 1970s can be traced back predominantly to institutional changes, rather than mere technological changes.

What should be noted here is that these changes Battilossi refers to were the outcome of a recursive relationship between the evasion of regulatory restrictions (which did not vanish even with the take-off of financial deregulation, and were renewed with re-regulatory or self-regulatory practices) and financial innovations. Financial innovations were reflected in information systems and these further created requirements for information and communication technology platforms. The range of uses of technologies also changed. Financial innovations leading to releases of new financial instruments or of financial products and services designed to attract a wide public, required a new philosophy of the development of technological infrastructure. Through these processes, not only were bank employees transformed into skilled users of technologies but customers and consumers had to use credit cards, ATMs and later their PCs, often for credit-based or stock and derivatives exchange-dependent transactions. For the IT specialists this meant that, in conjunction with every product and service item, they had to develop – in-house or with outsourcing to external companies – computer applications mapping out financial and operational features or platforms for trading and transactions (Fincham et al. 1994; Regini 1999). Financial deregulation and the connection between computational techniques, data processing and telecommunications technologies needed for data transfer, combined with significant shifts in the language of financial communication, have revolutionized the use of information technologies and their organizational impact for the financial sector.

On the basis of this mixture, from computational, processing and communications perspectives, information and communication technologies have impacted on various dimensions of the financial structure. Powerful computational techniques have indeed made the creation of complex financial instruments possible and thus led to the emergence and evolution of derivative markets. The eruptive evolution of telecommunications has immensely facilitated the delocalization and furthered the globalization of these markets. Online information systems have diminished the cost of information processing and databases have made access quicker, more efficient and flexible. Other technologies have made data transfer more secure and thus have contributed to trust in operations relying on branch automation, as well as on alternative electronic networks and transaction and payment systems (ATMs, EFTPOS (Electronic Funds Transfer at Point Of Sale), web banking and mobile banking) and to electronic transnational financial networks. This also made new entries to the market easier, a significant factor in the globalization of markets, and made possible the detachment of the calculation of risk exposure from the face-to-face collection of information (although this does not apply to certain forms of investment like venture capital). EFTPOS, ATMs, telephone banking and web banking have all, to various degrees, detached transactions from banking hours and geographic limitations. These developments have made finance (insurance included) the foremost Information and Communication Technologies (ICT) purchasing sector.[2] This coevolution of the financial markets with modalities of adoption and configuration of information and communication technologies has also radicalized the connection between organizational design, management and the adoption of technologies. The adoption of information and communication technologies in finance has radically transformed approaches to organizational issues; for technologies, either as artefacts or as pieces of knowledge and procedures, had to be integrated into organizational technologies. A more extensive definition of organizational technologies will be given later in this introductory chapter. Here it suffices to say that organizational technologies in banking and finance are the outcome of the interplay between the organizational articulation of business strategies and technological solutions shaping the operational implications of the techno-organizational landscape.

This is not a landscape without significant risks. Operational failure is very probable. The consequences can be severe for individual customers, but also for the financial bases of the economy. Fraud and the misuse of the financial system are among the many possible domains of operational failures. The realization of the existence of such potential hazards has led to an immense market for security and anti-fraud information technologies. But as the 2007–9 credit crunch has shown, issues of operational and informational transparency, and the ability of information systems to cope with these, can be of high priority. The pertinent problems are not solely intra-organizational, but inter-organizational as well. In most cases the latter are related to what we call counterparty risk originating in the eventuality of non-fulfilment of inter-organizational contractual obligations. The fact that financial commitments are increasingly acquiring a cross-border character and thus are bound to intrasparencies related to the enforcement of contracts, has led to the separation of the locus of risk-creation from the locus of risk-bearing (Dymski 2008). This implies a multitude of lender strategies and subsequent operational activities that are very difficult to keep track of. This poses both bank management and regulatory problems. From an organizational point of view it is very important to stress here that counterparty risk is not solely due to moral hazard, but to techno-organizational inefficiency and operational failures as well. The latter aspect is rarely discussed although it has to do with the technological intensity of our financial systems and of our economies as a result of the changes brought about by financial deregulation and the regulatory regimes of neoliberal re-regulation. But – as for instance the evolution of the mortgage, consumer loans and credit card business have shown, and especially the subprime business – utility banking and proprietary trading are tightly intertwined. Whereas the techno-organizational ground of utility banking makes the circulatory system of the economy possible down to its smallest blood vessels, the techno-organizational backstages of proprietary trading constitute the indispensable organs without which the heart of the leverage-dependent financial system would simply cease working.[3]

But even without going into this, the problem with trading operations, and the risks they imply, remain. Contrary to widespread views, understanding trading is impossible without understanding back offices. Back-office operations have to do with the less visible and without any doubt the less prestigious side of banking (Lépinay 2007). As Emanuel Derman reports, at Goldman Sachs 'almost no partners came from information technology or research, whose contributions, while substantial, did not carry a clear dollar value' (Derman 2004: 175). Worse still, in many cases, those who in reality are indispensable for setting in motion and making operationally viable the supposedly heroic acts on the trading floors, were ignored or even despised. As has been observed in studies of back offices of trading rooms, traders go in for an impressively messy way of dealing with data entry and paperwork-like procedures. For the most part they underestimate and thus disregard the importance of middle and back offices that have to control flows of goods and services necessary for the achievement and settlement of deals (Lépinay 2007: 267–8). Furthermore, trading operators have to cope with contractual complexities that go beyond front-office transactional complexities. What many people don't know is that organizational technologies in the field of rocket scientist-led operations are by no means up to the expected standard.[4] In the case of standardized financial products and financial instruments, clearing and settlement can be made within hours and value date issues can be handled on the basis of business decisions and have nothing to do with technological and logistical constraints of reconciliation and payment. But in the cases of financial products that rely on complex contracting, settlement could last even more than 30 working days and this work can involve various operators, among whom are lawyers who can play a significant role and undertake time-consuming tasks. Under such circumstances automation is difficult and the discrepancies between trading speeds and clearing and settlement speeds can assume dramatic dimensions, also implying high risks.[5]

Paul Krugman, and along the same lines the British House of Commons Treasury Committee, have drawn our attention to the grander style implications of operational messiness, this time as an inherent aspect of derivatives backed or of proprietary trading and one of the causes that accelerated the impact of the (2007–9) credit crunch. The House of Commons Treasury Committee (2009) has pointed to the fact that financial complexity does not reduce risk, as most financial engineers think, but rather obscures risk. According to the authors of this report, complexity was the result of the diffusion of risks among mostly end non-bank investors through the prevalence of the 'originate-to-distribute' model (issuing loans and then selling these and their risk exposure to investors) that gradually substituted the 'originate-to-hold' model (issuing loans and holding them to maturity) as the dominant banking practice. As we now know, this was working well up to the point that trust in the initial loan makers, and subsequently in banks buying the risk of such loans, was intact. But it stopped working when this trust was disrupted. One root of the 2007–9 crisis, then, triggered off by subprime lending, was the transformation of revenue-generation strategies of many dominant banks from holding to distributing risks, a practice that involved separating loan making from risk-taking (House of Commons Treasury Committee 2009; King 2008; Dymski 2008). When risk-taking had to be reconnected to loan making, because of defaulting mortgages, the operational side of the problems caused by securitized demand side economics came to the fore.[6] In this situation, as Krugman points out, one reasonable strategy would have been to reduce the cost of the foreclosures by renegotiating payments. Yet this was impossible because risks and ownership of securities were shifted to numerous organizations without mutual obligations for the management of necessary information on risks. Mortgages made by loan originators were then sold to financial institutions, which pooled them according to the various levels of risk exposure they entailed into tranches of Collateralized Debt Obligations (CDOs) sold to investors. As Krugman (2009: 167–8) writes:

> The actual management of the loans was left to loan services, who had neither the resources nor, for the most part, the incentive to engage in loan restructuring. And one more thing: the complexity of financial engineering supporting subprime lending, which left ownership of mortgages dispersed among many investors with claims of varying seniority, created formidable legal obstacles to any kind of debt forgiveness. So restructuring was mostly out and this meant that securities backed by subprime mortgages turned into very bad investments as soon as the housing boom began to falter.

As the House of Commons Treasury Committee stresses, by quoting Sir Tom McKillop and Lord Turner, when trust was disrupted,

> [nobody knew] where this distributed risk was and then a freeze took place. There was a complete lack of confidence, you did not know who you could deal with and the whole thing cascaded from there [...] the majority of the holdings of the securitised credit, and the vast majority of the losses which arose, did not lie in the books of end investors intending to hold the assets to maturity, but on the books of highly leveraged banks and banklike institutions. The new model left most of the risk still somewhere on the balance sheets of banks and bank-like institutions but in a much more complex and less transparent fashion.
> (House of Commons Treasury Committee 2009: 33)

Securitization made this situation unmanageable; nobody knew how a potential or a real run could be stopped. Banks that were able to find whom one could deal with, could also find ways of renegotiating credit repayment protocols. This constitutes an information problem and consequently a problem for the technological backing of information systems. It is necessary, then, to ascertain the nature of the relationship between information flows, as well as clearing and settlement procedures, on the one hand, and information and communication technologies on the other. For instance, derivatives operations are not automated and this makes everything worse. Or sometimes there is a compartmentalization because of organizational silos, which makes horizontal interactions and their coverage by information and communication technologies impossible. Such issues can be revealed if we try to create network topologies facilitating understanding of how money is moving around within and between organizations.

For hard-core financiers, the perception of such hazardous conditions is for the most part driven to the margins. Are they right? Should the financial economist view these incremental issues as contributing nothing significant to systemic risks? The answer would be yes, if maturities and liquidity did not really matter that much (as one could assert by adopting the point of view of traders and those espousing the idea of perpetual leverage). However finance can be regarded as a game of interconnections between liquid and illiquid assets, or between assets with varying maturities.[7] If only the side of trading of illiquid and long-term maturity assets matters, then organizational issues related to operations providing for the liquidity and maturity of assets can be disregarded. But even trading operations can fall victim to this perspective. We tend not to realize the extent to which trust in banking and in financial institutions implies also trust in their organizational efficiency and technological reliability. Once there is awareness of this, gaining an understanding of the techno-organizational foundations of financial operations becomes a high priority.

Computerization and organizational technologies

Misconceptions about the techno-organizational dimensions of finance have also led to misunderstandings concerning the role of computers. As Donald MacKenzie shows in Chapter 4, it is more the interrelationship between model-driven practices and technological configurations that has brought about significant changes. The role of technologies in finance is not restricted to their enabling, prosthetic character. Much more important is their impact on representations, skills and tacit knowledge, as well as on attitudes to financial objects and on the understanding of market dynamics. MacKenzie, mainly referring to the trading and valuation of assets, stresses that the 'scientization' or 'technologization' of finance creates rules of thumb on the basis of altered representations and tacit knowledge, depending on the shaping of the information they use.[8] This shaping of information always involves black-boxing, that is, disregarding the internal structure of tangible or intangible devices (we can conceptualize complex financial derivatives or risk management models as intangible devices). Also, abstract models of information system architectures used by their managers can be regarded as intangible 'devices' constituting the maps with which managers and IT specialists 'navigate' in both the internal and the external environments of banks or in electronic financial networks, as we will see in the last chapter of this volume. MacKenzie shows in his chapter how one can open the black box of finance in order to see its internal techno-organizational construction. He refers to Callon and Latour's argument that the macro-actors of social life are micro-actors grown large through their capacities to mobilize and command black boxes. Doing this also implies referring to the external surface of the black boxes and leaving their internal workings to micro-actors who are then enframed in local responsibilities defined by the boundary of the black box. As long as power relations make the reproduction of certain configurations of black boxes possible, there is no need to try to look through their surface, or to open them. The idea made fruitful here with reference to the case of finance is that the contents of black boxes are of paramount importance, but in moments of crisis, that is, if a black box ceases to function as such, it does not transform inputs into appropriate outputs, and thus the power of macro-actors or operational standards can be put in jeopardy. MacKenzie's remarks provoke two interrelated questions. The first is about how contents and functions of black boxes shape the contexts in which they are embedded. The second question has to do with the opposite causal direction: how do contexts of black boxes shape their internal content and the workings this implies? This can be a highly relevant point of departure in attempting to understand computers, computing and their uses in finance.

This recursivity between context and content mediated by black-boxing really matters. It is in this framework that changes in knowledge, skills and attitudes create the architectural conceptions and the ideational dynamics that remodel the meaningful use of artefacts or the configurations of functionalities. The deeper we go into the black boxes of finance, it becomes clear that artefacts, models and architectural solutions are for the most part and with relatively few exceptions not proprietary to this sector.[9] Their accommodation in financial environments, if they are not first invented as instruments of financial operations, requires putting them somehow in perspective in order to bring to light the qualities that make them fit for adoption in a different context of use. In Chapter 8 we will see that this recursivity between context and content of 'devices' takes a specific form in the phase of late neoliberalism. In this era, interrelationships between financial risk management and the assessment of organizational profiles culminate in attempts to hedge various risk-laden aspects of organizational contexts, by abstracting from the content of the organizational units' operational features. Risk management, and further organizational management in late neoliberalism, end up blocking the trajectory leading from context to content. This does not mean that under these circumstances the content is not influenced by context. It rather means that this relationship is mostly removed from the observations and from the variables that have to be consciously and deliberately manipulated. Black boxes can then be seen only from their external features. And even if black boxes are opened, if this externalization of perspective prevails, the new data do not alter information, and so do not alter knowledge, as the new signals do not change in the slightest the ideational terms of observation. This lack of ability to differentiate context from content, and the ontological framing this implies, creates a stronger version of black-boxing that also changes the modalities of manipulation of devices and of the artefactual character of systems. In other words, as is argued in Chapter 8, this context-oriented hedging of risks emerging from the content of the black boxes (which diverts attention from any kind of understanding of operational lines of communication and command, as well as from qualitative aspects of organizational analysis), is characteristic of the way in which problems of manageability of banks are tackled in the late phase of neoliberalism. We discuss the issue of what will be called 'techno-organizational gestalts'. Complex instruments like Structured Investment Vehicles (SIVs) and CDOs can function as techno-organizational gestalts. Data mining systems, the use of Enterprise Resource Planning systems (ERPs) and Service Oriented Architectures (SOAs) can have the same function as well.

At a more mundane level, context redefines all possible technological objects and artefacts that can be accommodated within the organizational setting of back offices or branch networks. Context also defines the paths we can follow to envision the internal workings of the black boxes populating banks. For instance credit and debit cards are not more than magnetic tape and data transmission technologies combined, if viewed in terms of packaged device technologies. But if they are viewed in terms of the architecture of the interrelations of functionalities in which they are embedded, the discussion takes a quite different course and goes well into areas where databases, user interfaces and transactional networks matter. Similar considerations apply to bank branch automation. The combination of a wide range of banking technologies with office automation technologies does not only influence productivity (eventually also in the negative direction as productivity paradox theorists have shown). They have also radically altered the organizational dynamics of the branches and of the branch networks. In many respects they have also changed the relations of branch networks to other banks and firms belonging to non-banking industries. This should attract our attention to the fact that ICTs in finance are not predominantly related to risk management and derivatives models. Technologies for financial networks – a main part of which are the less fancy branch networks and branch automation systems, as well as the so-called alternative electronic networks (ATMs, EFTPOS, web banking, telephone banking, mobile banking) and all the hidden underlying systems needed – are equally decisive in shaping the technological landscape of the financial sector. Among the most visible of all these are the ATMs, which are part of the fusion of three elements: the culture of retail banking, the cash culture and the culture of everyday life especially in urban settings.

Of course ATMs can be used for cashless transactions, but this is not what they are primarily built for. Cash-dispensing is a central characteristic of their role within payment systems. Departing from this, Bernardo Bátiz-Lazo and Claudia Reese pose in Chapter 6 the question of whether 'the future of the ATM is past'. They give their answer based on material gained from the study of the British case. The way they handle this material also considers the recursive relationship between context and content; this time between business context and the content of the artefactual dimension of technology. But what is additionally included at the contextual level is the role of the producers and vendors of ATMs and of their congenial systems. The authors show how organizational aspects of banking related to this medium (which complements and also can make redundant conventional brick and mortar branch networks through self-servicing) rely on the interaction between three processes: between manufacturers (i.e. producers and vendors); retail financial intermediaries (i.e. organizational users); and retail customers (i.e. ultimate end users). This interaction according to Bátiz-Lazo and Reese shapes the perception and the meaning of the machines, their functionality and consequently also the construction of shared networks extending on a transnational scale. It is also this interaction that allows us to see the future of the technological solution. It seems that this solution appears as indispensable in the framework of deregulated financial service providers. How else could the staff of the branches and other points of sale stop dealing with low-added value transactions and concentrate on marketing and sales? The transformation of the business context has been a challenge in this sense. But the network character of the solution itself presented banks with a different challenge as well: they had to cope with new electronic network security issues and with security issues related to the artefacts that made interfaces possible: the screens, but mainly the cards. ATMs were also a factor requiring shifts within the IT divisions: they had to cope with the development of new applications, and new forms of collaboration with external IT firms.

What we can learn from this study of ATM-based technologies is that it makes sense to adopt a transposed perspective. This is however not the usual way of doing research in the history of technology. What makes these developments less visible for many historians of technology is the fact that they are not considered to be as noteworthy as technological developments drawing on the technical features of tangible devices. In finance this neglect of context makes things more difficult. Very few machines are peculiar to banking, as already stressed. And the ones that are proprietary to the sector, although they have revolutionized the front desk and its relations to back offices, do not have the sophisticated technological configurations one might expect. Not the visible machines, but rather the invisible and intangible series of applications and their interconnections make up the sophisticated part of this technological world. In most cases the vast number of paths and modalities of interoperability, the database structures, the data mining systems, as well as the appropriate end user interfaces constitute the realms of problems technologists of banks have to cope with. For instance, among the most difficult technological problems peculiar to banks are software problems related to data cleansing and data mining, and the congenial software design and software engineering problems related to Customer Relationship Management (CRM). To a great extent these technologies are related to database software problems. Others are related to the technological infrastructure and the design of topologies of electronic financial networks with sophisticated telecommunications backbones. All these problems make clear the complexity of software and system development projects.

Computers in banking and finance are becoming interesting in this respect, when they start playing a role in connection with database and telecommunication technologies, and thus as devices that not only calculate and push around data but also pull data and configure it in order to create information and knowledge through often sophisticated end user–computer interfaces, as in the cases of scoping devices of dealing rooms used by traders (Knorr Cetina and Grimpe 2008). What has made computing extremely interesting in banking and finance is the fact that it has had to mirror dynamic and human-reflexivity-dependent configurations of information stocks, information flows and decisions taken with the help of these information flows. Computer-based technologies even altered the culturally determined responses to rapidly changing economic and financial environments, which defined both intra- and inter-organizational environments.

The communicative aspect of computing came to be related also to the centrality of databases. The idea of a fast and stable way to electronically transmit funds to any member bank and its respective customers (the rationale for the Society for Worldwide Interbank Financial Telecommunication (SWIFT)) was translated through databases and especially in their relational version into equivalent informational objects, but from a different perspective: not from that of information flows, but rather from that of information stocks. Stocks of information had to attain the characteristics that would facilitate the management of flows between various stocks, as well as between stocks and terminal points of system–end user interfaces. As David Gugerli in Chapter 5 shows with his study of the Swiss banks, this databank philosophy allowed the crossing of information available or generated in various divisions of financial organizations. His analysis of the role of the development of databases and their introduction in the banks as a main component of critical information infrastructures illustrates in the most lucid manner arguments that have been taken up earlier in this introduction. The flexibility databases implied made them the main instrument for the management of new financial products and services that, with the progressive spread of the impact of deregulation and globalization, began to define banking. The potential for recombination within distributed networks allowed bankers to cope with both new problems of customer relationship management and problems of asset-liability management relying on the assessment of the profitability of highly heterogeneous business units and organizational divisions. Through this, organizational patchworks could be made more easily manageable without necessary recourse to procedural system architectures. Pull technologies allowed for management without strong coupling, and without crises due to coordination problems stemming from asynchronous processes.

At this point it is crucial to define organizational technologies. We can understand these as durable configurations of technological knowledge, technological processes and technological artefacts that emerge from organizational agendas and create filters that redefine organizational agendas, discourses and representations among participants in organizational settings.[10] In this sense, organizational technologies are in most cases solution technologies arising from the perception of risks and opportunities in given circumstances. Most of those who use the term 'solution technologies', and who are more often practitioners than theoreticians, understand by this a dynamic but systemic configuration that is relevant in a business or more generally in an organizational context. In this sense ERP systems (like SAP) cannot be regarded as typical solution technologies. The purpose of such integrated software packages is to have one solution for everyone with only incremental corrections in terms of customization or parameterization but without moving too far away from the philosophy of the initial model. ERPs are top-down organizational technologies that bring about a re-disciplining of organizations (Pollock et al. 2003; Pollock and Williams 2007, 2009; Kallinikos 2004a). They can be contrasted with bottom-up solutions combining human and non-human resources with the aim to configure or to reconfigure technological modules (hardware and software).[11] Organizational solution technologies cannot be regarded only as means of disciplining organizations. This does not mean that power games are not relevant as a crucial aspect of understanding the shaping of organizational technologies. But it is simplistic to view all possible techno-organizational measures as disconnected from any agency aiming at the creation of added value that might challenge social and political relationships in organizations. The purpose of organizational technologies is primarily the transformation of risk objects into objects of certainty. 'Risk objects' is a term introduced by Michael Power: in his words, '"Risk objects" are essentially ideas about harm with implicit causality and may become the focus of "socio-technical" networks understood as "seamless webs" of elements and actors engaged in strategies for institutionalizing or de-institutionalizing particular objects of knowledge' (Power 2007: 25). Risk objects are often a counterpoint to the desire for objects of certainty: ideas about harm create uncertainties. If the perception of risk objects creates anxieties, certain actors in specific organizational settings are likely to try to cope with the situation by reducing uncertainty.[12] They imagine durable systems, objects that give a sense of usability without uncertain outcomes. These are, then, objects of certainty created as a reaction to the perception of what Michael Power defines as risk objects. Organizational solution technologies are a tactical response to imagined durabilities that could constitute techno-organizational architectures as objects of certainty. This interplay between risk objects and objects of certainty is what we should focus on in order to understand the evolution of the techno-organizational landscapes in finance.

Where does techno-organizational strategy come from?

Are bankers really preoccupied with techno-organizational strategies? Perhaps they are, but more in terms of wishful thinking and the managerial mythologies formulated by consultancies and vendor companies. In reality what happens in the banks has to do less with proactive and more with reactive approaches, originating in the perception of risks. This risk aspect, this sense of a need to transform risk objects into objects of certainty, is crucial for understanding the factors driving bank managers to technological investment and to the endorsement of plans for information system development. The belief in technologies, which prevails in the top echelons of financial organizations, is not in most cases the result of explicit planning. Hitt et al. (1999) have shown that most banks combine a standardization of the way they manage their IT projects with weak processes for identifying opportunities to invest in IT (Hitt et al. 1999: 95; see also Peters et al. 2002). Here again vendors and system-integrator companies play a crucial role (Hitt et al. 1999: 132–4). Bankers apparently go through hard times when they must decide on technology and, it seems, rarely have a clear techno-organizational vision. But despite their doubts there are strong reasons for spending on IT. One of the hardest decisions is to cut down IT budgets. Investing in technology in the era of liberalized financial markets is not primarily related to the reduction of costs, as was the case in the early phases of the computerization of banks. IT expenditure is necessary not only for building comparative advantages; it is indispensable for keeping up with the requirements for competitive parity (Llewellyn 2003). As already stressed, this has to do, among other things, with standards set within the inter-organizational environments of finance. It is interesting that the movement of top managers away from direct involvement in strategic technological decisions has in many cases occurred in tandem with the abandonment of the old productivity and cost-saving approach. Accounting oriented managers were more familiar with weighing technology as a factor in lowering the cost of production. Especially after the 1970s, when the technological and organizational landscape of financial organization became much more complex, investments started requiring multifaceted organizational decisions.

Contrary to mythologies promoted by consultancy companies, aiming at mitigating the anxieties of bankers, whenever the latter realize connections between techno-organizational processes and financial risks, IT investments cannot follow durable methods of planning. Furthermore organizational solution technologies in banking and finance do not constitute a realm of unconstrained creativity for information systems designers or for planners of IT investment. These complex systems have been built stepwise and on the basis of many ad hoc decisions dictated by adaptation to changing economic environments or to specific business needs. The shifts and the more radical changes in their architectures and in their recursive relationship to artefactual parameters and practices, are the outcome of the rearrangement of patterns and interweaving of orders. Drawing on David Stark's argument (Stark 2009: xv), we could say that instead of thinking of change or of techno-organizational innovation as replacement, it can be more relevant to examine even the insertion of new elements in conjunction with processes of recombination and reconfigurations of elements. The coexistence and coevolution of various layers – the intertwining of obsolete and futuristic components in the same system and the problems of system integration these represented – was one of the main sources of complexity and thus of the manageability of information infrastructures. Banking information systems have a long and complex multilayered history, and the impact of these successive phases remains embedded in many systems components still in operation.[13]

Moreover, a multitude of intra-organizational rearrangements were set in motion by responsible managers in order to reach the stage of the successful adoption of technologies. Innovations take place on the basis of a combination of research and development, operations and marketing related both to financial and IT products. Individuals who take up the role of 'system integrators', either in-house or in the IT companies – who not only pull together the operations, information technology and marketing functions but also manage the portfolio of innovations – are key players in this context. Sometimes, top managers collaborate with the internal IT specialists and with the external IT companies. In this case the characteristics of forms of social and organizational coordination can have implications for innovation processes. We can find various examples of the way managers decide on integrated software packages for branch automation or for alternative financial electronic networks with significant organizational impact. Purchases of software related to procedures dictated by the need for compliance with regulatory frameworks (e.g. Basel II, Sarbanes-Oxley, International Accounting Standards, Anti-Money

Laundering Regulations etc.), or of software related to risk management and complex financial instruments, give interesting stories on the background of techno-organizational decision making. The specifics of these processes remain a *terra incognita* for most academics. Real decision processes in this field take place within frameworks of social interaction often resulting in tense emotions and erratic psychodynamics. Some take place inside, others predominantly outside the organization and are the outcome of marketing and sales efforts of external companies. The same hierarchical levels are not always involved. And the reports related to these decisions are not always easily accessible. Yet what we know is that the higher one goes up the hierarchical ladder, the more attitudes to IT become reactive rather than proactive and strategic. The only managers who are proactive, and on the basis of a better understanding, are those in a lower echelon who very often try to exert pressure on the higher echelons by writing and disseminating proposals. This often takes place under the influence of IT companies or in combination with external promotional efforts. But as expected the lower-echelon managers have less negotiating power in this situation. However banks, as networks of operational units, very often depend more on lower echelon decisions at least in matters of implementation of plans for information system development. For the most part top managers select from among scenarios presented by middle managers. One might say that the attention to technological and organizational issues is more typical for middle and lower IT managers, or for managers of other operations divisions. Top managers are more aloof. And when it comes to technology they adopt a strongly consequential approach and rarely a procedural one, which might push them to look inside the black boxes of organizational sub-units.

In an era where cost issues have been subordinated to issues of competitive parity and intra-firm and inter-firm coordination, technology for top managers has acquired a different meaning for bankers. Equilibrating configurations of techno-organizational black boxes to create certainty out of risk has become a priority. This quest for certainty creates in many circumstances the illusion of the instrumental value of technology. It seems that many bankers view information technologies as the means by which risk objects can be smoothly transformed into objects of certainty. This allows them to overcome their Hamlet-like emotions when confronted with risky decisions. Jocelyn Pixley elaborates on this in Chapter 3. Her focus is not on operational architectures of techno-organizational systems, but on predictive models. The connection she draws between the need to cope with uncertainty and the technological rationalization of emotions-driven decision making in banking is crucial in this respect. For Pixley, this need to make uncertainties invisible by disguising them with the durability of technologies explains why the financial sector has invested in risk models, and continues to do so. Her central point is that the financial sector invested in information and communication technologies because of the pressing need to cope with uncertainties that arose after the deregulation of the 1970s. Beyond the sociological, social-psychological and decision-theoretical arguments, what this chapter brings is an historical perspective on technological change. The view presented here is that the reversal of the pre-1970 regulatory regime dictated an imperative of distrust and extrapolation from past data (a problem that was not so acute in the Bretton Woods environment). This was one of the reasons why after deregulation a vast amount of capital was poured into IT for financial predictive models.

But these emotionally driven intentions as presented by Pixley did not produce any more precise and operational understanding of the techno-organizational ground. As a consequence, what we see is not so much a coherent technological strategy but rather a constellation of blended tactical solution technologies. Strategy and innovation seem to be trapped in a fractal world. This is one of the main conclusions that can be drawn from Chapter 7. In this chapter Susan Scott starts from the question of the characteristics of techno-innovation in the era of deregulated financial services. More specifically, Scott is interested in revealing the sources of innovation and the ways these are managed, as well as its expected and unexpected consequences. One of the conclusions compatible with the image created earlier in this introduction is that techno-innovation in finance is loosely coordinated without having a homogenizing effect. The latter, as Scott shows, is not necessarily a source of inefficiencies. Organizational solution technologies originating from system development in banking and finance can rarely be traced back to technological strategies conceived exclusively in their ranks. The reason for this is that technological practices in banks and other financial organizations are reactive rather than proactive. The more they are reactive, the less they are also the prime movers of technological innovations. In particular, reactions to crises lead to the adoption and quick configuration of available technological components (both tangible, like equipment and intangible, like software and expertise) that can be delivered by IT companies. In this context, predicting crises and creating the appropriate technological configurations that might help to cope with these can be the craft of IT or consultancy companies. As some researchers have found, banks are mostly preoccupied with solving short-term problems. They tend to react to needs for technology dictated by perceived risks of short-term operational bottlenecks or even of operational breakdowns, rather than responding to the requirements of strategic planning towards technologically defined competitive advantage. In this context one of the main questions is whether they will opt for in-house development, or for purchasing products and services from external providers.

The technological reinvention of banking and finance after the turn of the 1970s has created new sources of risks that can be traced back to the recursive relationships between quasi-strategic architectural fixity, mythological rationalization, and reactive practices of tinkering and crisis management. The cases discussed by Susan Scott in Chapter 7 illustrate in a vivid way the fact that solution technologies of the real world of banking and finance had to do with this kind of complexity. This creates the ground for understanding further aspects of these trends. The implication is that not only configurations of risks but engineering philosophies emerged out of these processes, and many of these engineering philosophies were integrated in technological products and services. All the major information technology companies, like IBM, Oracle, Microsoft, Unisys and so on, but also the major consultancies, created huge financial services technologies departments. And this had a counterpart in the rapidly growing IT divisions of banks, that could finally make their voice heard in the top clubs of managers and boards of directors. All these images of the new realities bring us to the idea that it is worth studying the under-investigated processes of the coevolution of financial operations and information technologies. This relationship between the internal and the external domain of technological solution-design and system development is of paramount importance. In-house efforts for system development, upgrading and maintenance are overshadowed in most cases by the more glamorous consultants and IT companies. The local knowledge of technological communities of practice, which interact with users or super-users working in organizational divisions commissioned to plan operations and who are impressively knowledgeable in technological matters, remains beyond the horizon of managerial and organizational narratives. The fact that very few projects can be effectively accomplished without external resources is common knowledge in the branch. But the fact that outsourcing or consultancy projects typically remain totally ineffective if there are no internal human resources to successfully absorb skills and expertise should attract our attention to a greater extent than is usually the case. Any design of solutions and their implementation, or any IT innovations emerging in banking and finance, are in most cases the outcome of collaboration between internal and external human resources. If these forms of collaboration last for years, which is very frequently the case, the results are very impressive coevolutionary processes that influence the business and organizational trajectories on both sides – in the banks and in the IT companies. R&D resulting in sophisticated solution technologies, as well as innovative software engineering projects, is rarely encountered outside such coevolutionary dynamics. The lack of such stories is mainly due to confidentiality disclosures that obstruct both the eye and the pen of those who might be willing to produce historical accounts of the shaping and evolution of IT projects in the financial sector. The information remains hidden or distorted even when the main focus of such projects is the customization of products and services accessible to every organization of the branch. There are countertendencies to this, such as technology users associations. Users associations (like Unisys Users Association, DB2 Users Associations etc.) to which belong members of staff from various organizations, otherwise in fierce competition, are a very interesting phenomenon in this respect. In the forums they organize, local knowledge is put on stage without fear that this could threaten competitive advantage. The idea of competitive parity on the basis of knowledge sharing prevails, rather than the idea of hiding proprietary information. These forums further work as opportunities for the advertisement of the technological strength of organizations, with significance not only for the markets of products and services but also for the labour markets for highly skilled IT personnel.

These forms of action, as well as the informal communication in trans-organizational project teams, create a special perspective. But this too does not solve the problem of fragmentation. One might think that this problem of fragmentation could be solved with detailed maps and diagrammatic representations. In Chapter 8 we discuss the limits of this approach and also its cognitive and operational consequences. Here we need to briefly discuss the limits of lining-up and enumeration of historically existing or potential technological objects, functionalities and system configurations. This volume is not an encyclopaedia or a dictionary of technologies in banking and finance. Neither could such a thing exist and be made useful to researchers or practitioners. Lists, inventories, reports and detailed maps are thus not appropriate for creating the ground of understanding. As Umberto Eco shows, making lists is the articulation of a twofold problem: of being unable to rely on rather stable driving cultural patterns and of being unable to define phenomena. Information systems of banks and information infrastructures of extended financial networks are not demarcated in physical or in virtual spaces by any clear limit behind which we can find an unambiguously enumerable set of a limited number of objects. Information systems and their architectures convey an etcetera: their only possible representations are like paintings with frames – however much they insinuate a plethora of objects, they do not seek to include everything. The forms of the pictures are derived by the conceptual movers signalled by the image, even if they are not depicted. As Eco writes, '[...] a landscape could obviously continue beyond the frame [...] but this doesn't mean that the painter wishes to suggest that it extends to infinity [...] nonetheless, there are other fugitive works that make us think that what we see within the frame is not all, but only an example of the totality whose number is hard to calculate' (Eco 2009: 38). Although the termination of the process of collecting and putting together ideational objects can remain vague, the representational form frames the conceptual perspective. What we try to do in this volume is to overcome both the hurdles of conceptual and definitional uncertainties by means of a transition from lists to forms.

The pragmatics, which mark out the conceptual frame, are placed in this volume in relation to the history of financial deregulation. In the following pages the main theme is the coevolution of financial markets with organizational technologies. Examining techno-organizational developments through this prism will make it easier to give answers to the question of why certain scenarios of the conversion of risk objects into objects of certainty have prevailed over others. This perspective will facilitate the placement of the technological objects we might spot at the right point within the techno-organizational landscapes of finance. It will also facilitate the establishment of a connection between the ways we understand technologies in finance and the ways we understand risks emerging from information systems and organizational processes.

Notes

1. In *Fool's Gold*, a widely read book on derivatives banking and the origins of the credit crunch, Gillian Tett presents the other side: of those who care not only about portfolios but also about organizational processes. According to one story, when Jamie Dimon, shortly after his appointment as the Chairman of J. P. Morgan, travelled to London he did not head to the city headquarters but to the bank's UK IT operations (Tett 2009: 113–14). In another story from the same bank Tett talks about Peter Hancock's idea of hiring a social anthropologist to study the organizational dynamics and especially the synergies among departments and the risks of segregation (Tett 2009: 7). Spotting such anecdotal evidence is not easy. Frei et al. (2000) deliver an explanation for this. The tension between investing in the alignment of labour, capital and technologically-backed production processes on the one hand, and investing in portfolio strategies on the other is typical of the banking industry.

2. The course of adoption of ICTs in the financial sector was then eruptive. According to statistics from the IT industry, more then 80 per cent of the value of IT products and services after 1980 has been purchased by banks, insurance companies and other firms of the financial sector. As Litan and Santomero (1999: vii) stress, 'information technology probably has affected the financial service industry more than any other sector of the economy except for the computer and telecommunications industries that are driving the IT revolution'.
3. The heroes were of course the front- and not the back-office people. Even the 'quants', the rocket scientists of finance, became less recognizable figures than front-desk operators and marketing people if they could not find the way, as he puts it, to glory and money through academia or through the establishment of renowned firms (Derman 2004: 125, 175, 245, 266–7). See also Dymski (2008).
4. This applies also to interbank trading. Contrary to the common view, information processing in banking is less sufficiently backed by computers than one might think. For various reasons that have to do with traditions and inertia in inter-organizational social networks, for instance communication networks for interbank markets in Europe, which are managed by each country separately, are for the most part phone based, with perhaps the exception of Italy where communication is screen based and fully electronic (De Masi 2009: 245).
5. These contractually complex financial instruments are preferable for the banks issuing and trading them, as the lack of transparency – the asymmetric information they imply – is also the source of higher yields. But there are also other issues connected to operational deficiencies in this field. As Tett (2009: 158–60) reports, the Federal Reserve and especially its New York branch recognized the need to act in order to counter back-office inefficiencies resulting in clearing delays. However supervisory authorities and regulators had to cope with a collective action problem since no one wanted to be the first to undertake the cost of restructuring and the risk of disruption of operations because of the necessary re-engineering of back-office systems. Telephone and faxes as means to confirm deals are still defining operations in the credit derivatives markets, although as Tett writes, they are supposed to be the epitome of efficient 'virtual' banking.
6. On this political-economic model that prevailed after the end of the 1980s, see Crouch 2008, also Harrington 2008.
7. It is relevant here to recall the view of John Maynard Keynes, according to which the values of illiquid assets can be regarded as estimates derived from illiquid ones. Further stock valuation is not a *prediction* but a convention, which serves to facilitate investment and ensure that stocks are liquid, despite 'being underpinned by an illiquid business and its illiquid investments, such as factories'. Keynes also establishes a correspondence between qualities of assets and operational requirements. In order to understand this we can refer to Keynes' distinction between three attributes that assets, including money, possess in various degrees (Keynes 1964 [1936]: 225–6): (a) attributes related to their assisting some process of production or supplying services to the consumer; (b) attributes related to the process of carrying them; (c) attributes related to the liquidity of these assets. There are costs corresponding to these three categories of attributes: production costs, carrying

costs and liquidity costs, or what Keynes calls liquidity premium. Portfolio management and especially complex-derivatives-based investment banking changed the character of the attributes of money assets. Production of these assets requires financial engineering that includes the development of mathematical and procedural models for hedging, valuation and contracting. Carrying processes require trading, maintenance of the models and back-office operations. Liquidity requires clearing, settlement and custodian operations. Each direction implies also the corresponding operating costs.

8. A similar idea has been developed by Michel Callon and his associates. They use the term 'market devices' (Muniesa et al. 2007).
9. The context–content issue introduced here by Donald MacKenzie's chapter is crucial also from a different point of view. Although the content of the black boxes related to the various technologies used in the financial sector is binding and exercises an influence on the shaping of structural constraints and of mindsets, the innovative force comes from the context-driven organizational solution technologies. Not paying attention to this context–content recursivity is one of the main reasons why the eventual innovative force of technologies, developed as a consequence of demands stemming from the financial sector, has not been extensively investigated. We tend not to pay so much attention to this causal direction. The question would then be whether in the case of the financial sector we can solely observe mere processes of adoption of the technological innovations that have emerged in other sectors, or whether the financial sector has brought about its own technological innovations, induced by financial innovations, which have had an impact on the overall development of ICTs during the last quarter of the twentieth century and the first decade of the twenty-first century. All indications lead to the conclusion that we cannot easily find any original contribution, except for the realm of system configuration and system integration. There are a few exceptions such as the cheque clearing machines or the ATMs, and perhaps also the ERMA Stanford Project, which were not adoptions of innovations occurring in other sectors. In trying to understand the impact of financial deregulation on technological change, as well as on the interplay of financial and technological innovations, we must think of solution technologies and the emergence of virtual spaces these bring about, rather than of device technologies, integrated software packages, or demarcated pieces of embedded software.
10. For a similar approach see O'Callaghan (2005) and the contributions in Yates and Van Maanen (2001).
11. For ideas related to the understanding of the importance of the bottom-up approach see Ciborra 2002, Orlikowski 1992, Orlikowski and Barley 2001. For the limits of this approach, see Kallinikos 2004b.
12. As Margaret Archer has discussed, it is not possible for all actors, in all possible situations, to overcome their anxieties by trying to rationalize their action. Any degree of autonomous reflexivity presupposes forms of mediation of structural and cultural properties and their discursive elaboration, for which actors must be qualified both by the experiential equipment and the situational parameters (Archer 2003: 210–54).
13. Processes of manual or mechanical calculation and traditional accounting recording started being gradually replaced by analogue, and later by digital

computer assisted operations (Cortada 1993, 2004; Yates 1993, 2005). These transformations implied, at the beginning (approximately 1930–60), a one-to-one mapping of existing processes onto configuration of activities aiming at manipulating hardware, and this was also the character of the software used, mostly Assembler and later COBOL. For instance back-office technologies were mapping out, without much novelty, the usual clerical work. Up to this point, computers did not imply any significant step beyond a punch card driven philosophy. Only when computers started to communicate, at first with central computers and with various dummy terminals and then later with distributed processing power in more complex network topologies, did modern IT architectures for banking and finance also start to emerge. These implied distributed functions, but also a different blend of human-to-machine and machine-to-machine interaction, with growing density of the latter. With the advent of outsourcing, service-oriented architectures, and cloud computing, both complexities and risks started rising especially because of the disconnection of data from processes. For an overview see contributions in Jessica Keyes' *Handbook of Technology in Financial Services* (1999). For a managerial approach see also contributions in Seyman 1998 and Gandy 1999.

Bibliography

Abdelal, R. (2006), 'Writing the Rules of Global Finance: France, Europe, and Capital Liberalization'. *Review of International Political Economy*, 13(1): 1–27.

Archer, M. (2003), *Structure, Agency and the Internal Conversation*, Cambridge: Cambridge University Press.

Balling, M., Lierman, F. and Mullineux, A. (eds) (2003), *Technology and Finance: Challenges for Financial Markets, Business Strategies and Policy Makers*, London and New York: Routledge.

Batiz-Lazo, B. and Wood, D. (2002), 'An Historical Appraisal of Information Technology in Commercial Banking', *Electronic Markets*, 12(3): 192–205.

Battilossi, S. and Cassis, Y. (eds) (2002), *European Banks and the American Challenge: Competition and Cooperation in International Banking under Bretton Woods*, Oxford: Oxford University Press.

Bodie, Z. (1999), 'Investment Management and Technology: Past, Present, and Future', in E. R. Litan and A. M. Santomero (eds): 343–373.

Callon, M., Millo, Y. and Muniesa, F. (eds) (2007), *Market Devices*, Oxford: Blackwell.

Ciborra, C. (2002), *The Labyrinth of Information: Challenging the Wisdom of Systems*, Oxford: Oxford University Press.

Cortada, J. W. (1993), *Before the Computer*, Princeton, NJ: Princeton University Press.

Cortada, J. W. (2004), *The Digital Hand*, Oxford: Oxford University Press.

Crouch, C. (2008), 'What Will Follow the Demise of Privatized Keynesianism?' *Political Quarterly*, 79(4): 476–87.

De Masi, G. (2009), 'Empirical Analysis of the Architecture of the Interbank Market and Credit Market Using Network Theory', in A. K. Naimzada and S. Stefani, A. Torriero (eds), *Networks, Topology and Dynamics*, Berlin and Heidelberg: Springer: 241–56.

Derman, E. (2004), *My Life as a Quant. Reflections on Physics and Finance*, Hoboken, NJ: John Wiley & Sons.
Dymski, G. (2008), 'Financial Risk and Governance in the Neoliberal Era', http://www.dymski.com/wp-content/uploads/docs/2008-09-10-Financial-Risk-and-Governance-in-the-Neoliberal-Era.pdf.
Eco, U. (2009), *The Infinity of Lists*, New York: Rizzoli.
Fiet, J. O., Norton, W. I. and Clouse, Van G. H. (2007), 'Systematic Search as a Source of Technical Innovation: An Empirical Test', *Journal of Engineering and Technology Management*, 24: 329–46.
Fincham, R., Fleck, J., Procter, R., Scarbrough, H., Tierney, M. and Williams, R. (1994), *Expertise and Innovation: Information Technology Strategies in the Financial Services Sector*, Oxford: Clarendon Press.
Fleck, J. and Howells, J. (2001), 'Technology, the Technology Complex and the Paradox of Technological Determinism', *Technology Analysis & Strategic Management*, 13(4): 523–31.
Freedman, R. S. (2006), *Introduction to Financial Technology*, Amsterdam: Elsevier.
Frei, F. X., Harker, P. T. and Hunter, L. W. (2000), 'Inside the Black-Box: What Makes a Bank Efficient?' in P. T. Harker and S. A. Zenios (eds), *Performance of Financial Institutions: Efficiency, Innovation, Regulation*, Cambridge: Cambridge University Press: 259–311.
Gandy, A. (1999), *Banking Strategies and Beyond 2000*, Chicago, IL: Glenlake.
Gart, A. (1994), *Regulation, Deregulation, Reregulation: The Future of the Banking, Insurance, and Securities Industries*, New York: John Wiley & Sons.
Germain, R. D. (1997), *The International Organization of Credit. States and Global Finance in the World-Economy*, Cambridge: Cambridge University Press.
Greenspan, A. (2000), 'Technology and Financial Services', *Journal of Financial Services Research*, 18(2/3): 109–13.
Harrington, B. (2008), *Pop Finance: Investment Clubs and the New Investor Populism*, Princeton, NJ: Princeton University Press.
Harvey, D. (2005), *A Brief History of Neoliberalism*, Oxford: Oxford University Press.
Hendrickson, J. M. (2001), 'The Long and Bumpy Road to Glass-Steagall Reform: A Historical and Evolutionary Analysis of Banking Legislation', *American Journal of Economics and Sociology*, 60(4): 849–79.
Hitt, L. M., Frei, F. X. and Harker, P. T. (1999), 'How Firms Decide on Technology', in E. R. Litan and A. M. Santomero (eds): 93–136.
Holland, C. P., Lockett, G. and Blackman, I. D. (1997), 'The Impact of Globalisation and Information Technology on the Strategy and Profitability of the Banking Industry'. Proceedings of The Thirtieth Annual Hawaii International Conference on System Sciences.
Horvitz, P. M. and White, L. J. (2000), 'The Challenge of New Electronic Technologies in Banking: Private Strategies and Public Policies', in P. T. Harker and S. A. Zenios (eds), *Performance of Financial Institutions: Efficiency, Innovation, Regulation*, Cambridge: Cambridge University Press: 367–87.
House of Commons Treasury Committee (2009), *Banking Crisis: Dealing with the Failure of the UK Banks*, Seventh Report of Session 2008–9.
Ingham, H. and Thompson, S. (1993), 'Structural Deregulation and Market Entry: The Case of Financial Services', *Fiscal Studies*, 14(1): 15–41.
James, H. (2002), 'Central Banks and the Process of Financial Internationalization: A Secular View', in Battilossi and Cassis (eds): 200–17.

Kallinikos, J. (2004a), 'Deconstructing Information Packages: Organizational and Behavioural Implications of ERP Systems', *Information Technology and People*, 17(1): 8–30.

Kallinikos, J. (2004b), 'Farewell to Constructivism: Technology and Context-Embedded Action', in C. Avgerou, C. Ciborra and F. Land (eds), *The Social Study of Information and Communication Technology*, Oxford: Oxford University Press: 140–61.

Keyes, J. (1999), *Handbook of Technology in Financial Services*, Boca Raton, FL: Auerbach.

Keynes, J. M. (1964 [1936]), *The General Theory of Employment, Interest, and Money*, San Diego, CA; New York; London: Harvest Book, Harcourt.

King, M. (2008), Speech by Mervyn King Governor of the Bank of England, Edinburgh, 20 October 2009, http://www.bankofengland.co.uk/publications/speeches/2009/speech406.pdf.

Knorr Cetina, K. and Grimpe, B. (2008), "Global Financial Technologies: Scoping Systems That Raise the World", in T. Pinch and R. Swedberg, R. (eds), *Living in a Material World. Economic Sociology Meets Science and Technology Studies*, The MIT Press, Cambridge MA: 161–189.

Krugman, P. (2009), *The Return of Depression Economics and the Crisis of 2008*, New York and London: W. W. Norton.

Lépinay, V-. A. (2007), 'Parasitic Formulae: The Case of Capital Guarantee Products', in M. Callon, Y. Millo and F. Muniesa (eds): 261–83.

Litan, E. R. and Santomero, A. M. (eds) (1999), *Brookings-Wharton Papers on Financial Services 1999*, Washington, DC: Brookings Institution Press.

Llewellyn, D. T. (2003), 'Technology and the New Economics of Banking', in M. Balling, F. Lierman and A. Mullineux (eds): 51–67.

Macey, J. R. and O'Hara, M. (1999), 'Globalization, Exchange Governance, and the Future of Exchanges', in E. R. Litan and A. M. Santomero (eds): 1–23.

MacKenzie, D. (2001), *Mechanizing Proof: Computing, Risk, and Trust*, Cambridge, MA: The MIT Press.

MacKenzie, D. (2004), 'Social Connectivities in Global Financial Markets', *Environment and Planning D: Society and Space*, 22: 83–101.

MacKenzie, D. (2005), 'Opening the Black Boxes of Global Finance', *Review of International Political Economy*, 12(4): 555–76.

MacKenzie, D. (2006), *An Engine, Not a Camera: How Financial Models Shape Markets*, Cambridge, MA: The MIT Press.

Mazlish, B. (1993), *The Fourth Discontinuity: The Co-Evolution of Humans and Machines*, New Haven, CT and London: Yale University Press.

Millo, Y., Muniesa, F., Panourgias, N. S. and Scott, S. V. (2005), 'Organised Detachment: Clearinghouse Mechanisms in Financial Markets', *Information and Organization*, 15: 229–46.

Mishkin, F. S. and Strahan, P. E. (1999), 'What Will Technology Do to Financial Structure', in E. R. Litan and A. M. Santomero (eds): 249–77.

Morisi, T. L. (1996), 'Commercial Banking Transformed', *Monthly Labor Review*, August Issue: 30–6.

Mulligan, C. B. and Sala-i-Martin, X. (2000), 'Extensive Margins and the Demand for Money at Low Interest Rates', *The Journal of Political Economy*, 108(5): 961–91.

Muniesa, F., Millo, Y and Callon, M. (2007), 'An Introduction to Market Devices', in M. Callon, Y. Millo, F, Muniesa (eds): 1–12.

O'Callaghan, R. (2005), 'Technological Innovation in Organizations and Their Ecosystems', in W. H. Dutton, B. Kahin, R. O'Callaghan, A. W. Wyckoff (eds), *Transforming Enterprise: The Economic and Social Implications of Information Technology*, Cambridge, MA: The MIT Press: 1–12.

Orlikowski, W. J. (1992), 'The Duality of Technology: Rethinking the Concept of Technology in Organizations', *Organization Science*, 3(3): 398–427.

Orlikowski, W. J. and Barley, S. R. (2001), 'Technology and Institutions: What Can Research on Information Technology and Research on Organizations Learn from Each Other?' *MIS Quarterly*, 25(2): 45–165.

Peters, S. C. A., Heng, M. S. H. and Vet, R. (2002), 'Formation of the Information Systems Strategy in a Global Financial Services Company', *Information and Organization*, 12: 19–38.

Pixley, J. (2004), *Emotions in Finance: Distrust and Uncertainty in Global Markets*, Cambridge: Cambridge University Press.

Pollock, N. and Williams, R. (2007), 'Technology Choice and its Performance: Towards a Sociology of Software Package Procurement', *Information and Organization*, 17: 131–61.

Pollock, N. and Williams, R. (2009), *Software and Organizations*, London and New York: Routledge.

Pollock, N., Williams, R. and Procter, R. (2003), 'Fitting Standard Software Packages to Non-standard Organizations: The "Biography" of an Enterprise-Wide System', *Technology Analysis & Strategic Management*, 15(3): 317–32.

Power, M. (2007), *Organized Uncertainty*, Oxford: Oxford University Press.

Pryke, M. and Allen, J. (2000), 'Monetized Time-Space: Derivatives – Money's "new imaginary?"', *Economy and Society*, 29(2): 264–84.

Regini, M. (1999), 'Comparing Banks in Advanced Economies: The Role of Markets, Technology, and Institutions in Employment Relations', in M. Regini, J. Kitay and M. Baethge (eds), *From Tellers to Sellers. Changing Employment Relations in Banks*, Cambridge, MA: The MIT Press: 319–30.

Reifner, U. and Herwig, I. (2003), 'Consumer Education and Information Rights in Financial Services', *Information & Communication Technology Law*, 12(2): 125–42.

Rusinko, C. A. and Matthews, J. O. (2000), 'Evolution of a Technological Community: A Case Study of Financial Derivatives', *Journal of Engineering and Technology Management*, 14: 315–36.

Seyman, M. R. (ed.) (1998), *Managing the New Bank Technology*, Chicago, IL: Glenlake.

Shiller, R. J. (2008), *The Subprime Solution*, Princeton, NJ and Oxford: Princeton University Press.

Scott, S. V. (2000), 'IT-Enabled Credit Risk Modernisation: A Revolution Under the Cloak of Normality', *Accounting, Management and Information Technology*, 10: 221–55.

Spiegel, J., Gart, A. and Gart, S. (1996), *Banking Redefined. How Super-Regional Powerhouses Are Reshaping Financial Services*, Chicago, IL; London; Singapore: Irwin.

Stark, D. (2009), *The Sense of Dissonance: Accounts of Worth in Economic Life*, Princeton, NJ and Oxford: Princeton University Press.

Stiglitz, J. E. (2003), *The Roaring Nineties*, New York and London: Norton.

Swary, I. and Topf, B. (1992), *Global Financial Deregulation: Commercial Banking at the Crossroads*, Oxford: Blackwell.

Swire, P. P. (1999), 'Financial Privacy and the Theory of High-Tech Government Surveillance', in E. R. Litan and A. M. Santomero (eds): 391–442.

Sylla, R. (2002), 'United States Banks and Europe: Strategy and Attitudes', in S. Battilossi and Y. Cassis (eds): 53–73.

Sylla, R. and Wright, R. E. (2004), 'Networks and History's Generalizations: Comparing the Financial Systems of Germany, Japan, Great Britain, and the United States of America', *Business and Economic History On-Line*, 2, http://www.thebhc.org/BEH/04/syllaandwright.pdf.

Tett, G. (2009), *Fool's Gold*, New York: Free Press.

Thakor, A. V. (1999), 'Information Technology and Financial Services Consolidation', *Journal of Banking & Finance*, 23: 697–700.

Wallman, S. M. H. (1999), 'The Information Technology Revolution and Its Impact on Regulation and Regulatory Structure', in E. R. Litan and A. M. Santomero (eds): 206–27.

Werr, A. and Stjernberg, T. (2003), 'Exploring Management Consulting Firms as Knowledge Systems', *Organization Studies*, 24(6): 881–908.

Willcocks, L. P. and Lacity, M. C. (eds) (1998), *Strategic Sourcing of Information Systems*, Chichester: John Wiley & Sons.

Williams, R. H. (2000), 'All That Is Solid Melts into Air: Historians of Technology in the Information Revolution', *Technology and Culture*, 41: 641–668.

Yates, J. (1993), 'Coevolution of Information Processing Technology and Use: Interaction Between the Life Insurance and Tabulating Industries', *Business History Review*, 67: 1–51.

Yates, J. (2005), *Structuring the Information Age: Life Insurance and Technology in the Twentieth Century*, Baltimore and London: The Johns Hopkins University Press.

Yates, J. and Van Maanen, J. (eds) (2001), *Information Technology and Organizational Transformation: History, Rhetoric, and Practice*, London: Sage.

Zelizer, V. (1994), *The Social Meaning of Money: Pin Money, Paychecks, Poor Relief and Other Currencies*, New York: Basic Books.

2
The Eurodollar Revolution in Financial Technology: Deregulation, Innovation and Structural Change in Western Banking

Stefano Battilossi

> *In the world of finance, the impact of the Eurocurrency system is comparable to that of coke smelting in the development of iron and steel, the steam engine in the development of railways, and the computer in information processing.*
>
> T. M. Podolski, *Financial Innovation and the Money Supply* (London: Basil Blackwell, 1986): 113

Introduction

Modern financial theories based on the economics of information suggest that banks arise as a response to existing frictions in the process of acquiring information and making transactions. Bank intermediaries ameliorate such frictions through brokerage (which enhances the matching of borrowers and lenders by overcoming information asymmetries) and portfolio transformation (banks acting as delegated monitors and providing liquidity insurance). The way banks perform these functions – their 'financial technology' – changed dramatically in the 1970s on a global scale. We define financial technology as a body of knowledge that specifies the whole range of activities creating economic value in financial intermediation, encompassing product, process and organizational technologies. Financial innovations occur in each of these areas and improve the efficiency with which intermediaries perform their basic functions by expanding opportunities for risk sharing, lowering transaction costs and reducing asymmetric information and agency costs (Merton 1995: 463).

The transformations of the 1970s reversed four decades characterized by the absence of significant innovations in the banking industry, as well as by the pervasive regulation of the latter by the state – a regime of financial 'repression' or 'restriction' articulated in 'a set of policies, laws, regulation, taxes, distortions, qualitative and quantitative restrictions, which do not allow financial intermediaries to operate at their full technological potential' (Roubini and Sala-i-Martin 1995). An 'explosion of financial innovations', both in instruments and strategies, altered radically the features of financial decision making (Ross 1989: 541). At the same time, financial intermediaries began successfully to press in favour of a gradual withdrawal of the state as financial regulator. As a consequence, a twofold process of liberation of existing financial technology and a rapid shift forward of the frontier of financial technology characterized the two decades between the late 1960s and the early 1980s. How were financial innovation and financial deregulation related to one another? How did technological change, and in particular information and communication technologies originating mainly outside the financial sector, contribute to this epoch-making shift? And how did technological and institutional changes interact in reshaping the global financial structure?

We explore some of these issues by focusing on possibly the most important and far-reaching change in financial technology that took place in the 1970s: the rise of liability management (also referred to as the 'marketization' of banking), a process of innovation based on the development of wholesale interbank markets, both domestic and international. This innovation dramatically changed the concept of liquidity in banking, forced banks to implement totally new strategies of active liability marketing and required a new interactive banking management of the structure of assets and liabilities.

Such fundamental change originated in the emergence and explosive growth of so-called Eurocurrency (mostly Eurodollar) banking. The Eurodollar market was once highly controversial. Particularly during the period of financial instability from the late 1960s and lasting throughout the 1970s, the astounding expansion of the market raised fierce arguments of both theoretical and political relevance. Its capacity for creating potentially unlimited international liquidity, and transmitting inflationary pressures on a worldwide scale, came under severe scrutiny from both economists and politicians. The market was also blamed for its role as a source of funds for speculation and short-term capital movements, with destabilizing effects on the international monetary system. It was often regarded as a sort of 'unregulated juggernaut "out of control"' that undermined the national sovereignty of monetary authorities and increasingly frustrated their capacity to control domestic money supply. Such debate, however, seemed to generate more heat than light. The nature of the Eurodollar market was long considered an intriguing 'mystery story' (Machlup 1970).[1] Even 20 years after their first appearance, some argued that 'the size of the external, or Eurofinancial, markets is matched only by the aura of mystery and controversy they have generated', so that 'they continue to appear to be an enigma even to those who operate in them continually' (Dufey and Giddy 1978: 2). Over time however this aura of mystery, together with general concerns about the markets' unbridled expansion (and possible sudden contraction), gradually faded away, as did many of the old controversies. As Ralph Bryant later argued, the Eurodollar market has to be considered a key manifestation, but certainly not the only one, of increasing financial interdependence of national economies. In this sense, it contributed to exchange rate instability, transmission of inflation, increased the riskiness of financial intermediation and injured control over monetary and credit aggregates. Still it would be totally incorrect to identify Eurobanking as 'the villain chiefly responsible for these problems' (Bryant 1983: 14).

This chapter outlines the historical development of the Eurodollar market from its origins to the early 1980s and the implications of this for international banks of industrialized countries. Though the Eurodollar market was only one segment of the overall market for Eurocurrencies, its relative size, the dominant influence of its interest rate in determining the structure of Eurocurrency rates and its role as the core of Eurobusiness for a large majority of international banks in the 1960s and 1970s justify the choice of focusing on it. As a matter of fact, the dollar-denominated segment was permanently the largest one of the Eurocurrency market, and currency diversification by banks was a function of the degree of confidence in the dollar. Between 1964 and 1984 the Eurodollar market share (i.e. Eurodollars as a percentage of all Eurocurrencies) fluctuated within a range of 72 per cent and 84 per cent, recording a sizeable decline only after 1985 due to the deteriorating value of the dollar. Moreover, the Eurodollar rate and the dollar forward exchange rate have been demonstrated to be the pivotal factors that determined the whole spectrum of Eurocurrency rates.[2]

The chapter covers the initial phase of the 'Golden Age' of international banking (1960s–70s), brought to an end in 1981–3 by the global recession that followed the second oil shock, the debt crisis of developing countries and a shift of international finance away from bank intermediation towards financial markets (securitization). More specifically, the argument is that the development of the Eurodollar market has to be considered an evolutionary process that induced a structural change in Western banking. The first section defines Eurobanking by presenting a concise outline of its institutional evolution from an international interbank money market to a more complex banking activity involving interrelationships with the emerging international capital markets. The second section briefly reviews some key issues within the theoretical debate as to the nature of Eurobanking (the multiplier as opposed to the portfolio approach) and the implications of this for alternative explanations of the astounding growth rate of international financial intermediation. The third section elaborates on the relative importance of real-sector and institutional factors (international trade and business cycle, regulation and capital controls, arbitrage) in different phases of the market's history. The fourth section illustrates the role of the Eurodollar business as a factor of structural innovation in Western banking both at a systemic level (from regulated, oligopolistic, disintegrated banking systems towards a less regulated, competitive, integrated financial environment) and at a microeconomic level ('marketization' of banking, and asset and liability management). The fifth section concludes the chapter.

The Eurodollar technology: The rise of an international money market

In the financial jargon of the 1960s 'Eurodollar' became the popular name of dollar-denominated short-time wholesale deposits held by banks located outside the US – foreign branches and subsidiaries of US banks included – principally in European financial centres (hence the prefix 'Euro').[3] As such Eurodollars did not represent any significant financial product innovation: they were merely dollar time deposits that happened to be booked in banking offices outside the US. Nor was the practice of banking with foreign currency deposits new at all in the old continent. Operations in foreign currency deposits were well known in London before the First World War, and similar transactions denominated in sterling and dollars had been also negotiated in Berlin and Vienna in the late 1920s, before being brought abruptly to an end by the 1931 crisis.[4] Thanks to a gradual relaxation of foreign exchange controls during the 1950s, the practice of taking dollar deposits to finance international trade re-emerged in Western Europe; by 1960 some European banks were well known in international financial circles for actively engaging in bilateral interbank transactions in dollars.[5]

What was really innovative and unprecedented was the creation of a true international market for wholesale dollar deposits, which rapidly established itself as the centre of a network linking all major Western economies. It was after the general return to external convertibility of all major Western currencies in 1958 that the practice of trading in dollar time deposits gained momentum and scope. Technological innovations in data processing and communications (transactions were arranged over the telephone or by Telex) played a critical role in the process. Beyond the impact of technology, however, it was the rapid erosion of information barriers (so that all market participants could get all information available at low cost, and agreed on the implications of current information) and the consequent comparative advantages in transaction costs that made possible the evolution of trading from bilateral to multilateral, from correspondent banking to transaction banking. This led to the establishment of an almost perfectly efficient market.[6] In the initial stages, the information pooled by brokers in the City of London was vital, but soon large banks created autonomous units of dealers as a means of improving their ability to monitor the market's mood.[7]

As far as the market structure is concerned, prime depositors (also indicated as 'lenders') were large corporations (both US and non-US) with international and multinational activities, commercial banks located in main financial centres of the western hemisphere (including countries beyond the Iron Curtain and Arab countries),[8] central banks (mainly outside of Europe) and, limited to the early period of the market, international financial institutions such as the Basle-based Bank for International Settlements (BIS).[9] Final users (or 'borrowers') were mainly large international corporations, which used Eurodollar short-term facilities as an alternative to finance their international trade. Large commercial banks and other banking institutions located outside the US, mainly in Western Europe, played as intermediaries between depositors and borrowers. The City of London immediately emerged as the main trading hub. Here the initial dominance of merchant banks and British overseas banks declined rapidly. Due to the binding regulations (such as the imposition of an 8 per cent cash reserve ratio and a 28 per cent liquid assets ratio), UK clearing banks also found themselves with a structural disadvantage in Eurobanking until the 1971 banking reform, and had to enter the Eurodollar business through specialized wholesale subsidiaries and participation in consortium banks. By the late 1960s foreign branches or subsidiaries (including consortia banks) of major commercial banks from industrialized countries had already conquered the market leadership, with foreign branches of large American money-centre banks in a dominant position (Battilossi 2002; Ross 2002).[10]

As both depositors and borrowers were often resident in countries other than the country in which Eurobanks were located (although in London a sizeable portion of the business occurred among banking offices based in the City), Eurodollar banking is usually defined as external intermediation. This definition, officially adopted by the Bank for International Settlements and other institutions to provide a statistical representation of Eurocurrency aggregates, is to some extent analytically misleading, in that it suggests that Eurobanking is a kind of 'special' phenomenon, radically different from 'ordinary' banking. In fact, although Eurobanking was the emerging frontier of international financial intermediation from the 1960s, it originated from – and was closely linked to – traditional international banking, either cross-border or cross-currency, mainly channelled through the foreign exchange markets (Mayer 1985).[11] Moreover traditional international banking also expanded rapidly and kept providing the largest portion of actual means of international payments – that is, short-term credits for trade financing and hedging forward against exchange risk (McKinnon 1977: 4–5). As a consequence, 'there is no compelling reason for isolating one aspect of international banking and analyzing it independently of the rest of the nexus of financial relations linking nations together' (Bryant 1983: 10–11).[12]

Important facets of the Eurodollar market were its multi-tier structure and the large portion of business accounted for by interbank dealings. The tiering of the market reflected different creditworthiness and risk assigned by investors to different banks, with large commercial US banks and more generally dollar-based institutions (such as Canadian banks) in the top ranking positions as prime takers at marginally lower rates than second- and third-tiering banks. Tiering used to become more pronounced in times of liquidity strains or confidence crisis, such as in 1974 after the collapse of Bankhaus Herstatt (a German bank) and Franklin National Bank (a New York institution ranked seventeenth among US commercial banks).[13] A sizeable part of funds allocated in the Eurodollar market operated through interbank redepositing – sometimes also misleadingly termed 'pyramiding' – with very narrow spreads (between 0.125 per cent and 0.0625 per cent per annum equivalent) between 'bid' rates (the rate at which banks are ready to borrow in the market) and 'offer' rates (the rate at which banks offer to lend funds in the market). This meant that a chain of several banks, whether located in a major financial centre (such as London) or in different countries,

Figure 2.1 Eurodollar and interbank shares of total Eurocurrency market
Note: Dollar-denominated deposits and interbank liabilities as per cent of estimated gross size of all Eurocurrencies.
Source: Sarver 1988. Data from Morgan Guaranty Trust.

could serve as intermediary between original depositors and final borrowers. As shown in Figure 2.1, the incidence of interbank transactions on total Eurobanking grew from 30 per cent of the total Eurocurrency market, in the mid-1960s, to 50 per cent in 1980.[14]

The relative volume of interbank activity turned out to be even larger when figures were limited to BIS reporting countries. In the early 1980s about 70 per cent of foreign currency assets and liabilities (both within-border and cross-border) was accounted for by lending between banks. The figure would be slightly smaller (about 60 per cent) if measured on the base of the 'inside area' positions – that is, positions of reporting area banks vis-à-vis banks in major financial centres, which represented the 'hard core' of interbank market.[15] It is worth noting also that a substantial part of interbank business in the 1970s and 1980s was 'inter-office', as it took place between offices of the same bank: a practice that enabled large multinational banks to internalize the functions of the interbank market.[16]

The enlarging scope for interbank dealings provided the base for the emergence and the expansion of Eurocapital markets. Since the early 1970s, a rapidly increasing demand for medium- and long-term dollar loans by large international corporate and sovereign borrowers induced

Eurobanks to extend the maturity of part of their lending business.[17] Fixed-interest loans with medium-term maturity (2–3 years) provided by individual Eurobanks in the early phase of the Eurocredit market gave soon way to innovative bank products such as flexible-term loans with longer maturity (stretching up to 4–8 years). These credits were provided at floating rate on a roll-over basis (determined as a fix spread over the costs of funding in the market and adjusted every three or six months to prevailing short-term Eurodollar interbank rate, or London interbank offer rate [LIBOR]) by specialized institutions such as consortia banks or by international bank syndicates, sometimes under the coordination of merchant banks.[18] The Eurocredit market was closely linked to the Eurodollar market, since Eurobanks secured in the latter a large amount of funds used to finance their Euroloans portfolios. Occasionally, when short-term interest rates became higher than long-term rates, borrowers used to temporarily redeposit part of the proceeds of syndicated loans, pending use, in the Euromoney market. The Eurodollar market had also important links with the Eurobond market, where international bank syndicates engaged in managing, underwriting and placing bonds issued by corporate and sovereign borrowers.[19] In fact, investment banks, securities firms and commercial banks acting either as managers of new Eurobond issues or market makers of the secondary market financed part of their underwriting commitments by borrowing in the Eurodollar and other Eurocurrency markets.[20]

Understanding the new technology: Multiplier v. portfolio approach

From its origins to the early 1980s, and in spite of occasional and short-lived setbacks, international banking as a whole expanded at a breathtaking pace both in volume and scope (as shown in Figure 2.2).

Figures reported in Table 2.1 show that the gross size of the Eurocurrency market, traditionally measured as the outstanding external positions (i.e. foreign currency liabilities or assets vis-à-vis non-residents) of reporting banks in 15 OECD countries and other selected Eurocurrency offshore centres grew at an average annual compound rate of 26 per cent in the period from 1964 to 1985, passing from $20 billion to $2600 billion equivalent (at current prices and exchange rates).[21] Even when adjusted in order to allow for double-counting arising from interbank operations (i.e. growth of net size)[22] as well as the secular upward trend of inflation, these figures remain striking.[23]

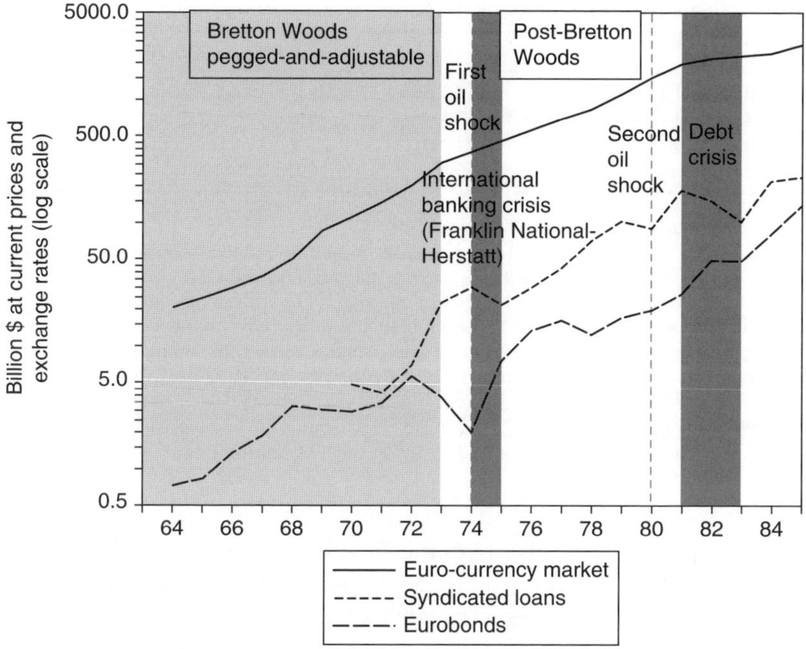

Figure 2.2 Emergence and expansion of Euromarkets, 1964–85
Note: Eurocurrency Market: estimated gross size of Eurocurrency Market including interbank deposits (foreign currency liabilities of banks from reporting countries vis-à-vis non residents: year-end amount outstanding).
Source: Sarver 1988. Data from Morgan Guaranty Trust Syndicated Euro Credits, Fisher 1988. Data from Euromoney; not available prior to 1970 Euroboards, Fisher 1988. Data assembled from statistical sources not always consistent.

Their growth rate largely outpaced that of domestic banking, and showed a slowdown only in the early 1980s as a consequence both of short-term factors (the global recession and the debt crisis of developing countries) and structural changes such as the adoption of more prudential attitudes by international banks and general displacement of international bank credit due to increasing 'securitization'.

What explains such remarkable performance? Why did banks expand their external intermediation so rapidly? This question became a key issue in the original Eurodollar debate. Early attempts to explain the growth of the Eurodollar market pointed to the existence of an endogenous credit creation process.[24] Theoretical investigation was urged, out of widespread concern over what was regarded as a potentially unconstrained ability of the market to create credit with global inflationary consequences.

Table 2.1 International banking, trade and world output

	1964–72	1972–80	1980–5	1964–85
International banking (net)[a]	33.6	26.7	12.9	25.8
International banking (gross)[b]	34.0	28.6	10.8	26.1
International trade[c]	12.0	21.2	0.4	12.4
World output[d]	9.6	15.0	4.7	10.4

Notes: Compound annual growth rate (per cent).

[a] BIS series for net size of Eurocurrency market (excluding interbank redepositing among banks in the reporting area) of Eurocurrency market; data from BIS. BIS reporting area included only G10 countries in the 1960s and early 1970s and was gradually extended to cover all European countries and US banks' branches in selected offshore centres.

[b] Morgan Guaranty series for gross size of Eurocurrency market (including interbank redepositing). Differs from the BIS series since it defines the reporting area to cover a larger number of countries and banks.

[c] International trade in goods and services (world excluding Soviet bloc); data from IMF.

[d] Gross domestic product (world excluding Soviet bloc); data from IMF.

Source: Bryant (1987): 22.

According to the multiplier hypothesis, Eurodollar growth was supposed to be a function of some credit or deposit multiplier because a proportion of funds lent out by banks to non-bank borrowers was redeposited with them. This implied that the Eurobanking system could be compared to a certain extent to a domestic banking system based on fractional reserves. This hypothesis however proved less than satisfactory, since it tended to misrepresent basic institutional features of Eurobanking and was unable to reach clear-cut conclusions. No Eurobanking system existed as such as a closed or autonomous system (since it was an open system linking national systems together), and Eurobanks used to hold reserves not with central banks but with other commercial banks. Moreover the excessive attention paid to original lenders and final non-bank borrowers meant that the critical importance of interbank market was overlooked. At the same time, empirical estimates of the actual base of the multiplier, and of the size of the multiplier itself, proved difficult and subject to large discrepancies. Finally, redepositing by non-banks suffered substantial leakage towards national systems – so that the multiplier, if any, could be in any case only a minor factor of the Euromarket's growth.[25]

Severe inconsistencies of multiplier models were mainly emphasized by supporters of a different view, the so-called portfolio approach. Moving along the lines drawn by Gurley and Shaw and Tobin, the 'new view' set an original theoretical framework in which banking (and non-banking) intermediaries and primary securities markets were seen to compete for deposits and loans by issuing liabilities and purchasing claims from borrowers. Thus their ability to expand their balance sheet (i.e. their stock of assets and liabilities) depended ultimately on the portfolio preferences of wealth-holders, influenced in turn by particular attributes (relative return, riskiness, liquidity) of the liabilities issued.[26] The portfolio approach has proved particularly helpful in shedding light on both the nature and the operating mechanism of Eurobanking. First, it has correctly emphasized that Eurodollars, as short-term yield-earning time deposits, did not represent 'money' in its narrowly defined sense (i.e. means of payment),[27] although like other money market assets with a high degree of liquidity they could be considered as 'near money' (close substitutes for money held in anticipation of payments and readily liquidated). Since Eurodollar deposits were close though imperfect substitutes of domestic deposits and money market assets, Eurobanks could expand their balance sheets by competing with other intermediaries and markets in attracting dollar funds from wealth-holders.[28] Thus credit expansion in the Eurodollar (external) market – as a time-deposit system fundamentally different from a checking account system – was made possible by a process of substitution of near money for money; a process in which a given stock of money increased in velocity. This occurred within a growing worldwide dollar-denominated credit market. As Gunter Dufey and Ian Giddy put it, the market was 'a growing slice of an expanding pie' (Dufey and Giddy 1978: 107–30; also Niehans 1982: 17–19).

Explaining Eurodollar innovation: Real factors v. deregulation

The strong theoretical appeal of the portfolio approach derives primarily from the fact that, by shifting attention towards institutional features of the system, it helped to bring to light new factors such as the interest rate linkages between domestic and external markets, the fundamental role of the Eurodollar market as a channel for international capital flows and the economic forces behind supply of deposits and demand for loans. As a consequence, explanations of the growth of the market have paid increasing attention to the impact of real-sector forces (business cycle, credit conditions) and to institutional factors, such as arbitrage and regulation, which affected the banks' behaviour in the market.

Real-sector-led explanations of the market's growth point to the expansion of international trade (and to the increasing multinationalization of industrial companies) as the main driver of international financial intermediation; and view cross-border financial activity as the financing counterpart of trade or intracompany transactions (Bryant

1987: 62–4). As a matter of fact, early theoretical interpretation of the Eurocurrency market also focused on trade influences (the need to maintain working balances in foreign currencies, and particularly in dollars for the financing of international trade), suggesting that high transaction costs involved in moving between domestic and foreign currencies had encouraged traders to hold balances denominated in international currencies. Subsequent econometric research provided further evidence of a relationship between Eurocurrency deposits and the growth of international trade, arguing that the international holdings of currencies were related to trade transactions. More specifically, Eurodollar deposits acted as substitutes for forward exchange contracts, since transaction cost advantages existed in making a large spot purchase of dollars and investing it in the Euromarkets at different maturities to coincide with payments abroad rather than making a number of forward contracts (Swoboda 1968; Makin 1972; also Johnston 1983: 76–81).

Among real-sector factors, large demand for Eurocredits by corporate (including state-owned) companies and sovereign borrowers with large investment programmes proved a driving force behind the expansion of the market from the late 1960s. A further shift followed the oil shocks of 1973 and 1979 due to increasing demand for external finance by governments of industrialized and developing countries, matched by petrodollar recycling (the channelling through the Euromarkets of the cash surplus of oil-exporting countries).[29] (See Figure 2.2.) As far as Eurobanking can be considered a satisfactory proxy for international banking as a whole, however, the growth rate of its net size (i.e. excluding interbank redepositing) also demonstrates that international financial intermediation expanded at a remarkably faster pace than world output and international trade from 1964 to 1985 (see Table 2.1).[30] Some other factors have therefore to be considered.

Among these, all studies dealing with the economics of the Euromarket have emphasized the lack of regulatory constraints as a crucial factor in its expansion (Dufey and Giddy 1978: 133–5; Johnston 1983: 86–7; Bryant 1987: 66–8). Both in the US and in Western Europe domestic banking was subject to tight regulation – either imposed by national monetary and supervisory authorities, mainly in the form of discriminatory credit allocation, reserve requirements, interest rate ceilings on deposits and loans, prudential capital-to-asset ratios, barriers to entry and market segmentation – or enforced by private interbank cartel arrangements. Compared with the modest opportunities for growth offered by domestic intermediation, the Eurodollar market in London was conspicuous for its totally unregulated and competitive nature: British monetary authorities guaranteed free access and allowed the foreign currency business of both UK and foreign banks to develop outside binding regulations imposed on the domestic (sterling) sector, as a means of reviving the role of the City as an international entrepôt centre.[31] Moreover in spite of the gradual relaxation of exchange controls after the return to external convertibility in 1958 (which actively contributed to the booming Eurodollar market), the widespread presence of capital controls – until 1973 in the US and West Germany, until 1979 in the UK and well beyond the 1980s in France and Italy[32] – imposed additional costs on international financial transactions[33] and limited to some extent the expansion of banks' international business. Similar regulatory discrimination also had an impact on different segments of the Euromarkets. The absence of government and foreign exchange authorities controls, a less detailed offering prospectus, tolerance for a scarce attitude to disclosure and fiscal exemptions, together with low interest rates and underwriting costs and substantial economies in transaction costs (relative to raising capital piecemeal in each individual country), prove critical factors that accounted for the rapid expansion of Eurocapital markets.[34]

During the 1960s and 1970s Eurobanking, harmed by regulatory constraints when conducted from home-based head offices, was therefore increasingly attracted into entrepôt financial centres such as London and Luxembourg or small offshore centres. Banks interested in an internationally oriented and growth-oriented strategy successfully circumvented domestic regulation and tax regimes by developing a multinational structure, thus increasingly moving external intermediation – which turned out to be sometimes purely domestic intermediation in disguise[35] – out of their domestic jurisdiction (see Table 2.2).

Also related to the growing internationalization of banking was an increasing presence of foreign banks in New York and other US banking centres. This was mainly motivated by their desire to gain direct access to the US domestic market. Additional incentives were provided before 1978 by a regulatory discrimination in favour of foreign banks relative to US banks.[36] These were reinforced by the introduction in 1981 of International Banking Facilities, which lifted regulatory constraints on the international business of banks in the US (either domestic or foreign), for the first time enabling New York to compete with London in attracting Eurobanking (Lees 1976; Buttrill White 1982).

The overseas expansion of American banks was particularly striking. Only eight US banks were operating overseas branches in 1960; this had risen to 163 by 1984.[37] Multinationalization of American banking was actively, though involuntarily, promoted by US government and

Table 2.2 Foreign banks in selected OECD countries, 1960–81

Host country	1960 banks[a]	1973 banks[a]	1981 banks[a]	1960 assets[b]	1973 assets[b]	1981 assets[b]
United Kingdom	51	129	229	Ö	Ö	60.2
West Germany	24	77[c]	148	0.5	1.4[c]	3.6
France	33	76	131	7.2	14.1	17.4
Italy	2	15	38	Ö	Ö	2.3
Belgium	14[d]	38	56	8.2[d]	28.6	46.8
The Netherlands	—	27	40	Ö	Ö	18.0
Luxembourg[e]	3	56	102	8.0	77.6	85.5
Switzerland	8[f]	99	107	Ö	11.4	11.6
USA	—	124	459	Ö	3.4	13.4
Japan[f]	34	38	94	Ö	1.6	2.5

Notes: [a] Number of foreign banking organizations operating in the country through branches or majority-controlled subsidiaries (year-end data).
[b] Foreign banks' assets as a per cent of total assets of all banks operating in the selected countries.
[c] 1970.
[d] 1958.
[e] Belgian-owned banks excluded.
[f] Foreign branches only.
Source: Pecchioli, 1983.

monetary authorities through monetary policy and balance-of-payments control programs. During the credit crunches of 1966 and 1969, the use of binding regulation (in the form of interest rate ceiling on interest rates payable on time deposits and negotiable Certificates of Deposit (CDs) – the so-called Regulation Q) induced American banks to resort to the Eurodollar market through their London-based and overseas branches in order to channel these funds back to the US.[38] By doing so, they successfully opposed disintermediation threats brought home both by Eurobanks and new competing domestic money markets (such as that on commercial paper). In the same period heavy bidding for Eurodollars by US banks was also a consequence of rising demand for Eurodollar loans from US corporations' subsidiaries in Europe, since voluntary and mandatory capital control programs enforced by the Johnson administration limited their parents' ability to transfer funds out of the US and curbed US banks' lending abroad. Such factors exerted a major expansionary impact on the Eurodollar market, which accounts for its extraordinary growth rate in the second half of the 1960s (Kane 1983: 28–50; De Cecco 1987).[39]

Demand from US banks and corporations however rapidly declined after 1970 when US monetary authorities relaxed monetary policy, discouraged Eurodollar borrowing by imposing marginal reserve requirements on borrowing by parent banks from their overseas branches and enhanced the competitiveness of the domestic market by lifting Regulation Q ceilings on large deposits and CDs. Moreover the shift towards financial liberalism promoted by the Nixon administration led in 1974 to the removal of the capital controls introduced in the 1960s.[40] However, in spite of a marked decline in the forces that had fostered the market's growth, Eurobanking kept expanding. This apparently paradoxical result shifts our attention to other forces (beyond real-sector developments and regulation) of critical relevance for the market's growth as well as for its working: the structure of interest rates and the arbitrage process.

Historical series give empirical evidence of strong covariance of interest rates in the Eurodollar market and in the US. Even more significantly, the Eurodollar rate also commanded a permanent premium both on bank time deposits and relevant money market instruments, as shown in Figure 2.3, which illustrates the trend of Eurodollar and relevant US

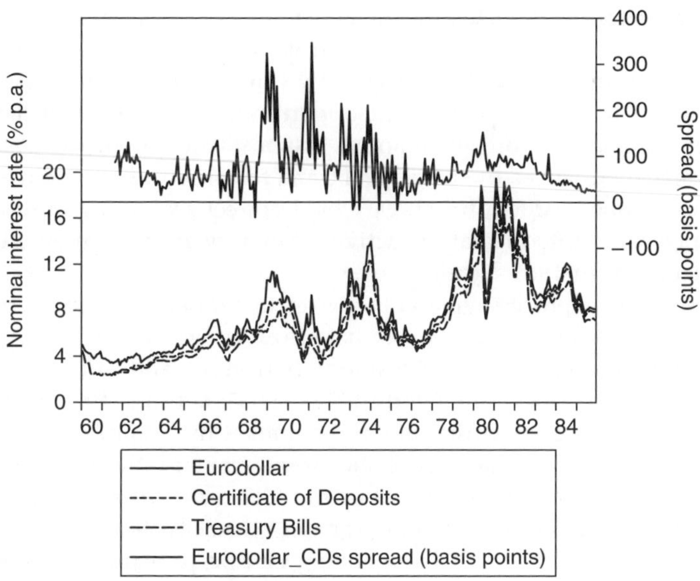

Figure 2.3 Eurodollar and US money market rates
Note: Monthly nominal interest rates (per cent per annum) of three-month Eurodollar deposits in London, US commercial banks' three-month CDs and three-month US Treasury Bills.
Source: OECD Monetary and Financial Statistics.

money market rates and the nominal differential between LIBOR and the nominal interest rate on three-month CDs in the US.[41]

This close concordance of Eurodollar and US rates variations suggests the existence of a causal relationship between monetary conditions in the US and the Eurodollar interest rate.[42] This can be partly accounted for by the relative size of the US money market and monetary aggregates as compared to the Eurodollar market, and the absence of currency risk. Recent literature on the economics of the Euromarkets however agrees that both premium and covariance can be ascribed to increasingly efficient arbitrage.[43]

It seems clear, then, that the revolutionary impact of innovations in communication technology upon banking must be stressed time and again. The technology-led revolution in the delivery of financial services (information processing and transmission, confirmation of transactions, electronic funds transfer and accounting) critically contributed to the reduction of economic distances between national financial systems. This dramatically enhanced responsiveness to opportunities for cross-currency and cross-border arbitrage, both on the part of suppliers of funds (cross-border and currency ladling in search for higher expected yields on foreign financial assets) and final users (borrowing funds internationally to profit from more favourable loan terms than those available domestically).[44] Banks were particularly well positioned to exploit such profit opportunities as major vehicles for information about foreign financial systems. This privileged position was further enhanced by the general trend towards multinational banking (mentioned earlier), which gave banks direct access to information, arbitrage and intermediation activities in foreign and international markets (Bryant 1987: 64–6).

The arbitrage process represents the key factor of supply-and-demand models of the Eurodollar market based on interest parity theory and portfolio adjustment by depositors, borrowers and intermediaries (Marston 1974; Dufey and Giddy 1978: 130–5; Gibson 1989: 49–67).[45] Such models emphasize the role of the market in the process of financial integration as a channel for short-term capital movements as well as the role of the Eurodollar rate as the focal price in an increasingly interdependent financial system (Argy and Hodjera 1973).[46] In fact the emergence and growth of Eurobanking can be principally accounted for by the emergence of new international arbitrage channels. For dollar-holding investors (either US or non-US resident), an American bank or the US money-markets were natural outlets for their funds; and for dollar borrowers, an American (or at least dollar-based) bank was the natural source of lending. Thus, apart from depositors in search of anonymity for political, fiscal or other reasons – and assuming that factors such as familiarity, business hours and communications played a marginal role in a market where transactors were large banks, public entities and international corporations with advanced communication technology – Eurobanks had to offer competitive conditions in order to compete with US banks. This implied offering higher returns on dollar time deposits (thus increasing the attractiveness of Eurodeposits relative to US time deposits and other money market assets) and charging lower interest on Eurodollar loans relative to standard lending rates (prime rate) in the US.

As a consequence, Eurobanks operated permanently on a narrower spread than banks in the US domestic market and in most parts of national markets. As has been pointed out, profit in interbank business could be as small as 1/8 of one per cent or even less, although it was substantially higher in medium- or long-term lending to non-bank borrowers. Still Eurobanking was profitable due to its institutional features. Eurodollar borrowing by banks was in fact exempted from reserve requirements and other regulatory constraints; administrative costs were low (because of economies of scale) and transaction and information costs only marginal, thanks to communication technology and an efficient brokerage system.[47] Eurobanks were therefore prepared to shift most benefits of lower operating costs to depositors and borrowers in the form of higher returns on deposits and lower rates charged on loans respectively.

The ability to attract depositors and borrowers out of the US domestic market into the external market through arbitrage channels, was therefore the key factor in the continued expansion of Eurobanks' business. Under favourable conditions and in the absence of binding capital controls, moreover, they could also induce cross-currency arbitrage, attracting depositors and borrowers from non-US markets in search for higher returns and better conditions than those obtainable domestically. A sizeable though minor part of Eurodeposits came in fact from Western European investors switching out of domestic currencies into dollar positions when the differential between the Eurodollar rate and domestic rates, adjusted for covering against exchange rate risk, proved profitable.[48]

Beyond the creation of new arbitrage channels for depositors and borrowers, however, Eurobanks have also to be analysed as arbitrageurs themselves. A number of analytical studies have suggested arbitrage induced by banks' portfolio behaviour (rather than by depositors) accounts for the covariation of Eurodollar and US rates.[49] As a matter of fact empirical analysis of the determination of the Eurodollar rate demonstrated that, in the absence of restrictions on free flow of capital, Eurocurrency rates have been tied within narrow margins to the level of US money market rates by the arbitrage activity of US banks in the efficient interbank market. An incentive for Eurodollar arbitrage was provided by the fact that Eurodeposits, as reserve-free substitutes for domestic bank deposits, allowed banks to reduce their overall holdings of reserve (in a fashion similar to other non-bank innovations such as repurchase agreements, money market funds and commercial paper), thus providing 'avenues for the growth of credit that are not directly constrained by the supply of reserves to US banks' (Frydl 1982: 13). Arbitrage mainly took the form of balance sheet-expanding outward arbitrage, which implied raising funds in the US CDs market (or in the commercial paper market through bank holding companies) and moving them offshore to invest them at a slightly higher return with Eurobanks, until domestic and external interest rates adjusted to remove arbitrage incentives or banks reached internal arbitrage constraints (such as perceived risk, capital-to-asset and return-on-assets ratios).[50] Eurodollar arbitrage made the domestic and external dollar money market increasingly integrated and efficient, thus tending to limit the interest rate differential.[51]

The existence of a large interest rate differential between Eurodollar and domestic time deposits for long periods in the history of the market, especially in the second half of the 1960s and in the early 1970s, as Figure 2.3 shows, may cast doubts on the efficiency of bank arbitrage in maintaining interest parity. However other factors have to be taken into account. One is the impact of US capital controls and bank regulation up to the early 1970s. In fact during the 1966 and 1969 credit crunches New York banks borrowed heavily on the Eurodollar market through their European branches, whereas Regulation Q ceilings prevented free adjustment of domestic CDs rates to rising Eurodollar rates (Formuzis 1973; Marston 1974). Eurodollar arbitrage was moreover impaired by capital controls that prohibited US banks from exporting abroad funds raised domestically, and tight credit conditions in the US account also for the Eurodollar rate remaining mainly above prime rate until the early 1970s. Unusually large Eurodollar differentials therefore reflected increased market segmentation. After this exceptional period, however, easing of monetary policy by the Fed and the removal by the Nixon administration of Regulation Q ceilings on CDs in 1970 made the US domestic market more competitive. With gradual relaxation of capital controls (lifted at the end of 1973), interest rate linkages between the internal and the external sectors were strengthened, US banks turned into net lenders to the market and the arbitrage process became much more efficient, responding even to marginal changes in liquidity and interest rate. Figures in Table 2.3 suggest that this was reflected in a clear trend towards a structural reduction in the interest differential between the Eurodollar and the US money markets (Marston 1995: 50–7).

In explaining the Eurodollar differential, changes in perceived risk have also to be taken into account. Depositors used to consider Eurodollar deposits structurally riskier than US deposits, since they were uninsured, held by banks with no direct access to the Fed discount window and located outside the legal jurisdiction of the US. Moreover riskiness varied from bank to bank: deposits placed with European branches of large American banks were almost perfect substitutes for domestic deposits, whereas the 'tiering' of the market reflected differences in risk associated with different categories of banks. Finally, perceived risk was also influenced by rumours of government intervention (mostly in the form of additional regulation, since vulnerability to sovereign risk stemming from restricted transferability or blocking of repayments was generally regarded as unlikely), confidence crisis – such as the already mentioned episodes of 1974 involving Herstatt Bank and Franklin National Bank – and increasing instability of the international monetary system (such as the rising concerns about dollar exchange rate deterioration throughout the 1970s).[52]

Over time however changes in the perception of Eurodollar risk by agents may have contributed to a structural reduction of differential. While rapid dissemination of both theoretical and practical knowledge of the Euromarkets eroded information barriers to arbitrage, the resilience of the market itself throughout the financial turmoil of the late

Table 2.3 Interest differential between the Eurodollar[a] and US markets[b]

	Pre capital control (1962–5)	**Capital control (1966–73)**	**Post capital control (1974–85)**
Number of observations	48	96	144
Average differential (in basis points)	66	103	66

Notes: [a] LIBOR on three-month Eurodollar deposits.
[b] Nominal interest rate on three-month US CDs.
Source: OECD Monetary and Financial Statistics.

1960s and early 1970s, in spite of recurring worries within international banking circles about the possibility of its sudden contraction, disappearance or collapse, allowed depositors to gradually downgrade the additional perceived risk. After the crisis episodes of 1974 raised the alarm, most banks autonomously upgraded internal controls and extended their responsibility for branches and affiliates' exposure under the 'principle of corporate liability' typical of the US legal tradition.[53] At the same time, as a result of closer cooperation among central banks within the BIS – epitomized in the Basle declaration of 1974 on lender-of-last-resort assistance to the Euromarkets in the case of liquidity crisis, and the 1975 supervisory guidelines known as the 'Basle Concordat' – monetary authorities enforced improved monitoring and tighter prudential supervision.[54] After two decades of development, large liquidity (as a direct function of size), increased integration, closer substitutability and the full manifestation of the information effect (i.e. the fact that market participants had to complete a learning curve to adjust their portfolio strategies) made Euromarkets even more attractive to both depositors and borrowers, who perceived the risk of conducting business in the external markets as being only marginally greater than in national markets. This is likely to have contributed to a secular decline in the interest-rate incentive required to attract depositors and borrowers from the domestic to the external market, thus making the arbitrage schedule more elastic.[55]

Eurodollars and structural innovation in banking: The shift to liability management

The revolutionary impact of the Eurodollar market on Western financial systems can hardly be overemphasized. Eurobanking brought epochal structural change to banking in industrialized countries. In a traditional world of closed and disintegrated national systems dominated by regulation, oligopolistic structure and collusive behaviour, barriers to entry, market segmentation and lack of innovation, suddenly a fast-growing unregulated enclave of wholesale business emerged based on international integration, free access, keen market competition and technological as well as financial innovation. Eurobanking therefore represented, to large commercial banks of Western countries that generally enjoyed little scope for domestic expansion, an unprecedented and largely unexpected opportunity for growth. This opportunity however brought with it also major challenges.

Up to the mid-1960s, risk implied in engaging in Eurodollars remained low and Eurocurrency banking was a fairly simple business that could easily be run by banks through their traditional international functions, normally a small department that offered services related to trade finance and dealt with correspondent banks. Over time commercial banks learnt how to use the international interbank market for domestic purposes too; that is, to adjust their reserve position in domestic currency in order to back loans to corporate customers (both in national or foreign currency), to support their traditional foreign-exchange banking activities and make these less dependent upon national regulations, and to undertake covered interest arbitrage in the foreign exchange market (i.e. covering in the Eurodollar market forward transactions undertaken on behalf of corporate customers). Eurodollars were also increasingly used by banks in forward calculations, thus enhancing their ability to deal in foreign exchange transactions. Currency risk remained modest, and so was liquidity risk, due to the prevalence of interbank business and short-term self-liquidating transactions with non-bank borrowers (McKinnon 1977: 17–18; Davis 1979: 82–6).[56]

The 1970s however brought home an abrupt shift in riskiness. Increasing multinationalization implied the implementation of efficient procedures to monitor and control a growing number of foreign branches and subsidiaries usually responsible for sizeable business, although leaving them adequate scope for independent decisions. Volatile exchange rates increased currency risk, as a larger share of the balance sheet being denominated in foreign currencies created scope for exchange fluctuations to cause sizeable losses. This forced banks to develop more sophisticated procedures for monitoring and controlling currency exposures. Even more importantly, a secular rise in the level of interest rates, compounded by unusual instability, also sharpened interest risk as sudden fluctuations in the cost of funding could severely affect profits from loans of longer maturity at fixed rates.

At the same time, the emergence of the Eurocredit business, the fall in lending margins (caused by the reversal of US banks' borrowing which left the market with high liquidity and excess banking capacity), keener competition, a general lengthening of credit maturities and the expansion and diversification of medium-term lending to sovereign borrowers contributed to substantially change the pattern of the Euromarkets' activity. By funding loans of long contractual maturity through short-term deposits, as well as mismatching or short-funding rollover deposit maturities in order to increase the profit yielded, international banks found themselves increasingly engaged in net liquidity creation (Kane 1983: 101–3; also Heinevetter 1979). All investigations of London Eurobanks, though adopting different methodologies, have provided clear evidence – briefly summarized in Table 2.4 – of increasing positive maturity transformation, and hence of net liquidity production.[57]

As a consequence, growth-oriented commercial banks were urged to develop new functions of liquidity management. Since Eurodollar borrowing by banks (apart from US prime-takers) usually relied upon small core deposits and was extensively financed in the interbank market, liquidity management functions on a cash flow basis became vital to ensure that maturing deposits could be repaid from the proceeds of maturing assets or replaced by fresh borrowing. Reliable access to wholesale market funding became a crucial factor for Eurobanking: in this phase, therefore, 'marketization'[58] meant essentially developing an efficient dealing room function in order to fund the expansion of international business through managing Eurodollar liabilities. At the same time banks proved reluctant to absorb the interest rate risk associated with rate volatility. The introduction of marginal pricing in roll-over lending at floating rates was an effective response in terms of active asset management; it adjusted assets to potential liabilities and separated interest risk from liquidity risk – although shifting interest risk to borrowers could harm the latter's ability to service their debts, and thus eventually turn into greater credit and default risk for banks (though shared with all participants in the syndicates) (Harrington 1987: 46–8).

The new concept of banking based on managed liabilities was bound to prove a far-reaching structural innovation. Unlike in traditional banking, where liability management was confined to a few long-run strategic decisions, banking in the Eurodollar system urged banks to implement totally new strategies for actively marketing liabilities and funding their growth by tapping wholesale financial markets. This implied a radical change in the nature of bank liquidity. The traditional

Table 2.4 Maturity analysis of all London banks

	< 8d	8d–<1m	1m–<3m	3m–<6m	6m–<1y	1y–<3y	=/>3y
	liabs–claims	liabs–claims	liabs–claims	liabs–claims	liabs–claims	liabs–claims	liabs–claims
1973[a]	19.1–14.9	19.5–18.8	26.2–24.8	20.9–20.9	8.8–8.2	2.5–4.8	3.1–7.8
1980[a]	21.1–16.3	18.9–15.3	27.9–23.1	19.7–16.7	7.5–7.4	3.2–6.6	1.7–14.6
1985[a]	22.4–16.4	21.0–16.4	27.2–22.1	16.9–14.4	6.2–6.5	2.6–6.8	3.8–17.4

Note: 'd' = days; 'm' = month; 'y' = year.
Liabilities and claims by maturity as per cent of total liabilities and assets in foreign currencies[a] year-average.
Source: Gibson 1989; data from Bank of England Quarterly Bulletin.

concept of a portfolio of liquid assets (reserves, government securities) that could be turned into cash at short notice and on predictable terms (by redemption, sale, or use as collateral for borrowing) was increasingly integrated by a new concept of liquidity based on issuing new liabilities to raise cash in financial markets. In Eurobanking the principle of a new interactive banking management of the structure of assets and liabilities found its first materialization. Eurobanking can therefore be considered the initial breakthrough in a transition towards an integrated management system based on matching assets and liabilities as to maturities, currencies and interest rates. Although in the 1960s–70s this process was mainly limited to international business of top commercial banks of industrialized countries, in recent periods bank intermediation undertaken on market-determined terms became an emergent feature of domestic financial systems.[59]

American banks pioneered this new way of banking. Eurodollar borrowing by US banks in the late 1960s was a pioneering experience of liability management, although the revival of the Federal funds market in the 1950s and the emergence of the market for bank CDs and commercial paper in the early 1960s can be regarded as equally crucial innovations (Kane 1979; Hester 1981). However it was the deepening and globalizing of the interbank market that made it possible for such structural change to have global implications. Eurodollar interbank trading – the efficiency of which was greatly enhanced in the 1970s by the establishment of international, interconnected private clearing systems such as CHIPS and SWIFT, and new advanced information services offered to interbank traders by Reuters and Telerate (Sarver 1988: 207–21) – performed four critical functions that allowed the market to absorb external shocks and continue to expand:

1 Liquidity smoothing: The stock of interbank liquid assets acted as a buffer between the inflow and outflow of funds from deposits and loans, thus reducing transaction costs by economizing on the volume of precautionary balances; Eurobanks held in fact very small reserves (in the form of negotiable assets), sometimes supplemented by stand-by facilities from US banks.
2 Liquidity transfer: As deposits of non-bank suppliers were channelled mainly to large banks of high name and credit standing, the latter acted as main intermediaries of the rest of the interbank system.
3 Currency transfer: This enabled banks to match the currency composition of their assets and liabilities through interbank trading – an

important function in the light of innovative bank products such as multicurrency trade facilities and Eurocredits with multicurrency options.

4 Finally, global liquidity distribution, which compensated excess demands and supplies between the Eurocurrency centres and a large network of local markets – turning the Eurodollar and Eurocurrency markets into a true global phenomenon.

(BIS 1983: 9–17; Johnston 1983: 98–103)

Conclusion

Between 1960 and 1980 international finance went through a true revolutionary process. This chapter contends that the emergence of Eurodollar banking lies at the very heart of such epoch-making structural change in financial technology, and attempts to disentangle the 'prime movers' behind it. Usually technological change, especially in the field of information and communication, is given a key role among the determinants of recent changes in the financial structure, mainly due to its impact on transactions costs and information asymmetries (Mishkin and Strahan 1999). This chapter finds that the Eurodollar story is no exception in this respect: there is little doubt that the fast growth of the international money market would have been impossible without the fall in transaction and communication costs and information barriers allowed by the emergence of a new global information and communication infrastructure. The key development from this point of view was certainly the spread of Telex networks as the main medium of intra- and inter-firm communication. Telex increased the speed and volume of transactions among international banks and favoured the erosion of information asymmetries between market participants. Together with later developments such as electronic storage and transmission of data, the global communication network was at the roots of new management information systems that enhanced both speed and volume in the transmission and processing of information within business organizations, both banks and non-banks. From the late 1960s, these technologies enhanced the emergence of new forms of business intelligence and management through which both financial intermediaries and corporate organizations increasingly monitored liquidity and took decisions about managing risk and raising capital on a transnational or even global scale. Beyond this first-order impact, information and communication technologies also helped to increase the liquidity and marketability of financial products related to the Eurodollar system, and favoured competition among financial intermediaries, which also had an impact on the growth of the market.

This chapter suggests, however, that beyond purely technological factors, institutional changes were the critical elements that made Eurodollar banking such a revolutionary innovation. In this respect, regulatory arbitrage was a key element in the process of internationalization of financial intermediaries. Likewise international asymmetries in capital and exchange controls, as well as in monetary policy-making, created huge and systematic profit opportunities from cross-border and cross-currency arbitrage in the money markets. This eventually generated the most radically innovative characteristic of Eurodollar banking, namely the development of active liability management. This structural change was bound to have profound implications, too, for the conduct of monetary policy, as it played a role in undermining the ability of monetary authorities to control – and even measure – monetary aggregates, and fostered the transition to inflation targeting as main monetary policy rule.

From the 1980s the process of financial innovation set in motion by the Eurocurrency system gained further momentum. The debt crisis of developing countries and the global economic recession paved the way to a marked slowdown in Eurocurrency banking growth rate. Many banks were then thought to have reached a ceiling in the internationalization of their assets and liabilities portfolio, especially in the light of repeated warnings by supervisory authorities against excessive reduction of capital ratios. The removal of capital controls as well as more efficient arbitrage and ever-intense competition further reduced the already narrow margins of Eurobanking, while demand for Eurocredits was declining relative to emerging securitization (Johnston 1980; Ball and Davies 1984; Campbell 1984). As a consequence, whereas in the 1960s and 1970s liability management had been mainly 'asset driven' (i.e. liabilities were managed to allow banks to expand asset portfolios), in the 1980s banks abandoned their strong growth-oriented strategies. A more selective attitude towards profitability and asset quality was then accompanied by a diversification of funding sources to reinforce the capital component of banks' liability side (floating-rate notes, note issuance facilities). Innovative strategies were also pursued that aimed at exploiting fee-generating business with no expansion of balance sheet, engaging in dealing of derivatives (such as currency and interest swaps) or assisting customers in their issues of Eurocommercial paper and Euronotes with syndicated and backup facilities, stand-by credit lines, guarantees (i.e. commitment banking). Moreover direct use of financial derivatives enabled banks to hedge more efficiently against price risk through off-balance sheet operations. Eurodollar contracts quickly became the most significant instruments traded in Chicago and London in terms of open-interest positions, and were also the contracts in which banks participated most actively. Both US and non-US banks became used to taking net long positions (net purchases) in Eurodollar futures to hedge against their acceptance of Eurodollar deposits as a more efficient substitute for interbank transactions, mainly because futures positions were not reflected in the banks' balance sheets, thus reducing the constraint imposed on banks by market and regulatory constraints on capital ratios (Frankel 1984; Bullock 1987).[60] These later developments in financial engineering, directly related to new information and communication technologies, are usually regarded as the 'core' of the financial revolution of the late twentieth century. This chapter argues that the revolution started much earlier and was driven less by technological factors than by institutional changes.

Notes

1. For a history of the early period of the Eurodollar market and a profile of its institutional features see Einzig 1964; Clendenning 1970; Bell 1973; Little 1975; and Mendelsohn 1980.
2. Marston 1976 provided evidence that bank arbitrage tended to keep Eurocurrency interest rates at interest rate parity with respect to forward exchange rates – that is, non-dollar Eurocurrency deposits can be regarded as covered Eurodollar deposits (i.e. Eurodollar deposits covered forward by swap contracts). A forward swap involves a purchase of spot dollars against non-dollar currency and a sale of dollars forward.
3. Maturities were ranging from call to one or more years, the standard maturity being three months. Minimum size of each deposit was in the region of US$ 1 million. It is worth emphasizing that the prefix 'Euro' is partly misleading. Although banks dealing with dollar deposits outside the US were, for the most part, located in Western Europe, a sizeable Eurodollar business was carried out from the very beginning by banks in Canada, Japan and the Middle East (i.e. Beirut financial centre). In the 1970s the importance of other Eurocurrency financial centres outside Europe, such as Singapore (the 'Zurich of Asia', where the bulk of the Asian-dollar market was located), Hong Kong, Manila and offshore centres (Nassau, Cayman Islands, Panama, Bermuda) grew rapidly.
4. Early references to such transactions are in Einzig 1964: 3–4; for an historical analysis see Cottrell and Stone 1989. These transactions can be regarded as the most straightforward historical antecedents of the Eurocurrency system, but their scale was too small to influence foreign exchange and money markets in London and New York, or the international financial system.

5. Holmes and Klopstock 1960; Altman 1961, 1963. The latter reported information from discussions held with central and private bankers in all the main financial centres of Europe.
6. On transaction costs in the Euromarkets, see Agmon and Barnea 1977; Frenkel and Levich 1975, 1977.
7. Apart from allowing banks to economize substantially, avoiding large information and transaction costs (especially in periods of increased volatility of interest rates), brokers make it possible for banks to approach the market on their own terms and to maintain anonymity in the early stages of the dealing (which was particularly helpful for the placement of deposits of unusual size and maturity). See BIS 1983: 7–9.
8. The well-known story goes that since the late 1940s Soviet bloc countries (including China) moved their dollar balances from New York to banks in London and Paris in order to avoid any risk of 'freezing'. The same happened with dollar balances of Arab countries after the Eisenhower administration froze assets held in the US by countries involved in the Suez episode of 1956.
9. On the BIS role see Toniolo 2005: 452–5.
10. Merchant banks and overseas banks used to claim the merit for having pioneered the Eurodollar business in the late 1950s (see Fry 1970 on George Bolton, chairman of Bolsa), and indeed Eurodollar dealing was known in the City of London's financial circles as 'the merchants' market'. However Schenk (1998) provided evidence that one British clearing bank took dollar deposits since at least the mid-1950s.
11. Cross-border business implied banking in domestic currency with non-residents (e.g. British banks using sterling facilities to finance international trade of European customers). Cross-currency business was banking in foreign currencies with residents (e.g. Italian banks using dollar facilities to finance international trade of their domestic customers).
12. Data assembled by Bryant (1983) for 15 industrial countries show that Eurocurrency assets (claims on foreign residents denominated in foreign currencies) accounted for 56 per cent of total claims with international characteristics in the early 1980s.
13. In November 1974 the nine levels of tiering included: (1) four prime US banks, (2) the rest of the top US banks, (3) second-tier US banks from major financial centres, (4) Canadian and some minor West Coast US banks, (5) London clearing banks and regional US banks, (6) wholly owned US banks in Europe, (7) consortium banks, (8) Italian banks, (9) Japanese banks. See Sarver 1988: 28–30.
14. This is measured as the difference between gross and net size of the market estimated by *World Financial Markets*, published by Morgan Guaranty Trust of New York.
15. Such figures need some qualification, in that they include not only pure interbank activity but also transactions that are not arranged in the interbank money market (such as credit granted among banks), and, as mentioned earlier, 'inter-office' business. Moreover the magnitude of interbank relative to non-bank business is overestimated due to the fact that non-bank transactions giving rise to interbank deals may not appear on the banks' balance sheet (such as in the case of a forward foreign exchange sale to a non-bank

customer, while the bank may hedge the risk arising from the forward sale through lending and borrowing in the interbank market). See BIS 1983: 17–22. A different study (Ellis 1981) found a rather constant percentage, around 70 per cent, for the period 1973–80.

16. Some large, multinational banks were reported to privilege inter-office business as a general rule, resorting to the interbank market only when they could obtain a better rate. Other banks concentrated their interbank business at a few dealing branches or offices located in major financial centres (to which other branches direct funds) in order to centralize control of the business. BIS 1983: 15–17.
17. Most Eurocredits (over 90 per cent) used to be denominated in dollars, at least initially, in the 1960s and 1970s. However in some cases contracts gave borrowers the right of choosing other currencies for each rolling-over period, provided that banks were able to obtain the currencies in the market for the maturities required.
18. In fact Eurobanks committed themselves to providing borrowers with a succession of short-term loans over a medium-term period: see Mendelsohn 1980: 71–86. For financial innovations related to the emergence of the Eurocredit market, see Dufey and Giddy 1981.
19. Eurobonds were bonds mainly denominated in dollars and Deutsche Marks and placed by international bank syndicates with investors in different European countries. See Kerr 1984; Fisher 1988.
20. This proved especially true when low short-term interest rates in the Eurodollar or Eurocurrency markets created wide yield curves and large profit opportunities on Eurobond investments. Banks were therefore induced to borrow extensively in the short-term market to finance their voluntary holdings of Eurobond.
21. BIS began to publish regular statistics on the Eurodollar and Eurocurrency markets in 1964. Originally the BIS data included in the Eurocurrency aggregates only claims and liabilities in foreign currencies vis-à-vis foreign (usually both bank and non-bank) residents of banks in the Group of Ten countries. Estimates provided by Morgan Guaranty Trust of New York since the early 1970s are more comprehensive as they include some non-European centres.
22. This is the meaning of the 'net' measures of international banking operations provided by the BIS and other financial institutions. For a detailed illustration of Eurocurrency statistics and related methodological problems in measuring Eurocurrency markets, see Dufey and Giddy 1978: 21–34; Johnston 1983: 35–55.
23. In evaluating the rapid growth of banks' international liabilities and claims, the effects of a secular acceleration of inflation since the 1960s, reflected in a sharp rise in the nominal value of funds intermediated by banks, have to be taken into account. Pecchioli (1983: 16) argues, however, that the expansion in the volume of international business has been on an average markedly greater than the rise of global measures of inflation.
24. A different and hotly debated issue in the 1960s was whether there was a causal relationship between the continued deficit of the US balance of payments and the Eurodollar growth. Theoretically however the causal link has proved tenuous at best; moreover, econometric investigations have demonstrated that the rate of Eurodollar growth was not related to trends

of the US payments deficit. Nonetheless the US balance-of-payments deficit explanation re-emerged after the 1973 oil shock: see Frydl 1982: 14–15.
25. For a critical review of the multiplier debate, see Dufey and Giddy 1978: 135–54; Mayer 1979; Johnston 1981: 8–27; De Cecco 1987.
26. Theoretical foundations of the 'new view' were provided by classical studies by Gurley and Shaw 1960 and Tobin 1963. A concise review can be found in Spencer 1986: 15–30. For the application of this framework to Eurocurrencies, see Crockett 1976; Freedman 1977.
27. Eurodollar deposits cannot be used as means of payment (cheques cannot be drawn on them). This is the fundamental reason why Eurobanks relied on clearing balances (demand accounts) held with New York banks for making and accepting payments.
28. Whether investors, by adjusting their portfolio of domestic and foreign assets, conform to a stock-adjustment or a flow-adjustment model is a matter of debate. See Johnston 1983: 87–98.
29. Oil-exporting countries and other non-oil developing countries showed a marked preference for Eurodollar deposits as investments with a high degree of liquidity and shorter maturities (not available from US banks). See Johnston 1983: 144–59.
30. Bryant 1987: 72–3, related this result to the Goldsmith–Gurley–Shaw proposition that financial intermediation tends to grow faster than output in the earliest stages of economic development, suggesting that this proposition may be validly extended to the world economy as a whole.
31. See Forsyth 1987: 144–49; Helleiner 1994: 83–4; Burn 1999. In domestic banking, a cartel arrangement set interest rate ceilings on deposit and loan base rates (linked to Bank rate), while the Bank of England imposed quantitative and qualitative limits on banks' sterling portfolios.
32. For a description of national capital controls and their impact on international capital flows, see Mills 1972; OECD 1978; Artis and Taylor 1989 (for the UK); Dooley and Isard 1980 (for West Germany); Marston 1995: 45–69.
33. In the form of either costs of transferring funds, or opportunity costs of keeping funds invested in domestic assets at lower returns.
34. For a detailed institutional analysis of the Eurobond market, see Kerr 1984; Fisher 1988.
35. As in the case of US banks' overseas branches accepting Eurodollar deposits from and making Euroloans to foreign subsidiaries of US corporations; or Luxembourg-based branches or affiliations of German banks doing Eurodollar business with foreign subsidiaries of German companies.
36. Before 1978 foreign banks in the US were regulated only at state level and exempted from Federal Reserve requirements, interest rate ceilings and restrictions on interstate banking. In 1978 the International Banking Act gave foreign banks the same regulatory status as domestic banks.
37. An analytical narrative of the invasion of London by US banks is provided by Sylla 2002. For a quantitative analysis, see Brimmer and Dahl 1975; Goldberg and Saunders 1980; Darby 1986.
38. Regulation Q was an interwar regulatory device that imposed a ceiling on interest rates payable by banks on time deposits; it was also applied to CDs in the course of the 1960s. Deposits from foreign governments and international institutions were exempted. See Friedman 1975.

39. On the crucial relevance of the 1966 and 1969 credit crunches for financial innovation in the US see Woynilower 1980.
40. Helleiner 1994: 111–22.
41. LIBOR is the London interbank offer rate, a compound average of 'offer' rates in the London market.
42. The existence of market imperfections – for example, the possibility that Eurodollar rate adjusted more quickly to changing credit and market conditions than interest rates in the US domestic markets – is a matter of debate. For the capital control period (1963–73), market segmentation makes it difficult to detect the existence of market imperfections. For the post-capital control period, Giddy et al. supported the view that Eurodollar rates were more sensitive to changing market conditions. Kaen and Hachey (1983) found no evidence of the presence of such a phenomenon and tended to deny any unidirectional causality from the Eurodollar to the US money market. They suggested that a reasonable position would be that domestic markets responded relatively more quickly to changes in external market conditions than vice versa.
43. For a discussion of short-term interest-rate determination in the Euromarkets and empirical analysis, see Dufey and Giddy 1978: 48–106; Johnston 1983: 110–43; Gibson 1989: 68–104.
44. Arbitrage includes asset and liability portfolio adjustment in response to changes in relative yields or costs, as well as transactions of simultaneously borrowing cheap funds and relending them at a higher return.
45. The interest parity theory states that, under conditions of equilibrium and efficient markets, the differential between interest rates on assets of the same degree of risk, that are denominated in different currencies, will equal the forward discount/premium between the two currencies. See Frenkel and Levich 1975, 1977; Marston 1995: 70–104.
46. Financial integration is defined by the sensitivity of capital flows to interest rate changes, as well as by the portfolio stock adjustment caused by such flows. For a review of different approaches to financial integration and efficient markets, see Gibson 1989: 33–40.
47. Empirical estimations are in Frenkel and Levich 1975, 1977; Agmon and Barnea 1977.
48. The basic condition for such cross-currency arbitrage was the absence of an adverse forward exchange rate of the domestic currency vis-à-vis the dollar, which could offset partially or totally the nominal differential in favour of the Eurodollar. Investors with liquid funds denominated in domestic currencies usually invested in Eurodollar deposits on a covered basis, that is, by purchasing a forward exchange contract to cover against the exchange risk.
49. While non-banks are supposed to be stock adjusters to changes in interest rates, banks are regarded as flow adjusters, that is much more sensitive to interest. Empirical estimates of arbitrage margins can be found in Kreicher 1982 and Marston 1995: 53–7.
50. Bank holding companies were established in order to circumvent regulations on liabilities banks were allowed to issue: see Hester 1981. Although outward arbitrage usually expanded a bank's balance sheet, this was not an absolute necessity. Domestic funding could also be used to replace maturing Eurodollar interbank liabilities, leaving the balance sheet's size unchanged.

51. Excessive borrowing in the domestic market could however offset the incentive to arbitrage by lowering a bank's credit standing, thus raising its funding costs. See Khambata 1986: 159–62.
52. A discussion on the sovereign risk and jurisdictional issues related to Eurodollar (and Eurocurrency) banking is in Dufey and Giddy 1984: 577–88. On the 1974 crisis, see Kane 1983: 116–25.
53. For a legal discussion and historical background of this issue see Heininger 1979.
54. On cooperation among central banks in supervising international banking and the 'Basle Concordat', see OECD, 1985: 48–72. See also Dufey and Giddy 1978.
55. See Kreicher 1982: 10–23; Johnston 1983: 110–42. On the learning curve and the information effect, Dufey and Giddy 1978: 54–5.
56. In the same case, banks engaged in deliberate position-taking based either on pure arbitrage (commanded by covered interest differentials) or speculation (expected change of interest rates and foreign exchange rates: e.g. by riding the yield curve to profit from anticipated interest rate movements; or by performing currency arbitrage to profit from anticipated variations of exchange rates).
57. For a detailed discussion of available data on maturity mismatching in the Eurocurrency market, alternative methodologies and a review of existing literature see Gibson 1989: 146–59. His results for the period 1973–85 are broadly consistent with previous studies. It is worth mentioning that Bank of England data are likely to contain a disproportionate amount of interbank data as a consequence of the importance of London as an interbank centre. As maturity mismatching in the interbank market is considered to be lesser than average in the whole Euromarkets, figures might underestimate actual mismatching.
58. The expression is used by Bingham 1985.
59. An overall assessment can be found in OECD 1985: 24–37. For a general review of asset and liability management, see Harrington 1987; Wilson 1988.
60. A general review of financial innovations and their impact on banks' asset and liability management and the international interbank market is provided by BIS 1986; Harrington 1987: 43–81; BIS 1992.

Bibliography

Agmon, T. and Barnea, A. (1977), 'Transaction Costs and Marketability Services in the Eurocurrency Money Market', *Journal of Monetary Economics*, 3(3): 359–66.

Altman, O. L. (1961), 'Foreign Markets for Dollars, Sterling, and Other Currencies', *IMF Staff Papers*, 4: 313–52.

Altman, O. L. (1963), 'Recent Developments in Foreign Markets for Dollars and Other Currencies', *IMF Staff Papers*, 1: 48–93.

Argy, V. and Hodjera, Z. (1973), 'Financial Integration and Interest Rate Linkages in Industrial Countries, 1958–1971', *IMF Staff Papers*, 20(1): 1–73.

Artis M. J. and Taylor M. P. (1989), 'Abolishing Exchange Control: The UK Experience', *CEPR Discussion Papers* n. 294.

Ball, A. and Davies, A. (1984), 'International Banking Markets: End of an Era?', *Barclays Bank Review*, 59(2): 37–41.

Battilossi, S. (2002), 'Banking with Multinationals: British Clearing Banks and the Euromarket Challenge, 1958-1974', in Battilossi, S. and Cassis, Y. (eds), *European Banks and the American Challenge: Coopertaion and Competition in International Banking under Bretton Woods*, Oxford: Oxford University Press, 103–34.

Bell, G. (1973), *The Euro-Dollar Market and the International Financial System*, London: Macmillan.

Bingham, G. (1985), *Banking and Monetary Policy*, Paris: OECD.

BIS (1983), 'The International Interbank Market: A Descriptive Study', *BIS Economic Papers*, n. 8.

BIS (1986), *Recent Innovation in International Banking*, Report prepared by a Study Group established by the Central Banks of the G10 Countries, Basle.

BIS (1992), *Recent Developments in International Interbank Relations*, Report prepared by a Working Group established by the Central Banks of the G10 Countries, Basle.

Brimmer, A. F. and Dahl, F. R. (1975), 'Growth of American International Banking: Implications for Public Policy', *Journal of Finance*, 30(2): 341–63.

Bryant, R. C. (1983), 'Eurocurrency Banking: Alarmist Concerns and Genuine Issues', *OECD Economic Studies*, n. 1.

Bryant, R. C. (1987), *International Financial Intermediation*, Washington, DC: The Brookings Institution.

Bullock, G. (1987), *Euronotes and Eurocommercial Paper*, London: Butterworths.

Burn, G. (1999), 'The State, the City and the Euromarkets', *Review of International Political Economy*, 6(2): 225–61.

Buttrill White, B. (1982), 'Foreign Banking in the United States: A Regulatory and Supervisory Perspective', *Federal Reserve Bank of New York Quarterly Review*, 7(2): 48–58.

Campbell, K. (1984), 'Euromarkets: The Age of the Hybrid', *The Banker*, 134(703): 41–4.

Clendenning, W. (1970), *The Euro-Dollar Market*, Oxford: Clarendon Press.

Cottrell, P. L. and Stone, C. J. (1989), 'Credits, and Deposits to Finance Credits', in P. L. Cottrell, H. Lindgren and A. Teichova (eds), *European Industry and Banking Between the Wars. A Review of Bank-Industry Relations*, Leicester, London: Leicester University Press: 43–78.

Crockett, A. D. (1976), 'The Eurocurrency Market: An Attempt to Clarify Some Basic Issues', *IMF Staff Papers*, 23(2): 375–86.

Darby, M. R. (1986), 'The Internationalisation of American Banking and Finance: Structure, Risk, and World Interest Rates', *Journal of International Money and Finance*, 5(4): 403–28.

Davis, S. I. (1979), *The Management Function in International Banking*, London: Macmillan,.

Davis, S. I. (1981), *The Euro-Bank. Its Origins, Management and Outlook*, London: Macmillan.

De Cecco, M. (1987), 'Inflation and Structural Change in the Euro-Dollar Market', in M. De Cecco and J. P. Fitoussi (eds), *Monetary Theory and Economic Institutions* London: Macmillan: 182–208.

Dooley, M. P. and Isard, P. (1980), 'Capital Controls, Political Risk, and Deviation from Interest-Rate Parity', *Journal of Political Economy*, 88(2): 370–84.

Dufey, G. and Giddy, I. H. (1978), *The International Money Market*, Englewood Cliffs, NJ: Prentice Hall.
Dufey, G. and Giddy, I. H. (1981), 'The Evolution of Instruments and Techniques in International Financial Markets', *SUERF Series*, n. 35-A.
Dufey, G., Giddy, I. H. (1984), 'Eurocurrency Deposit Risk', *Journal of Banking and Finance*, 8(4): 567–89.
Einzig, P. (1964), *The Euro-Dollar System: Practice and Theory of International Interest Rates*, London: Macmillan.
Einzig, P. (1973), *Roll-Over Credits: The System of Adaptable Interest Rates*, New York: St Martin Press.
Ellis, J. C. (1981), 'Eurobanks and the Interbank Market', *Bank of England Quarterly Bullettin*, 21(3): 351–64.
Fama, E. F. (1970), 'Efficient Capital Markets: A Review of Theory and Empirical Work', *Journal of Finance*, 25(2): 383–417.
Fisher, F. G. (1988), *Eurobonds*, London: Euromoney.
Formuzis P. (1973), 'The Demand for Euro-Dollar and the Optimum Stock of Bank Liabilities', *Journal of Money Credit and Banking*, 5(3): 806–18.
Forsyth, J. H. (1987), 'Financial Innovation in Britain', in M. De Cecco (ed.), *Changing Money: Financial Innovation in Developed Countries*, London: Basil Blackwell: 141–57.
Frankel, A. B. (1984), 'Interest Rate Futures: An Innovation in Financial Techniques for the Management of Risk', *BIS Economic Papers*, n. 12: 19–23.
Freedman, C. (1977), 'A Model of the Eurodollar Market', *Journal of Monetary Economics*, 3(2): 139–61.
Frenkel, J. A. and Levich, R. M. (1975), 'Covered Interest Arbitrage: Unexploited Profits?' *Journal of Political Economy*, 83(2): 325–38.
Frenkel, J. A. and Levich, R. M. (1977), 'Transaction Costs and Interest Arbitrage: Tranquil versus Turbulent Periods', *Journal of Political Economy*, 85(6): 1209–26.
Friedman, B. J. (1975), 'Regulation Q and the Commercial Loan Market in the 1960s', *Journal of Money, Credit and Banking*, 7(3): 277–96.
Fry, R. (1970), 'A Banker's World. The Revival of the City 1957–1970', in R. Fry (ed.), *Speeches and Writings of Sir George Bolton*, London: Hutchinson.
Frydl, E. (1982), 'The Eurodollar Conundrum', *Federal Reserve Bank of New York Quarterly Review*, 7(1): 12–21.
Gibson, H. D. (1989), *The Euro-Currency Markets, Domestic Financial Policy and International Instability*, London: Macmillan.
Giddy, I. H., Dufey, G. and Min, S. (1979), 'Interest Rates in the US and Eurodollar Markets', *Weltwirtschaftliches Archiv*, 115(1): 51–67.
Goldberg, L. and Saunders, A. (1980), 'The Causes of US Bank Expansion Overseas', *Journal of Money, Credit and Banking*, 12 (4): 630–43.
Harrington, R. (1987), *Asset and Liability Management by Banks*, Paris: OECD.
Heinevetter, B. (1979), 'Liquidity Creation in the Euromarkets', *Journal of Money, Credit and Banking*, 11(2): 231–4.
Heininger, P. (1979), 'Liability of US Banks for Deposits Placed in Their Foreign Branches', *Law and Policy in International Business*, 11(3–4): 903–1034.
Helleiner, E. (1994), *States and the Reemergence of Global Finance: From Bretton Woods to the 1990s*, Ithaca, NY: Cornell University Press.
Hester, D. (1981), 'Innovations and Monetary Control', *Brookings Papers on Economic Activity*, 12(1): 141–200.

Holmes, A. R. and Klopstock, F. H. (1960), 'The Market for Dollar Deposits in Europe', *Federal Reserve Bank of New York Monthly Review*, 42(11): 197–202.

Johnston, R. B. (1980), 'Banks' International Lending Decisions and the Determination of Spreads on Syndicated Medium-Term Euro-Credits', *Bank of England Discussion Papers*, n. 12.

Johnston, R. B. (1981), 'Theories of the Growth of the Eurocurrency Market: A Review of the Eurocurrency Deposit Multiplier', *BIS Economic Papers*, n. 4.

Johnston, R. B. (1983), *The Economics of the Euro-Market. History, Theory and Policy*, London: Macmillan.

Kaen, F. R. and Hachey, G. A. (1983), 'Eurocurrency and National Money Market Interest Rates', *Journal of Money Credit and Banking*, 15(3): 327–38.

Kane, E. J. (1979), 'The Three Faces of Commercial Bank Liability Management', in Micheal P. Dooley, Herbert M. Kaufman and Raymond E. Lombra (eds), *The Political Economy of Policy-Making*, Beverly Hills, London: Sage: 149–74.

Kane, D. R. (1983), *The Euro-Dollar Market and the Years of Crisis*, London: Croom Helm.

Kelly, J. (1977), *Bankers and Borders: The Case of American Banks in Britain*, Cambridge, MA: Ballinger.

Khambata, D. M. (1986), *The Practice of Multinational Banking: Macro-Policy Issues and Key International Concepts*, New York, London: Quorum Books, .

Kerr, I. (1984), *A History of the Eurobond Market: The First 21 Years*, London: Euromoney.

Kreicher, L. L. (1982), 'Eurodollar Arbitrage', *Federal Reserve Bank of New York Quarterly Review*, 7(2): 10–23.

Lees, F. A. (1976), *Foreign Banking and Investment in the US*, London: Macmillan.

Levich, R. M. (1979), *The International Money Market: An Assessment of Forecasting Techniques and Market Efficiency*, Greenwich, CT: Jai Press.

Little, J. S. (1975), *Euro-Dollars: The Money-Market Gypsies*, New York: Harper & Row.

Machlup, F. (1970), 'Euro-Dollar Creation: A Mistery Story', *Banca Nazionale del Lavoro Quarterly Review*, 25(94): 219–60.

Makin, J. H. (1972), 'Demand and Supply Functions for Stock of Eurodollar Deposits: An Empirical Study', *Review of Economics and Statistics*, 54(4): 381–91.

Marston, R. C. (1974), 'American Monetary Policy and the Structure of the Euro-Dollar Market', *Princeton Studies in International Finance*, n. 34.

Marston, R. C. (1976), 'Interest Arbitrage in the Eurocurrency Markets', *European Economic Review*, 7(1): 1–13.

Marston, R. C. (1995), *International Financial Integration*, Cambridge: Cambridge University Press.

Mayer, H. W. (1979), 'Credit and Liquidity Creation in the International Banking Sector', *BIS Economic Papers*, n. 1.

Mayer, H. W. (1985), 'Interaction Between the Euro-Currency Markets and the Exchange Markets', *BIS Economic Papers*, n. 15.

McKinnon, R. I. (1977), 'The Euro-Currency Market', *Essays in International Finance*, Department of Economics, Princeton University, n. 125.

Mendelsohn, M. S. (1980), *Money on the Move: The Modern International Capital Market*, New York: McGraw-Hill.

Merton, R. C. (1995), 'Financial Innovation and the Management and Regulation of Financial Institutions', *Journal of Banking and Finance*, 19: 461–81.

Mills, R. H. (1972), 'The Regulation of Short Term Capital Movements in Major Industrial Countries', *Board of Governors of the Federal Reserve System, Staff Economic Studies*, n. 74.

Mishkin, F. S. and Strahan, P. E. (1999), 'What Will Technology Do to Financial Structure?', *Brookings-Wharton Papers on Financial Services 1999*: 249–87.

Niehans, J. (1982), 'Innovation in Monetary Policy. Challenge and Response', *Journal of Banking and Finance*, 6(1): 9–28.

Officer, L. H. and Willet, T. D. (1970), 'The Covered Arbitrage Schedule: A Critical Survey of Recent Developments', *Journal of Money Credit and Banking*, 2(2): 247–57.

OECD (1978), *Regulations Affecting International Banking Operations of Banks and Non-Banks*, Paris: OECD.

OECD (1985), *Trends in Banking in OECD Countries*, Report to the Committee on Financial Markets, Paris: OECD.

Pecchioli, R. (1983), *The Internationalisation of Banking*, Paris: OECD.

Ross, D. (2002), 'Clubs and Consortia: European Banking Groups as Strategic Alliances', in S. Battilossi and Y. Cassis (eds), *European Banks and the American Challenge: Coopertaion and Competition in International Banking under Brettonw Woods*, Oxford: Oxford University Press: 135–60.

Ross, S. A. (1989), 'Institutional Markets, Financial Marketing, and Financial Innovation', *The Journal of Finance*, 44(3): 541–56.

Roubini, N. and Sala-i-Martin, X., (1995), 'A Growth Model of Inflation, Tax Evasion and Financial Repression', *Journal of Monetary Economics*, 35(2): 275–301.

Sarver, E. (1988), *The Eurocurrency Market Handbook*, New York, New York Institute of Finance: Prentice Hall.

Schenk, C. R. (1998), 'The Origins of the Eurodollar Market in London: 1955–1963', *Explorations in Economic History*, 35(2): 221–38.

Schenk, C. R. (2002), 'International Financial Centres 1958–1971: Competitiveness and Complementarity', in S. Battilossi and Y. Cassis (eds), *European Banks and the American Challenge: Cooperation and Competition in International Banking under Bretton Woods*, Oxford: Oxford University Press: 74–102.

Spencer, P. D. (1986), *Financial Innovation, Efficiency and Disequilibrium: Problems of Monetary Management in the United Kingdom 1971–1981*, Oxford: Clarendon Press.

Sylla, R. (2002), 'United States Banks and Europe: Strategy and Attitudes', in S. Battilossi and Y. Cassis (eds), *European Banks and the American Challenge: Cooperation and Competition in International Banking under Bretton Woods*, Oxford: Oxford University Press: 53–73.

Swoboda, A. K. (1968), 'The Euro-Dollar Market: An Interpretation', *Essays in International Finance*, Department of Economics, Princeton University, n.64.

Toniolo, G. (2005), *Central Bank Cooperation at the bank for International Settlements, 1930-1973*, Cambridge: Cambridge University Press.

Wilson, J. S. G. (ed.) (1988), *Managing Bank Assets and Liabilities*, London: Euromoney.

Woynilower, A. (1980), 'The Central Role of Credit Crunches in Recent Financial History', *Brookings Papers on Economic Activity*, n. 2: 277–339.

3

Tensions Between Economic Policies, Technology and Bankers' Professional Perceptions

Jocelyn Pixley

Introduction

'Risk management can never achieve perfection.' Alan Greenspan, former chair of the US Federal Reserve (the Fed) wrote this after the credit crisis broke. He still has faith in risk management, saying problems lay not with regulators' inaction, but with the people using products like derivatives, who became 'greedy' and dishonourably peddled them. He implies they lacked the integrity and reliability of 'the pharmacist who fills out the prescription ordered by our physician'.[1] This typical moral argument embodies one of the tensions explored here. The logic is that technical risk models would be perfect were it not for their abuse by people.

Such a technological determinism ignores the social and institutional contexts of financial markets, which inspired the creation of these models, also by people. The hope for near perfection of risk models, more seriously, refuses to contemplate fundamental uncertainty. This is my topic. My approach is based in the interpretative social sciences and the sociological tradition. It does not share the discourse and the quantification priorities of financial risk management, and it listens to senior financiers' concerns. From this, another picture emerges about the practicalities of risk management, and policies derived from contemporary economic theories.

This chapter aims to show such an alternative picture by looking at one of the causal directions of technical change, and specifically why the financial sector invested in the risk models, and continues to do so. In this view, technologies are developed and set in place *in response to* social demands – as happened in the financial sector, in a particular historical context. In considering these demands, I argue that the financial sector invested in computer technology because of banks' pressing needs to cope with newly created uncertainties. These uncertainties were not necessarily acknowledged. They arose from the competition and asset-inflation following deregulation from the 1970s. Instead of the former Keynesian controls by nation states (with their uncertainties such as wage inflation), banks faced re-regulation in favour of market rules. The financial industry kept changing continually in reaction to expanding international pressures. One change was a relentless drive to find technological fixes – not as mere aids but to predict the future.

Although some banking practices have remained as before, market (self) regulation was a reversion to pre-1930s rules. It was allied with this technical change in financial products in order to develop the capacity of statistical techniques. But what explains the creation of so many computer-generated risk models? This chapter suggests that cognitive and *emotional* rules changed to cope with market uncertainties, and these collective or shared rules drove the decisions to invest heavily in computer models. The former personal trust (with its certainties and caution) between central bankers, treasury officials and top financiers gave way to *impersonal distrust* built into financial products. What seemed like cognitive rules (emotional at heart), built less upon prudence than upon *caveat emptor* and *ceteris paribus*, became official decision rules, and required technical models to assay every conceivable detail of the past (assuming continuation in future). Such distrust and extrapolation procedures gave some comfort to investment and bank CEOs but – my studies of professional financiers show – never gave conclusive assurance, because the models continually failed in practice. The growth of impersonal distrust agencies that assessed *future* reputations, credit-worthiness, business confidence and likely profits from these risk models, was matched by ever more competition, with its distrust procedures of audits, market prices and performance benchmarks. Pension funds, which also expanded as never before, played a major role in this huge investment in external scrutiny. Tensions between data generated from within and outside banks detracted from bankers' professional judgements, and from banks' vital roles as intermediaries between borrowers and lenders, and did not encourage a proactive vision on the part of bankers (see Kyrtsis, introduction in this volume) or regulators, but rather anxiety. This alternative picture, then, is about how institutional actors cope with uncertainty. My questions are: (1) were coping strategies different before the 1970s? (2) Have financial risks and dangers changed since then? (3) Which of these strategies have driven technical change in the financial industry?

The chapter proceeds by noting important policy changes since the 1970s, to see how they reflected different uncertainties from the post-war era. Policies that conquered those previous uncertainties, however, gave an unfortunate, completely unfounded sense of certainty to the financial industry. The hope behind utilizing and expanding the power of information technology (IT) was that the future could be conquered. That hope culminated in 2004 with US Secretary of Treasury Henry Paulson convincing the Securities and Exchange Commission (SEC) to exempt 'non-bank' *investment banks* from maintaining reserves to cover losses on investments. A former Reagan administrator describes this 'greatest mistake' as one where 'in place of time-proven standards of prudence, computer models engineered by hot shots determined acceptable risk' (Roberts 2008).

This evident technophobia does not explain the change any better than the 'greed and abuse of technology' argument, exemplified by Greenspan's above. I suggest instead that apparently stable parameters (such as low inflation and predictable interest rates) had encouraged the idea that probability assessment was feasible, and a sound method to make serious financial decisions. These hopes to mathematize the future in fact developed during the previous Keynesian policy era. Albeit with different aims, it is fair to say that both policy eras hoped to gain certainty through over-reliance on either theoretical or inductive positivism and, since the 2007 credit crisis, both policy eras (having failed to predict the future) faced crushing blows to reputations.

This was disheartening in the case of Keynesian policymakers, since the actual theorists stressed that predictions are always difficult (especially when they are about the future, as the joke has it). Friedrich Hayek and Frank Knight were the anomalies among pro-market theorists for also emphasizing uncertainty, and Hayek later criticized the turn to maths and probability models in financial markets (Mirowski 1989). However, in the democratic era in which we live, the temptation for economic and political leaders to invest in quantitative methods to justify and try to legitimize these financial decisions (as purely technical ones) and to create confidence in financial relationships became uppermost. The deployment of such techniques was expensive (van Duyn 2009: 15). Policies that relied on economic theories purporting to control the future, without mention of inevitable uncertainty, played a major role in investment in IT.

One of the crucial differences in the Keynesian era was that when politicians made rash economic decisions they could be punished by their electorates. After that era, who could be blamed? When central banks (CBs) gained operational independence from governments (in the late 1970s–80s), effective responsibility for *taking* political (economic) decisions shifted although accountability (to electorates) remained with governments. Some (such as Bernie Fraser, former Governor Reserve Bank of Australia) argue that central banks became dependent on markets; that – in the expression the great post-war Fed chair, McChesney Martin, used to describe CB duties – they were no longer brave enough to take away the punch bowl before the party became riotous. (Galbraith 2008; Pixley 2004: 108). After their operational independence from treasuries, CBs were more anxious to maintain their reputations – with the market – and to avoid the public odium that would follow should they appear to cause a financial crash. Treasuries became timid and captured by neoclassical theory. Specialist technicians tried to reduce political decisions to technical and administrative ones, as I discuss. They were also unable to admit, frankly, in public, that uncertainty is ever-present and that, whatever the decisions, there would be winners and losers. This change was similar to that brought about by the UK's Bank Charter Act of 1844: where the gold standard was used just like the inflation targets of today. When the act set the Bank of England's management of the national currency on a quasi-public basis (the bank was still privately owned), that duty was defined, to Walter Bagehot's irritation, as an 'automatic, technical' matter rather than a 'public responsibility'. It also gave the bank distance from treasury to continue gaining profits from its lucrative role as the bank to the government. Back then, some prime ministers and presidents started alluding to their fear of the 'money power' – while others embraced it.[2]

Similarly with *automatic* wage–price inflation targets, central banks had no discretion and technical models prevailed. Pressure for low wage inflation was exerted by the financial industry even without formal targets, often leading to overzealous contraction (e.g. the ECB) to make money scarce or, since asset inflation was not in the remit, a fear that bold action might cause market panic.The latter fear fostered more credit-money. In answer to criticisms after the dot com collapse, the Fed claimed that it was impossible to *predict* an asset inflation.[3] Yet, after each crisis, there developed greater reliance on models of the future that denied uncertainty. Moreover, *before* each crash, few could admit that things might easily go wrong. Any public statement of uncertainty might itself cause a panic. Professionals know this tightrope, and all face anxiety and constant dilemmas. The unelected in the state and commercial financial world became responsible for *acting* in a more global economy, whether they wanted such political duties or not. When their actions failed, governments socialized their losses.

A brief contrast with the era before the 1970s, when most financial markets were national in scope, is given here only to show why banking faced different uncertainties and dangers then and now, and how the new uncertainties have played a significant role in driving investment in information technologies. This argument rejects the idea of a 'golden era' pre-1970s, and suggests that both economic orthodoxies denied uncertainty, though they did so in different ways. The turn to economic liberalism after the 1970s involved a new attempt at managing the future. Instead of the Keynesian focus on maintaining *business confidence* through state measures, the pro-market focus turned (against economists' predictions) *distrust*. While all policies have unintended consequences, now faceless organizations unpredictably 'lived down' to that distrust, as extensive reliance on predictive models (via IT) grew. Regulators were obliged to maintain this 'trust via distrust', which reduced their capacity to stop the music or take away the punch bowl.

Since 2007, quantitative models have failed again, as we know from the many reports. A mild foretaste of what was to come later in the crisis occurred when a Goldman Sachs probability model of 'extreme events' that were said to occur once every 100,000 years, *except in actuality*, became a straitjacket. The computer model lost 30 per cent of its value over a week (Tett and Gangahar 2007). It was not that people did not know about the dangers of models. The 1987 financial crisis was partially caused by too many firms selling portfolio insurance, another computer-driven model. The key problem was that 'synthetic portfolio insurance ... must buy as markets rise and sell as they fall' and the dynamic of these 'mechanistic and information-less trades' was copied by everyone else, under the assumption that portfolio trades expressed knowledge about the future (Jacobs 1999: 16, 297). Fischer Black, who invented the option pricing framework, argued in 1972 that this was a form of leveraged gambling that should be taxed (like gambling); he refused to become involved personally in options or, in 1994, in Long-Term Capital Management (LTCM), as his colleagues did. He was appalled that LTCM was 'loading up on risk' – taking on major risks, like heavy debts, that can bring down a whole corporation (Mehrling 2005: 138–9, 297–9).

So, it is timely to consider the human factors that created these apparently technical models. The human factors include differing sentiments, within increasingly impersonal, financial processes under a structure of competition geared to winning a futile game of predicting outcomes of promises and obligations (money). Neither technophobia and criticisms of lack of regulation, nor abuse of technology by 'Wall Street' greed,[4] give a satisfactory explanation.

Rules and uncertainties before the 1970s

As is well known, the post-war financial architecture was a Keynesian one structured by the Roosevelt reforms in the US from 1933 onward. It emphasized fiscal instead of monetary policy. Treasuries would aim to counteract peaks and troughs in the national business cycle and to maintain high levels of employment and public goods – and thus, indirectly through the multiplier effect, to maintain *business confidence* about profit expectations. During the Great Depression, Keynes argued that financiers were wary of lending for proposals for new social development, and few enterprising firms made such innovative proposals, because there was insufficient 'effective demand'. But if governments invested in some job creation, its effects on consumer spending, private sector development and jobs would *multiply* (Keynes 1936: 115–22). Fiscal cutbacks and higher taxes would likewise forestall or diminish a likely crash from a speculative and 'over-optimistic' boom. These allegedly 'automatic stabilizers'[5] were allied with the tight global controls over movements of capital that came with war-time legislation; and later, along with the 1945 Bretton Woods agreements of fixed exchange rates, and national accounts, these were used to scrutinize international imbalances. This architecture fostered mixed economies, equality and social development.

Inside the financial world, banks and other financial firms only competed mildly and were tightly supervised, with a mixture of government-owned, publicly listed, mutual or partner ownership. Salaries prevailed and long-term practices like relationship banking for economic investment were the norm, such as in the US with its anti-competitive state banking laws; countries had different ways to meet fairly similar ends. Generally government controls of exchange rates, and limits on ownership of foreign assets, gave some certainty. Moreover mass production techniques were still used mainly in industrial firms; this did not yet apply to services from fast food to finance, in the sense that quality professionalism was still the norm in elite investment/merchant banks and Main Street retail banks.

What were the major uncertainties? Many see the post-war era as a 'golden age' of employment stability and economic growth, perhaps boring and dull (and environmentally worrying, too), but offering security for many more in industrialized countries than ever before. Opinions differed, with warnings that government controls only paved the road to 'serfdom' as Hayek argued, and to unpredictable rent seeking. In banking, some suggest the local US banks were more risky than nationwide banks, others that they were better able to focus on business needs, so creating money for development (Rajan 2005; Roberts 2008; Schumpeter 1934). Moreover, few policymakers expected the rapid post-war growth. Demobilization and huge numbers of displaced people led many to believe that there would be a slump, not the economic boom led by the US and its Marshall Plan for Europe. Uncertainty centred on unemployment: the focus of that era. Keynesian technicians developed quantitative analyses of every conceivable measure of national economies in attempts to predict the future. Governments could fall if unemployment rose, although historical fears of inflation were uppermost among, for example, the Germans, with the Bundesbank renowned for fighting inflation.

Probably the greatest *economic uncertainty* came from the growth of popular *political demands* (a debate that cannot be explored in this chapter). In brief, the most widespread forms of social and political integration the world had seen, came to be *implicitly* regarded as an unnecessary uncertainty by economic leaders and their emerging theorists. Hayek's more explicit, fundamental position was that limitations on democracy were necessary – this was neoliberalism's major *disruption* (Berman 2003). Milton Friedman (1953: 4–11, 15) declared that the basis of economic policy should *not* rest on democratic debate about norms and ends, but on 'positive' predictions – those that are 'proven' correct after the fact. Hayek, *very differently*, argued (first) that since our knowledge can only be fragmentary, (second) blind market processes are preferable to 'false' democratic decisions, particularly those aiming for justice for minorities and women. His first, correct point on uncertainty does not logically lead to the second; but to Hayek, democracy was now a 'totalitarian system' of 'organized interests' (Hayek 1982: 2–3, Vol. I). In this text written during the 1970s, hope was at hand, he thought, in 'signs ... that unlimited democracy is riding for a fall' (Hayek 1982: 3, Vol. I). In regard to emerging demands for corporate social responsibility, Hayek was appalled (in *The Mirage of Social Justice*) that most people 'thought' in terms of organizational requirements (Hayek 1982: 133–4 Vol. II).[6] A 1970 article by Friedman called 'The Social Responsibility of Business is to Increase Its Profits' shared a similar anti-democratic view.[7]

Theorists usually need a social movement to promote, let alone establish their prescriptions. In industrialized countries wage–price inflation had seemed a 'price' that the large oligopolies could afford – in order to maintain their unionized workforces – but not so the competitive sectors (Hirsch 1978), nor the financial sector. Political leaders of all hues (e.g. Richard Nixon *and* Harold Wilson) acted erratically (unpredictably) to ensure their re-election. Nixon put the Fed in an awkward position when it appeared that his re-election took priority over the Fed's remit. Then *predictable*, cheap oil supplies were suddenly endangered when oil producers in the Middle East formed the OPEC cartel, in a sense aping their corporate colonizers.

Before all these alleged and real crises coalesced unpredictably in the 1970s, another factor was also creating greater uncertainty *inside* the relatively tame financial world. Hostile takeovers of firms started in the 1960s; some unpredictably collapsed. First, capital mobility returned when financial networks became global once again, after having been outlawed during World War II. Second, to avoid the US 'Regulation Q' introduced by the Kennedy administration, Eurodollar markets developed in the 1960s that could avoid currency controls.[8] Agents for so-called petrodollars also sought investment outlets. But until the 1970s at least, various factors restrained trading in financial markets. Equity markets, in particular, were national in scope (with, in 1963, only seven per cent of British shares owned by foreigners). Trading in shares was taxed quite heavily, and the British brokerage industry was regulated in a manner that made it highly fragmented. Also British brokers operated with minimal capital, and were often partnerships, as were many on Wall Street and elsewhere (Ford 2008).

Once capital mobility was again in play, governments found it far more difficult to manage their domestic economies and tame the business cycle. Keynesian commentators looked to the past to argue that global capital mobility – with fixed currency exchange rates *and* nationally independent macroeconomic policies – is a difficult or incompatible combination (Eichengreen 1998: 195; Quiggin 2002). Neoclassical theorists blamed the state (and rising democratic demands) for the mess, and Keynesian quants for failing to predict the future. Where they used statistics as modest 'sounding ropes', Milton Friedman (1953: 5–15) claimed predictions were possible through choosing the 'correct' parameters. Many governments attempted to defend their currencies and/or stem a flight of capital only to be beaten by the Forex market and bond traders. Arbitrage became more profitable than lending for development. Here lay one change in the type of uncertainty. Bankers moved from qualitative, proactive and discretionary judgement about the promises of borrowers to create new ventures, to using mathematical work on arbitrage (Mehrling 2005: 136–40). As currencies shifted erratically, businesses could not count on steady import or export prices and this was a further source of uncertainty. Job security thereupon clashed with firms' alleged new needs for human flexibility. Monetary policy returned to prominence, partly due to currency fluctuations, and fiscal policy became a bottomless pit of industrial and rural handouts as economies faltered and politicians dithered.

Rules after the 1970s: Constant changes

Among the numerous factors in the policy about-turn was an evasion of Keynesian rules and taxes, after the imperatives of World War II and recovery vanished. There followed constant changes, up to the present day, which threw up new uncertainties and dangers – differently borne – for the major economic sectors and populations. Unlike the Keynesian theorists, the neoclassical ones popularized a thoroughgoing uncertainty-denial through political slogans: *There Is No Alternative*. The market was claimed to be superior not only to state coordination but also to not-for-profit and mutually owned coordination. For example, the efficient market hypothesis propped up the new policymakers who necessarily believed that markets efficiently incorporated new knowledge. However, to expert financiers, the problem with the hypothesis was that market prices failed, in practice, to incorporate 'new' knowledge – often for over a year. Each asset inflation and unpredicted collapse showed this, and they became more frequent. In 2006 everyone *knew* that US housing prices had fallen, but market actors kept investing in populist mortgage products, using technical models' assumption of *rising prices* to mid-2007.

Despite considerable conflict over their merits, by the 1980s, Anglo-American policy changes were so far-reaching that they formed a new architecture. While the policies are well known, I cite them here to show which certainties changed. In 1971, President Nixon abandoned convertibility of the dollar into gold and devalued the dollar by ten percent. This reduced America's dominant economic role in maintaining a global system (Panić 2003: 240), and caused extreme uncertainty after the post-war currency stability. The change by central banks from full employment to 'fight inflation first', with Federal Reserve Chair Paul Volcker leading the way in 1978–80, along with the UK's 'big bang' in 1986, a policy that opened the City to foreign competition, created other major uncertainties and unexpected shocks and new potential *certainties* for the financial industry (Pixley 2009). Gradual lifting of the US 1933 and post-war financial controls created uncertainty, in dangers of job losses and faltering corporations. Yet new certainties in the corporate sector were provided by low wage–price inflation through unemployment and an emphasis on worker flexibility. The democracies were split over who should benefit from the new certainties. Anglo-Saxon countries, notably, elected governments that claimed legitimacy through promising share-owner democracy. Governments of right and left that abandoned full employment, offered their electorates so-called certainties of wealth accumulation and access to credit, and transformed large numbers of middle-income groups into modest *rentiers* and consumers of financial 'products', as pensions and state social security or insurance were now called. However for the financial industry, the modest savings of millions, and fees and commissions they charged, gave certainty.

Economic sociology's term 'the architecture of markets' (Fligstein 2001; although it avoided this crucial development in money for years) is useful to show that removing the Keynesian architecture did not mean an absence of rules and regulations. Instead, the new financial architecture imposed highly competitive rules and risk-taking incentive structures (Rajan 2005). Later rules developed to cope with uncertainties surrounding predatory practices in the financial sector, the increase in booms and busts and rising debts (Wade 2006). I expand on these points below.

When Nixon 'floated' the dollar in 1971, the result was that the NYSE became internationally dominant and foreign investment flowed back into Wall Street (Ingham 2002), after London and European markets had evaded currency controls. Many companies needed to hedge exchange-rate risks and so technologies developed to track currencies, derivatives being part of this new need. Then, in 1979–80, the US Federal Reserve under Paul Volcker targeted the money supply, which nearly brought the US economy to a standstill. Some argued this was to stem creditors' flight from the US dollar due to perceived excessive state debts of the Vietnam War. Others said workers' wages were too high (Smithin 1996). Whatever the case, the severity of this step meant new uncertainties for the finance sector – threatening recessions too deep even for moneymaking. Central banks used the non-accelerating inflation rate of unemployment (NAIRU) for their calculations. It was presented as a neutral, technical tool, whereas in fact it is a policy option, based on the efficacy, alleged by neoclassical economics, of *the lash of unemployment* for driving down wages and reducing job security. It still influences most central banks today and the NAIRU often had pro-cyclical effects, in prolonging a trough. Monetary policy is a sledgehammer. When central banks took counter-cyclical moves against troughs, in making money cheap again, for example with the Fed's low interest rate 'cure' for each collapsed asset inflation under Greenspan (and even Volcker), recovery created another asset boom and gave a sense of certainty and over-optimism to financial actors.

Serious architectural changes took place *within* banking. Anglo-American government controls against ownership of foreign assets broke down entirely once the rules preventing the entry of foreign banks and investment firms ended, in the UK with the 'big bang', and earlier in the US with the *same arguments* in 1975 about how local banks could not compete with allegedly global banks. Similarly in Australia in 1982, foreign bank competition opened in Australia on the grounds (argued by a Labor government) that the working class could gain fairer access to credit (Nevile 1997). Even state-owned entities had little choice but to get involved in Forex markets, hedging strategies like derivatives and credit ratings. This prompted demands for instant IT to provide data for models and for financial engineers to help the managers of everything from car manufacturers to universities cope with a foreign world. Banks, facing external competition, looked for other sources of profit than 'vanilla' mortgages. New uncertainties thus arose under this competition, as banks were forced 'to flirt continuously with the limits of illiquidity' (Rajan 2005: 1). Leverage became the norm for all 'products'.

In the US, with Alan Greenspan's support from 1987, another key change was the weakening of Roosevelt's 1933 Glass-Steagall rules about the separation of commercial from investment banking and the 1936 prohibition on retail banks from purchasing 'speculative securities'. When the 1998 Travelers merger with Citicorp was presented as a fait accompli, Glass-Steagall was rescinded altogether in 1999. The term 'full service banks' describes these changes. Also in 1987, the Federal Reserve permitted margin lending against mortgage-backed securities and (later) foreign bonds (Basel Committee 2000; Macdonald 2005). The positive nature of credit-money creation through lending for uncertain ventures is the banking sector's capacity to foster development (Schumpeter 1934). Was that lost, in the aim to defend market share through highly speculative, dangerously leveraged and much more uncertain, less prudent strategies?

Many central bank regulatory tasks were passed to new bodies, which copied the US system of prudential supervision by separate, often *weaker* regulatory bodies, such as the SEC. The Bank of England and Reserve

Bank of Australia eventually had less prudential duties than the US Federal Reserve. Prudential and systemic risks are, however, difficult to separate in logic, if a bank failure creates a systemic central bank concern.[9] Policies based on the nostrum that banks were just like any other firm ignored their vital role and the interconnections between banks, which also involved hedging strategies like derivatives contracts, sold 'over-the-counter' (OTC), away from the sight of regulators and formal exchanges (clearing houses). The uncertainties of guessing if a 'systemic' crisis might unfold – because the finance sector was borrowing and dealing internally, formally and 'informally' and with other corporate sectors – became a nightmare for regulators. Moreover, prudential requirements for commercial banks did not cover the many new financial firms (hedge funds, private equity firms), and 'financialized' corporations down to tiny municipal councils. But in this scenario, according to an IMF official, disclosure helps when financial positions are 'simple and static' (as they once were) but 'it is less useful when positions are complex and dynamic' (Rajan 2005: 5). Complex data was essential but within time-horizons that might last no longer than a day. New financial firms and weaker regulatory bodies gave rise to uncertainty, due to the possibility that one firm could act aggressively and, under higher competition, force others to join. This usually entailed investing in similar IT models for fear of losing market share. Under these circumstances, the volume turns into a huge mass of firms all seeking the same 'sure thing'. Once that fails, as any predictive model inevitably does, everyone tries to exit at once. The 1987 crash was only one example of the role played by financial actors who sought a technical fix, in this case synthetic portfolio insurance (Pixley 2004: 144–6).

Shareholder value came to dominate corporate aims, in banks as well. The idea that management interests should be 'aligned' with those of shareholders began with hostile takeovers in the 1960s and the registration of US companies in Delaware, which freed directors to take loans, options, stock bonuses and other 'incentive' schemes from their firms (Stretton 2000: 339). Share-price – and *how to evaluate* it – became a major source of conflict and of short-term uncertainty between fund management firms, company executives, accountancy firms, credit-raters and legal firms, with rising demands for every conceivable type of data to assuage suspicions – uncertainties – on all sides. Typically, commentators argue that 'technology has spurred deregulation and competition' and yet the evidence above suggests otherwise. There is however general agreement that changes in incentive structures are most pronounced in the US (e.g. Rajan 2005: 5, 37). Incentives on Wall

Street and in the City are not as dominant in Asian and European centres, where fixed salaries and/or job security still partially prevail. With one-year accounting of rewards for success, banking and investment officials do well purely from a rising market and luck (Pixley 2004: 88–9, 198–201).

The pro-market architecture created uncertainties of asset booms and busts, such as the 1980s banking and South American crises, the South East Asian financial crisis of 1997 and Russia's default in 1998. Orthodoxy called these 'sobering lessons' for liberalizing policies, yet preferable to what they perceived to be the 'financial repression' and 'confiscation' of Keynesian-type policies (McKinnon 1993). Taking the US and Australia as examples of large and small operators, the 1980s saw the US Savings and Loans (thrift) crisis; there were state bank failures and other dubious practices in Australia; and in 1998 panic erupted over US hedge fund LTCM. The dot com crash in 2000 was followed by the collapse of Enron, Andersen's and WorldCom, the mutual funds scandals in the US and, in Australia, the collapse of large insurer HIH, merely by 2002.

Such sobering lessons resulted in policies that, it was claimed, would change the architecture. In fact they further refined the competitive model without acknowledging uncertainty or changed inter-firm relationships. Instead, increased amounts of data were henceforward required in further calls for market actors to be fully informed, under the slogan of transparency. These included revised standards in accounting (despite the major difficulty of predicting future value), corporate governance rules and disclosure requirements (e.g. the US Sarbanes-Oxley Bill of 2002), risk assessments and more audits. Many rules were directed at preventing the most recent disaster, or shoring up a loophole that lay behind the last unforeseen scandal. Once audits of the 'fair value' of a firm's assets were required, intended to prevent corporate milking-dry of pension funds, some City analysts joked that British Airways was running a hedge fund for its deficit pension fund and to ward against currency, interest rate and credit shocks, with a small subsidiary that ran planes (Perry and Nölke 2006). This was why governments had to buy out derivative products in 2008: many large corporations *might* have failed, but it was 'a very good deal' for corporations to have this government support (Gapper 2009: 11). Sarbanes-Oxley required 'top executives to certify company accounts'; it made managers responsible for maintaining an 'adequate internal control structure and procedures for financial reporting'; and demanded that companies' auditors 'attest' to the management's assessment of these controls and disclose any 'material weaknesses' (*Economist* 2005). But under competition a disclosure of weakness is unlikely, and control structures ask staff to prove they are avoiding the previous poor practices, not necessarily newly devised ones.

More complex technical systems of risk management were required in Basel II, begun in 2004. This was not claimed to be a 'new architecture', because another boom with its requisite 'new' IT investment was already under way in creating unlimited credit-money for the 'masses' (now so insecure in most respects). Also that year the SEC permitted US investment banks exemption from maintaining reserves. Instead, what Basel II took to be a pressing need to preserve other actors' confidence in banks, was to be met by demands for more information, and a 'better' system of risk management. Basel II aimed to encourage 'banks to identify the risks they may face, today and in the future'. Despite these tedious pleas for more transparency (subverted by macroeconomic needs to keep 'western' consumerism fuelled by effective demand, now with debt not jobs), the problem about all data is that information can only be about the past, and banks did not know their risks (we are now told). Basel II's mid-2008 directive, *after* the crisis had started, gave more *discretion to regulators* because of 'uncertainty around the current realizable value of a position due to illiquidity' (Bank for International Settlements 2008). In effect, once trust evaporated, no one bought certain financial products. They had no 'value' since they could not be 'marked' to a dead market. Of course, past data should not be used intentionally to deceive (though temptations under competition do encourage such manipulation), but the past cannot *tell us anything* about unpredictable events.

The number of computer-aided models of possible future trends rose in every field of financial speculation. They have failed every three years. The argument that technological change is due to inventions by 'talented tinkerers' but sometimes found to have drastic effects *on society*, as technological determinists assume (e.g. Bell 1976: 20–1), is not convincing. Thousands of inventions have never seen the light of day in solid investment. With the recent government bailouts, the financial industry now sees that a potential certainty lies in assuming implicit government subsidies, whatever the risky effects *on* society that are *built into* a technical innovation that might be sold in the future. This practice, unfortunately, can prompt opposite ideas that the 'money power' rules. This is an equally unsatisfactory idea of determinism by the financial base. How, then, can this search for fractionally 'new', dangerous risk models be interpreted?

From personal trust to impersonal distrust

Self-regulation might seem efficacious if past data were the sole ingredient for managing future promises. The market-based architecture created new uncertainties, dangers and *seeming certainties*, as we have seen. As market decisions of buy/sell replaced political decisions of representative debate, the demand for information from market prices rose. *What does the market think?* became a common question that tortured thousands of analysts and forecasters, and daily TV reports. Would the bulls or bears win, to excess either way? Possibly more important, a change took place in the ways that financial actors made decisions. This section explores the new cognitive rules that replaced prudence and proactive professional judgement. *Caveat emptor* put the onus on the buyer to be suspicious, emotionally wary. *Ceteris paribus* became the fall back in the 'fine print' to blame the buyer for lacking the requisite wariness to the seller's claims about models of every past trend of anything from price movements to business confidence. Trends were said to predict the future, unless conditions in other respects changed, as they do. Since computers had become widely available, quantitative models became increasingly attractive.

After the Wall Street scandals of the dot com collapse (with its naïvety of imagining emails and online orders to be amazingly new, cheap, labour- and time-saving, even infallible sources of profits), the founder of Vanguard Group, the world's largest, still genuine mutual fund, John Bogle, described to US Congress how American financial services had changed since the 1940s: 'Over the half-century-plus ... the fund industry has moved from what was largely a business of *stewardship* to a business of *salesmanship*' (Bogle 2003; Pixley 2004: 130). Each financial centre was formerly enmeshed in smaller worlds, where centres hardly competed. UK commentators described the personal ties, trust and cosy club-like relationships between the City and regulators before competition was introduced: some claimed that banks took the national interest to heart.

And yet this story of before and after is not so simple. Even with relatively negligible global financial trading before the 1970s, so conducive to personal ties, the US system was already different to that in the UK and Europe. This was due to other Roosevelt reforms of the 1930s that introduced impersonal and external scrutiny. No one trusted Wall Street in 1933 and so the Administration called for firms to pay for external accountancy firms to inspect and sign off on their annual results, and agencies to rate their credit-worthiness. The Federal Reserve shared regulatory functions with the SEC. Again, a more impersonal element existed in the US system through these new external public and private agencies than, say, the UK. Moreover, while well-meant, the Roosevelt requirements were in effect distrust strategies that required a mountain of data to verify claims.

In contrast, even into the 1980s in the UK, the Bank of England governor could ask the major banking executives into his office – and this office was not only lavish, even large, but also they all knew each other. A handshake, a personal assurance, the Governor's 'raised eyebrows', all provided a personal form of social control among the key players (Pixley 2004: 95–102). Such an environment gave a sense of certainty – and they 'told' each other about their decisions, which gave them an advantage over the public. European practices were similar. New competitive regulations and global links put an end to all those certainties and ethics of stewardship or serving a national (even socially international) interest, notably where Anglo-American influence was most accepted.

The Roosevelt distrust policies do not, on their own, explain the later shift from prudence to salesmanship in the US. When combined with global finance competition over promises (post-1970s), a new set of cognitive rules emerged that became prerequisites for financial players to decide and to act. Under competition, there is no rational basis to assume that other players *will* be trustworthy. The drastic temptation to cheat becomes an ugly dilemma. But each firm must preserve its reputation: banking corporations have most to lose from any loss of credibility. In that process all firms use every means possible to foster, to craft a reputation. Trust shifted to distrust, and it spread from the US system of external auditors and raters. With *caveat emptor* a main plank in the new architecture, buyers had to be fully informed, to alleviate suspicions. So, paying for external scrutiny would, in fairness, be the responsibility of sellers. Failure to do so hinted ominously that a firm had something to hide from its buyers of shares and products, and this scrutiny spread worldwide.

In addition, after the 1970s, the new architecture was based on one theoretical entry point: self-interest. When accountancy firms or credit agencies made a faulty prediction, a typical accusation was that their interests were *in conflict* with buyers. The question of who was manipulating data – whether a Moody's or a PricewaterhouseCoopers agent by the seller, or the firm itself, or both in collusion – became difficult to resolve, let alone cases of plain bad luck. This possibility (uncertainty) was neglected by the other plank in the new architecture, the traditional economist's escape clause in any forecasting from past trends, *ceteris paribus*. If enough data were collected and subjected to rigorous probability testing, trends could tell us something about the future, other 'things' (parameters such as housing prices, interest or bond rates) remaining the same. In my view this escape clause should not be acceptable in reports. Probability only applies to *known chances* (a dice game, a horse race – as pointed out in the 1920s by Frank Knight), and does not apply to investment and lending. Reports, extrapolations and correlations from past data became more voluminous, implying causation but with *ceteris paribus* in the fine print. From being a mere aid, probability is now a straitjacket. If the information is useless, why is it used? Enron's legal prospectus and accounting reports were hundreds of pages long, another escape using volume of data.

Karl Mannheim (1936) described various 'ideal-types' of political practice in Europe. But what about economic practice? By the 1980s financial markets were no longer small in scope and the number of actors – firms and regulators – was so extensive that few could know each other in person. The economic world already consisted of huge organizations that had to compete and grow in order to survive. Moody's and PWC became global firms as beneficiaries of the rise of audits and ratings. Although English became the dominant language of global finance, cultural and policy differences did not vanish. The major central banks became operationally independent of governments. This created a huge expansion of unelected public and private bureaucratic regulators into *economic politics* in a semi-anarchic sphere, so that countries and financial centres distrusted their opponents' motives. Yet they used similar IT products in many cases, signed off by the usual suspects.

Various 'ideal-types' are relevant to economic practice. The bureaucratic mind, Mannheim (1936: 118) argued, tended 'to turn all problems of politics into problems of administration' . This is because, whether a firm is scrutinized by PWC or the UK's Financial Services Authority (for example), the laws and regulations must be taken as given. Their duties are not to query why certain policies are in place, or whether they represent partial views. They seek administrative answers to their prescribed duties. A democracy requires that bureaucrats may not query the social problems of policies imposed by their elected masters. But if bureaucrats are *deciding policy* in the name of operational independence or external scrutiny, yet in an overall architecture that is not their job to criticize, their responses are constrained. Failures are explained as aberrations from the normal structure of competition. Specialist reasoning, in the name of democratic transparency, becomes incomprehensible. Central banks and credit-rating agencies are a fraction of the bureaucracies that generate data, models of the future and deploy all this to justify *political decisions*. Recent continental thought tries to address the impasse between public discourses and 'semantically closed systems' used by specialists (Grodnick 2005). In the financial arena, specialists must translate their assessments into public presentations. When proved wrong, they are blamed, not the financial architecture that rests on the possibility of apolitical predictions.

Mannheim contrasts this bureaucratic mentality with the conservative politician who, far from concealing the political sphere, sees it sharply and looks back to 'history' to define politics as an unending source of 'irrationalism' and emotions (Mannheim 1936: 122). A third ideal-type, middle-class (bourgeois) 'intellectualism', always had an optimism that irrationalism and the 'emotional element' could be removed, such as modern nationalism (or semi-modern city-state xenophobia). But, Mannheim (1936: 123) claims, because such intellectuals 'sanction competition' and socio-economic divisions, this 'creates a new irrational sphere'. People like Robert Shiller who sanction competitive markets in further aspects of life *and* cite 'irrational exuberance' or animal spirits as *the cause* of asset inflations (but not busts or *normality*), straddle all three views. A crucial point to make here is that uncertainty is not an issue of irrationalism. Uncertainty is compounded by competition, and cannot be conquered but only managed rationally by emotions (confidence, trust, distrust). Competitive sports are, for example, adored by spectators for the very reason that the outcome is always uncertain. But excitement is always tempered when uncertainty *matters*, that is, when there is vulnerability to awful loss from poor outcomes. This point is always ignored in financial booms although professional financiers who are frank stress that mistakes are bound to be made about the future.

Alan Blinder, former deputy chair of the Fed, describes the anxieties in using probabilistic models:

> BLINDER: Confidence really depends on the issue. When you're talking about macro-economic forecasting in monetary policy ... everybody knows these forecasts are inaccurate. Even the best forecast is inaccurate, so nobody really has that much confidence. You're making the best judgement that you can on the modes of probability distributions that you *know* are dispersed. What's the best you can do? Go for the mean or the median and act on that basis. But I wouldn't use the word 'confidence'. Everybody knows their forecasts could be quite wrong, but you have to make the best guess that you can.
>
> (From permitted transcript of interview with the author, March 2002, Princeton University)

Blinder was Deputy to Greenspan and his view of models is at odds with Greenspan's claim that risk management cannot achieve 'perfection' or that 'history tells us' a specific future event. All history can 'tell us' is that events erupt unpredictably, and many events are unimaginable before they occur. In the same interview, Blinder was critical of Greenspan's habit of claiming predictive success, seeing this as reducing the office of the Federal Reserve chair to the status of a guru (cited in Pixley 2004: 119). Even so, the performative aspect of the status of high office, amidst the current intolerance of uncertainty, makes it unlikely that a central bank chair would announce a policy change was based on a mere guess.

In the private sector, everyone remarks on their lack of time. Banks cannot explore the nature of decisions under stress, as pointed out by the Chair of the Board of a German bank, just before the crisis:

> I don't think about uncertainty – only intuitively. I look at the options, such as the likelihood of a good venture and the economic strengths of a client. Then the market has its own view which has to be factored in. The market price of money dominates decisions to lend. Other risks like portfolio risk may mean that the bank needs to diversify even if I don't like the various risks. Decisions are driven by market opportunity and five years is too long to think ahead; even one year is fraught with whether mergers might take place. But decisions are made within 30 seconds with 60 different proposals and sometimes one hour to decide them all.
>
> (Interview 20 March 2007, Germany)

It is no wonder that data from models and market prices are reduced to a number, a score, a triple-A rating, and divided by multiple categories of risk. Executives must move on, to decide on the next proposal by using the same set of allegedly quantifiable risks: even if Boards 'do not like' certain risks. One cause of this lack of time is that Boards of Directors and Executives spend nearly a third of their time being scrutinized by their owners. Are they indeed owners? They are fund managers primarily (and analysts) who, also under similar policies (monthly performance benchmarks), are merely traders for huge numbers of direct/indirect shareowners (who have rights to some income stream and to buy or sell shares; and are not 'owners' of firms, per se). Fund managers' influence is extreme, not because of greed but because management requires short-term increases in share/fund value, and big pension funds can buy/sell a lot of shares. Their professionalism is measured by short-term profits because – under competition – prudent trustees and duties of stewardship are difficult to quantify, audit or evaluate on a mere quarterly or monthly basis.

All these incentive structures are based on rational distrust models. Bonus systems for traders or fund managers reward success, but do not require recompense for losses *or* a long tenure to fix up the mess when the market collapses. Turnover is rapid and poaching shows that banks must believe traders are talented, not simply lucky. Here the distrust is directed to profit at all costs, to enticing more customers; and the unsuccessful just get sacked, whether they were 'too' cautious, unlucky or fraudulent (Pixley 2009). So investment managers are assessed relative to other fund managers, and this competition produces 'perverse behaviour': regulators have been arguing this for years. For example (Rajan 2005: 3), two incentives are magnified when combined. Managers (traders) are, first, tempted 'to take risk that is concealed from investors', to appear to outperform their peers: these are called 'tail risks' that are assessed in the models as having low probability but terrible effects. (But tail risks are selected via *climates of feeling*, as I argue below.) A second incentive is that all managers 'herd' – the adage 'the trend is my friend' – as an insurance against underperforming their conforming peers. (Keynes said this years ago.) Both trends are reinforced under an asset boom, and stars take further risks to survive against individual or firm competitors. In 2005, the IMF official cited earlier warned that while banks were not yet ruled by such incentives, they could be generating 'the most complicated and most volatile portion of the risks they originate'.[10]

And such timid warnings and longer-term worries proved correct. Many banks started subsidiary hedge funds. Bear Stearns, the former US investment bank, spent nearly as much as the 1998 LTCM bailout, on 22 June 2007, to rescue its hedge fund that was 'collapsing because of bad bets on subprime mortgages' in America – in hope of retrieving the former definition of the situation, and to save its big customers (Creswell and Bajaj 2007). BNP Paribas, the large French retail bank froze its subprime (CDO) hedge funds two months later, on 7 August, thereby saving its *modest* retail customers (Nason 2007). This opposite tack *stopped the music*. Banks stopped lending to each other because no one challenged BNP Paribas's new definition of the situation: the IT models were suddenly defunct. Then the world knew that some ordinary banks had taken huge risks, because not one bank knew how many might be insolvent.

Such relations of trust and distrust are not individualistic when all financial institutions are in systemic competitive relationships: the

London interbank offered rate (LIBOR) is one enactment of those relations. Paribas said that CDOs could not be priced and this public bravery dramatically altered the *climate of feeling*. The action shows that the parameters of computer-generated models of the future always include implicit assumptions based on intangible and unmeasurable aspects of social life. The 'tail risks' – said to have low probability (Rajan 2005: 19–20) even if with catastrophic effects – included the possibility of collapsing house prices or a central bank raising interest rates suddenly. But these risks are not 'extremely' improbable. This only shows how a collective mood frames *the human and fallible choices* built into IT-generated risk models. Central banks were so constrained to provide transparency and *predictability to the market* that the financial sector assumed the uncertainty of a surprise interest rate change was licked. Southern England experienced a calamitous house price collapse only 12 years before the technicians put 'falling house prices' into the tail risk. More alarmingly, US house prices were declining *before* Bear Stearns et al. invested in subprime mortgages.

Terms like Keynes's 'animal spirits' and Minsky's 'tranquility of success', therefore, are approximations. The typical emotions in finance, my evidence shows, are formed through *esprit de corps* and climates of feeling. In an impersonal world, the *presentation of trust* through corporate disclosures, with training for public relations sessions and crafted press releases, depends on good performance. Whether credible or not, the implicit/explicit parameters set not by the gods, but mere officers of public and private organizations, dictate which categories of past data will be selected. Eventually one firm *acts* on the basis of rising doubts (e.g. Paribas) and suddenly the competition to lend turns into a game to lend the least. It is interesting that executives' hopes and fears for their firm's or bureaucracy's status are most evident in publicly available US Federal Reserve transcripts, which document major worries about the reputation of the Fed, the duties of office and fears of attracting blame. But it is fair to say that collective moods and climates of fear or optimism define what will be in the contents of a bell curve and what will be relegated to its tails. Such moods arise from collaborations and conflicts among corporations and bureaucracies. And the more aggressive the competition, the less questioning there is of these ephemeral notions about how the future may pan out. Regulators can jawbone all they like, to no avail: each new IT model is often, by then, on a railway track to disaster.

At the decline of the dot com boom – the boom when most faith was placed in technology's magical capacity to control future outcomes – some firms promoted certainty as a product. This was salesmanship. For example, BT Funds Management had a full page advertisement in February 2000 in a major Australian paper, with the heading 'How future-proofed is your portfolio?'[11] It asked investors whether they were 'at risk of being left behind', and supported its idea about 'the technology-based shift in production and distribution that's revolutionising business models around the world', with evidence of 'visionary' BT investments. For example, Wells Fargo 'left its competitors in its dust by leading the conversion of bill payments from lick-and-stick to click'. The advertisement claimed that every BT fund had 'a portfolio constantly being future-proofed' so it is 'rich with truly adaptive businesses and weeded-free of companies slow ... to ... get ... it'. Indeed BT warned that unless all companies became 'Internet companies', in five years' time 'they won't be companies at all'. A *caveat* in minuscule fine print hardly covers the mendacity implied in the entire advertisement, which threatens that certain firms will be losers, run by idiots. In trying to induce fear in investors through its authoritarian tone, the BT advertisement also projects an air of desperation. It offers a technology of trinkets that will determine one's happy future.

In a competitive architecture directed towards selling the *most* money (promises), the typical, day-to-day uncertainty facing financial institutions is fear of losing ground (not bankruptcy and not public responsibility to fund socially inspired, if risky, ventures). The fraught tensions between hopes for a purely rational – that is, predictable – economic sphere and the many efforts to gain elusive trust, through distrust strategies, have driven investment in collecting mountains of data. There is no returning to systems of personal trust. Nevertheless, money is not the commodity presumed by neoliberal policy regimes, but is created from credit–debt relations that are promises, always uncertain. How IT could be created that would include uncertainty is a different question, because choosing parameters from this overwhelming data requires prescience. Human beings are happy to gamble on sport's chances, but ironically far more risky financial competition (than ordinary gambling) was embraced in the 1970s on the faulty grounds that uncertainty could be reduced to probabilistic risk distributions and correlations with categories of past data. A firm didn't need to *buy* insurance but could *borrow to buy it* and all the other, less sturdy products of hedging against calamity. The grounds were faulty because no one can prove that a correlation is *the cause* of a previous event, and no correlation whatsoever can *predict* future human events. And risk must involve a set of *known chances*: two sixes in a dice game for example. Debt – not *too* much – is fruitful for creating development, but not for gambling. This has all been known for years and years.

Yet what would be the point of spending on a computer-driven risk model that does not claim to give predictability? The search for certainty, however futile, has driven the investment in IT, but information cannot enlighten us on the future. The best we have is some wisdom, and preferably modesty. Unfortunately, some banks are not modest and, for 30 years, have basked on the very hidden assumption (not built into the threadbare IT models) that however much money they lose, the state will bail them out. And this has happened time and again. In a more recent, equally futile move, some behavioural finance specialists were claiming in late 2009 that they could predict a panic (Lohr 2009: 12). Although emotions are indeed slightly more predictable than mendacious rationalisations, these behaviourists neglect uncertainty: namely that plans succeed or fail because of 'events, dear boy, events' (Pixley 2010). My conclusion is that some reduction of brutal competition would provide bankers with the bravery to act creatively and openly declare the uncertainties of lending for development. Banks (as Joseph Schumpeter said: 1934) need to foster innovation, not invent puerile innovations themselves. Is it possible to reward banking professionalism, proactive vision and gain accountability, and without stifling everyone with audits and compliance checks? Could banks compete over the extent of their prudent bravery in creating money from promises? This kind of competition would be unquantifiable and offer some long-term social development, accepting always that promises to create popular (not populist) enterprises can inadvertently fail.

Conclusion

There have been countless quantitative financial models, as we have seen, which are esoteric and remote from the practitioners who invested in them. In a way, their extraordinary impact on banking practices should not surprise bankers (since the money spent suggests banks were lured into, even believed in, building certainty into the models). Yet everyone expresses surprise at each failure. This paper draws on issues felt by those involved in everyday banking and investment decisions. Many are sceptical of, yet reliant upon, technical risk systems because of the competitive pace to sell obligations. While few make a promise to pay with the intention of breaking it, ventures fail and borrowers default – not, as a rule, on purpose. However the financial industry today is less bound by personal trust (and its converse: bitterness, betrayal) and firms themselves, by definition, cannot 'feel'. Cognitive and emotional rules of *caveat emptor* and *ceteris paribus* imposed specific behaviour and motivations on financial relations from the 1970s onwards. The architecture entailed a reversion to the pre-1930s regulatory regime, which dictated certain imperatives: to distrust and to extrapolate from past data. And so investment poured into IT for financial predictive models. How could a lay person criticize the huge industries involved?

The technology already existed and was created for different purposes – it was designed for state use in war and espionage, population control for good or evil, or to preserve full employment by post-war Keynesian policymakers. This is the hard lesson about contemporary life: we can show how the machine is socially constructed but how can we change it?[12] The crisis of 2007 onward was a series of unpredictable (if likely) events that again dashed the foolish hopes and deceptions that 'this' boom would last forever. It showed that quantitative models can never predict the future (their futility is particularly distressing to those who accept uncertainty), and that no one should neglect the human factors in large impersonal processes. Uncertainty (if it is quantifiable at all) is magnified or made more fraught by competition and vulnerability to catastrophic loss across the world. Loss is borne mostly by groups with the least capacity to bear it but who, in democracies, became share owners and mortgage-holders despite their insecurities and democratic claims being unmet. Although the financial sector assumed certainty from this populist development, it has equally scored many own goals.

Lack of acknowledgement of uncertainty has hounded every conceivable leader in virtually all social arrangements. But the aim to control life's vicissitudes, social and natural, is a modern arrogance of dominant economic sectors – the economics profession is thus a mere handmaiden to this arrogance. Such is the influence of a capitalist economy on democratic processes. A great joke in Eastern Europe under the Soviet command economy – which also relied on predictions – was this: 'Under capitalism man exploits man. Under communism, just the reverse.' Failed predictions are always a prelude to downfall, so the wonder is that there is such a temptation to predict. The risk assessments that tried to predict the future via probability perhaps depersonalized the futile project, but why for so long? Positivist verification, required from accountancy firms and global credit-rating agencies, became more elaborate as each 'sure thing' failed. Charges of blame and counter-blame became difficult to resolve because, under *caveat emptor*, each main actor avoids taking responsibility. Banks and financial firms – which *move in step* – end in law suits, bankruptcies and appeals for bailouts, instead of gaining respect for attempting to keep promises. These practices occur especially in Anglo-America and rest on newly 'financialized' populations, anti-inflation and pro-market policies. Such centres have a mind-set in which centres can be rigid (resistant) but we must be flexible. Risk models use a range of macro-concepts showing past trends to extrapolate into the future. Human discretion is always fallible but let us not forget that the very same 'discretion' and intuition are built into the use of IT Maybe we need more bankers to take an intuitive and openly declared punt that does not hide behind technical models. Unfortunately – given the rise of an impersonal world, and the global conflicts over which economic sector, finance centre or nation state can demand, and then inevitably lose, *certainty* – the difficulties do seem like an iron cage.

Notes

1. Cited in, and commentary from, Goodman 2008. The first citation is from Greenspan's recent book and the second from his speech at Georgetown University in the first week October 2008.
2. Bagehot, cited in Kynaston 1995: 22, also Gladstone cited in Kynaston 1995: 15; Jefferson cited in Galbraith 1975: 28–9. The US Federal Reserve System is still partly privately owned (12 cities have Federal Reserve banks which represent all 'districts' in the US). Although not-for-profit, each is owned by key district private banks and their presidents rotate in serving on the Federal Open Market Committee. Potential problems of their voting habits used to be denied by the Fed's own website, but are not mentioned now: http://www.federalreserve.gov/pubs/frseries/frseri3.htm.
3. This is only correct in the sense that no one can ever predict when an actual collapse will occur, but there are many ways to know that assets may be dangerously inflated, and that debt looks unsustainable, as I discuss later.
4. Although Frank Partnoy's *Infectious Greed* (2003: 109) charges Alan Greenspan with championing the removal of regulations, he assumes that mild punishment for transgressors simply increased the individual greed and corruption in financial markets.
5. Caporaso and Levine (1992: 101) provide an excellent summary of Keynesian political economy, and criticize post-war Keynesian economists for alleging that administrative decisions ('automatic mechanisms'), and not political decisions, would ensure economic stability. Few doubt that unemployment payments and 'public works' (Keynes 1936: 119) provide some stability to maintain 'effective demand' and potentially build up bankers' confidence to invest in development (see also Schumpeter 1934), but Keynes took the argument further. Against orthodox economics he said that such equality *maintained* a capitalist economy, not inequality and a reserve army of labour (despite what individual employers might argue about a disciplined workforce). He stressed that what might seem in the interests of individual

share owners was not serving the collective interests of private enterprises, let alone a social purpose (Caporaso and Levine 1992: 110, 116–7). The democracies, ever since, when faced with a severe collapse of employment, have always reverted to Keynesian public spending policies, even when pro-market governments are in power and even if the spending is on the military and on tax cuts for the wealthy (as in the alleged 'trickle-down effect').

6. Hayek thus disagreed with Friedman's view that predictions were possible but agreed with him regarding corporate social responsibility. Hayek invoked the 'private vices – public virtues' pro-market line against organizational thinking about social justice: arguing that it threatens an 'Open Society' ruled by the 'morals of the market'. All morality is presented as inadvertent because 'in fact we generally are doing most good by pursuing gain' through the invisible hand of the market (Hayek 1982: 145–6, Vol. II).
7. This article was published in *Sunday Times Magazine*, and was based on Friedman's *Capitalism and Freedom* of 1962: cited in Bell 1976: 292.
8. Martin Wolf (2007) argues that 'Regulation Q', which forbade the payment of interest on deposits, 'promoted' the first main post-war offshore financial market.
9. Such a debate came to the fore when the Fed engineered a bailout of a hedge fund on 'systemic grounds' – LTCM, in 1998.
10. Rajan only proposes that bank and fund managers should risk their personal investments while admitting that LTCM did exactly that.
11. *Sydney Morning Herald* Good Weekend section, 4–5 February 2000. BT was originally a firm called Bankers Trust which had, in the US, previously collapsed.
12. Langdon Winner (1993) asked this question, using a frame showing Charlie Chaplin in *Modern Times*, totally stuck in the machine. Winner's caption reads: 'It's OK Charlie. The machine was socially constructed.'

Bibliography

Bank for International Settlements (2008), 'Basel II', www.bis.org, downloaded 10 November.

Basel Committee on Banking Supervision (2000) 'Credit Ratings', *Working Papers* 3, Basel: BIS.

Bell, D. (1976), *The Coming of Post-Industrial Society*, New York: Basic Books.

Berman, S. (2003), 'We Didn't Start the Fire: Capitalism and its Critics', *Foreign Affairs*, 82(4): 176–81.

Bogle, J. (2003), Statement to US Congress: 12 March 2003, Washington, DC.

Caporaso, J. A., and Levine D. P. (1992), *Theories of Political Economy*, Cambridge: Cambridge University Press.

Creswell, J. and Bajaj, V. (2007), '$3.2 Billion Move by Bear Stearns to Rescue Fund', *New York Times*, 23 June.

Economist, The (2005), 'Sarbanes-Oxley: A Price Worth Paying?' 19 May.

Eichengreen, B. (1998), *Globalizing Capital*, Princeton, NJ: Princeton University Press.

Fligstein, N. (2001), *The Architecture of Markets*, Princeton, NJ: Princeton University Press.

Ford, J. (2008) 'A Greedy Giant Out of Control', *Prospect Magazine*, Issue 152.
Friedman, M. (1953), *Essays in Positive Economics*, Chicago, IL: University of Chicago Press.
Galbraith, J. K. (1975), *Money: Whence It Came, Where It Went*, Boston, MA: Houghton Mifflin.
Galbraith, J. K. (2008), 'The Collapse of Monetarism and the Irrelevance of the New Monetary Consensus', Levy Economic Institute, *Policy Note* 1.
Gapper, J. (2009) 'Clearing Up the Future of Futures', *Financial Times*, 1 October.
Goodman P. (2008) 'Taking Hard New Look at Greenspan Legacy', *New York Times*, 8 October.
Grodnick, S. (2005), 'Rediscovering Radical Democracy in Habermas's Between Facts and Norms', *Constellations*, 12(3): 392–408.
Hayek, F. A. (1982), *Law, Legislation and Liberty*, London: Routledge & Kegan Paul.
Hirsch, F. (1978), 'The Ideological Underlay of Inflation', in F. Hirsch and J. Goldthorpe (eds), *The Political Economy of Inflation*, London: Martin Robertson.
Ingham, G. (2002), 'Shock Therapy in the City', *New Left Review*, 14: 152–8.
Jacobs, B. I. (1999), *Capital Ideas and Market Realities: Option Replication, Investor Behaviour, and Stock Market Crashes*, Malden, MA: Blackwell.
Keynes, J. M., (1936 [1964]), *The General Theory of Employment, Interest, and Money*, New York: Harbinger Book.
Kynaston, D. (1995), 'The Bank of England and the Government', in R. Roberts and D. Kynaston (eds), *The Bank of England*, Oxford: Oxford University Press and Clarendon.
Kyrtsis, A-. A. (2010), 'Introduction: Financial Deregulation and Technological Change', in this volume.
Lohr, S. (2009), 'It's Imperative to Engineer Better Risk Modelling', *Australian Financial Review*, reprinted from the *New York Times*, 14 September.
MacDonald, S. B. (2005), 'The Rise and Fall of the Glass–Steagall Act', *Financial History Magazine*, 83: 12–15.
Mannheim, K. (1936), *Ideology and Utopia*, London: Routledge & Kegan Paul.
McKinnon, R. I. (1993), *The Order of Economic Liberalization*, Baltimore, MD: John Hopkins University Press.
Mehrling, P. (2005), *Fischer Black and the Revolutionary Idea of Finance*, Hoboken, NJ: John Wiley & Sons.
Mirowski, P. (1989), *More Heat Than Light. Economics as Social Physics: Physics as Nature's Economics*, Cambridge: Cambridge University Press.
Nason, D. (2007), 'Central Banks Act in Bid to Arrest Slump', *The Weekend Australian*, 11–12 August.
Nevile, A. (1997), 'Financial Deregulation in Australia', *Labour and Economic Relations Review*, 8(2): 273–82.
Panić, M. (2003), *Globalization and National Economic Welfare*, Houndmills: Palgrave Macmillan.
Partnoy, F. (2003), *Infectious Greed: How Deceit and Risk Corrupted the Financial Markets*, London: Profile.
Perry, J. and Nölke, A. (2006), 'The Political Economy of International Accounting Standards', *Review of International Political Economy*, 13(4): 559–86.
Pixley, J. F. (2004), *Emotions in Finance: Distrust and Uncertainty in Global Markets*, Cambridge: Cambridge University Press.

Pixley, J. F. (2009), 'Time Orientations and Emotion-Rules in Finance', *Theory & Society*, 38(4): 383–400.

Pixley, J. F. (2010) 'The Use of Risk in Understanding Financial Decisions' *The Journal of Socio-Economics*, 39(2): 209–22.

Quiggin, J. (2002), 'The Fall and Rise of the Global Economy', *Evatt Foundation*: 2, http://evatt.labor.net.au/publications/books/12.html.

Rajan, R. G. (2005), 'Has Financial Development Made the World Riskier?', Paper on www.kc.frb.org/PUBLICAT/SYMPOS/2005.

Roberts, P. C. (2008), 'A Futile Bailout as Darkness Falls on America', *Counterpunch*, 8 October 2008, http://www.countercurrents.org.

Schumpeter, J. A. (1961 [1934]), *The Theory of Economic Development*, Cambridge, MA: Harvard University Press.

Smithin, J. N. (1996), *Macroeconomic Policy and the Future of Capitalism: The Revenge of the Rentiers and the Threat to Prosperity*, Cheltenham: Edward Elgar.

Stretton, H. (2000), *Economics*, Sydney: UNSW Press.

Tett, G. and Gangahar, A. (2007), 'Why Computer Models Proved Unequal to Market Turmoil', *Financial Times*, 14 August.

Van Duyn, A. (2009), 'Hidden Costs Emerge from the Debris of Lehman Crash', *Financial Times*, 13 September.

Wade, M. (2006), 'Mortgage Now Lifelong Debt', *Sydney Morning Herald*, 8–9 April.

Winner, L. (1993), 'Social Constructivism: Opening the Black Box and Finding It Empty', *Science as Culture*, 3(16): 427–52.

Wolf, M. (2007), 'The New Capitalism', *Financial Times*, 19 June.

4
Opening the Black Boxes of Global Finance

Donald MacKenzie

Introduction

In this chapter, I shall describe and advocate a 'science-studies' approach to global finance.[1] 'Science studies' is the generic name for a collection of humanities and social-science specialisms that examine the contents and contexts of science and technology. These specialisms are diverse: some are historical, some philosophical, some sociological, some anthropological, some draw on literary theory.[2] They have no simple overarching theory or methodology, so it must be emphasized that what I am discussing is *a* science studies approach, not *the* science studies approach. References to other authors studying finance from a science-studies perspective will be found in an endnote,[3] but the topic is still a relatively new one for science studies, and the work done so far has only scratched the surface of what is possible. In advocating a science-studies perspective, in no sense do I wish to denigrate the contributions of other approaches. There is an exciting emergence or revival of interest in financial markets in economic sociology (e.g. Godechot 2001, 2007), anthropology (e.g. Zaloom 2006) and human geography (e.g. Leyshon and Thrift 1997); and of course international political economy has long been interested in finance (e.g. Mosley 2003). A science-studies approach is complementary to those of other disciplines, not in competition with them.

Why take a science-studies approach to finance? One reason is that the practice of high-modern finance is interwoven intimately with theory, in particular with modern financial economics. Is financial economics a science? If pressed, I would say that it was (although it is plainly a social science, not a natural science). Science studies, however, has found it productive to sidestep the question of whether or not fields are 'really' sciences, and focus instead on the 'boundary work' (Gieryn 1999) by which that status is granted or denied. It would, for example, be fascinating to study from this viewpoint 'chartism' or 'technical analysis', which will be discussed briefly below. Chartism is the analysis (often graphical, hence the name) of 'patterns' in time-series of prices. Although it has many practitioners in the markets,[4] chartism seems fated permanently to be given the status of 'astrology' with respect to the 'astronomy' of financial economics.

Another reason for taking a science-studies approach to finance is that it is a highly 'technologized' activity. Historically many financial transactions have been enacted with voices, hand signals and handshakes alone, and some still are (see MacKenzie 2004). But these have almost always been complemented by more permanent media.[5] Especially since the nineteenth century, traditional media such as pen and paper have been supplemented by new technologies such as the telegraph, telephone, and stock ticker: for a fascinating study of the last of these, see Preda (2006). As Preda emphasizes, it could be quite incorrect (and certainly contrary to typical science-studies approaches) to assume that such technologies simply facilitated and speeded up essentially unchanged market relations. Investors who watch a stock ticker, or view near real-time prices on electronic screens, may behave quite differently, may stand in different relations to financial markets, than those who act on the basis of word-of-mouth information, newspapers, or newsletters.

So finance is a 'scientized' and 'technologized' domain, but science studies offers no unitary approach to it. One way of thinking through what science-studies perspectives on finance might consist in is to ask what science studies' *heuristics* are: what rules of thumb do people in the field adopt when approaching a new situation or new topic? Given the field's diversity, these are of course numerous. One, for example, is this: discover what entities are taken to exist, and how their existence is stabilized via material and textual practices.[6] Another is to seek out controversies, for it is in them – in knowledge (or machines) in the making, rather than in stable, consensual knowledge or established technologies – that the processes of construction, and what is at stake in those processes, can most clearly be seen.[7] A third – this list is intended to be neither exhaustive nor mutually exclusive – is this: open the black box![8]

It is this last heuristic on which I shall focus. As far as I am aware, 'black box' was originally an engineers' phrase: roughly speaking, it describes a device whose internal structure can be disregarded. All the engineer needs to know is that the device transforms given inputs into predictable outputs: how it does this can be ignored. It can thus be treated as opaque, as if its contents cannot be seen.

Black boxes litter the societies of high modernity: increasing black-boxing may, indeed, be a passable definition of modernization. Many black boxes are of course the literal, or near-literal, black boxes of engineering. For most of us, the grey or white metal that surrounds our computer's central processing unit is a cognitive as well as a physical boundary. Similarly, we frequently lack knowledge about the engines of our cars (or at least the components thereof), our televisions, iPods, watches and so on. Somewhat more metaphorically, modern organizations are often black boxes: most of the time, we can interact perfectly satisfactorily with retailers, banks, the Inland Revenue or other arms of government while knowing nothing of the particular people we are dealing with, their family connections, allegiances and conflicts, and without having to offer them any special inducements.[9] Recognized expertise, too, is a black box: we routinely place our lives in the hands of surgeons, pilots and so on of whom we have no personal knowledge.[10]

Treating artefacts, organizations and expertise as black boxes is an inescapable aspect of daily life in high modernity: not to do so is to head for the hills of Montana with the survivalists. The point, however, of 'open the black box!' as a heuristic is that what may be inescapable as a practical matter is nevertheless unsatisfactory intellectually. Not to examine the contents of black boxes is to miss a critical part of how societies are constructed.

The heuristic cuts against what is, or at least what used to be (things seem to be changing in this respect), a widespread instinct in the social sciences. That instinct is to study the big issues: capitalism, militarism, patriarchy, racism, poverty, globalization and so on. Complementing the more common critique of science studies (that it is 'over-political', reading too much into what is simply the pursuit of better knowledge or more efficient machines)[11] is therefore the suspicion that it is apolitical, diverting its eyes from the big questions to study little technicalities.[12] To my mind, however, the suspicion is misguided: big issues often pivot on apparently small technicalities.

Though there are also clear connections to Michel Foucault's 'micro-physics' of power, within science studies the black box account of power has been elaborated most influentially by Bruno Latour, especially in a joint article with fellow 'actor-network' theorist Michel Callon (Callon and Latour 1981). What is it to be powerful, they ask? It is to sit on top of black boxes. No generals could succeed if they had to stand behind every soldier, gun in hand, to enforce compliance. No corporation could prosper if its top managers had to be in every office, looking over the shoulder of every employee. The general must be able to say 'the fifth battalion will advance over the ridge at 2 p.m.', or the manager to say 'close our branch in Toronto', and then not attend to 'the details'. Callon and Latour's argument is that the macro-actors of social life (including not just individuals, but also organizations and even 'structures') are micro-actors grown large through their capacities to mobilize and command black boxes.

The contents of black boxes are indeed 'details', but not 'mere details'. If a black box ceases to function as such – if it no longer reliably transforms inputs into appropriate outputs – then the power of a macro-actor can be disturbed. Among other things, this suggests why opponents of a particular form of social power might be interested in the opening of the black boxes on which it depends. It also indicates two of the questions that can be asked when black boxes are opened. How does the 'small' structure the 'big': in other words, how do the contents and functions of black boxes shape their contexts? And how is the 'big' inscribed in the 'small': how do the contexts of black boxes shape their contents?

This may seem very abstract; so let me give an example from a different sphere, from previous work on military technology. The black boxes examined by MacKenzie (1990) were nuclear missile guidance systems. Accurate nuclear missiles could be used not just in the counter-city strikes of 'mutual assured destruction' but also in counterforce strikes against an opponent's underground command posts and missile silos. Guidance systems thus helped structure the strategic environment of the cold war. Simultaneously, that environment (and many other factors, including inter-service conflict and the technological preferences of contractors) shaped the contents of guidance systems, not just overall but even in the 'technical detail' of components.[13] Understanding guidance systems – and in particular understanding the processes by which *knowledge* of missile accuracies was constructed – opened political opportunities for those disturbed by counterforce's dangerous temptations (see MacKenzie 1990: 409–23).

What might be equivalent black boxes to open in the context of global finance? There are many, and rather than seeking a comprehensive list – which would be very long – I shall discuss four.

Option pricing theory

The first black box to be considered is the most technical: option pricing theory.[14] An option is a contract that gives a right, but not an obligation;

for example to buy ('call') or to sell ('put') a given asset (such as a block of shares) at a given price on, or up to, a given future date. How should such a contract be priced? As the modern mathematical theory of finance began to be constructed in the 1950s and 1960s, several scholars studied the question either econometrically (examining observed option prices) or by applying the emerging 'random walk' model of share price changes.[15] This was solved by Black and Scholes (1973) and Merton (1973): they showed how (under certain assumptions, of which more below) the returns on an option can be replicated perfectly by a continuously adjusted portfolio of the underlying asset and cash. Offering identical returns, the price of the option and the cost of the replicating portfolio must be identical. If they are not, arbitrageurs (traders who exploit price discrepancies) will buy the cheaper and short sell[16] the dearer, until equality is restored. This reasoning yields to the Black-Scholes option pricing equation, a version of the heat or diffusion equation from physics. The characteristics of a particular option are entered as boundary conditions, and the equation is solved either analytically or numerically to yield an option price.

When published in 1973, the Black-Scholes equation described observed option prices only imperfectly (Black and Scholes 1972; Galai 1977). Over subsequent years, however, it became a much better description (Rubinstein 1985). The reasons are complex (see MacKenzie 2006), but include the equation's use by arbitrageurs to exploit – and thus reduce – discrepancies between observed prices and the model. It is an instance of an important theme developed by Michel Callon: the performativity of economics. Economics, he argues, does not describe an already-existing external world, but helps bring that world into being: it is performative, not simply descriptive. Performativity is a complex notion, but a basic meaning comes from the work of philosopher J. L. Austin on 'performative utterances', utterances that bring into being that of which they speak, as when an absolute monarch declares someone an 'outlaw' (see Austin 1962; Barnes 1983).

In principle, any belief about pricing, if widely enough shared, could be performative. 'Chartism', or 'technical analysis', is replete with beliefs about the patterns that can be seen in price charts and their implications for future price movements. From the perspective of orthodox financial economics, these patterns are simply read by undisciplined observers into what are actually random walks. Note, however, that if there are enough chartists perceiving the same patterns and seeing in them the same implications, chartist beliefs may be self-fulfilling. The *Guardian*, for example, described how a fall in the S&P 500 index in

September 2002 was temporarily reversed when the index reached 870, 'the point at which the index would have handed back exactly half of its recent 70 point "summer rally"'. According to some chart watchers, a 50% retracement is a signal that the market has bottomed, at least in the short term' (Hume 2002). The potentially self-vindicating nature of chartism is well understood by market practitioners. For example it allows those who know that being a chartist is potentially discreditable to distance themselves while still practising chartism, by saying in effect 'of course, *I* do not believe in it, but because others do, I must also attend to it'.[17]

The *Guardian*'s headline on the S&P's reversal – 'Hocus-Pocus saves the Day' – indicates the difference between the performativity of financial economics and that of chartism. The former has considerable cognitive prestige: by no means everyone agrees with its propositions, but its leading practitioners have won Nobel Prizes. While many traders (professional as well as lay) are chartists, chartism enjoys no similar wider authority. For example, as far as I am aware, no university teaches chartism.

The reasons for the contrast are many, but they include the fact that the key propositions of financial economics are tightly linked to an influential theoretical portrayal of markets. Among the assumptions of Black-Scholes-Merton option pricing theory, for example, are that shares can be purchased entirely on credit (at the same 'risk-free' rate of interest that cash can earn), that there are no restrictions on short selling, and that a portfolio can be adjusted instantaneously and without incurring transaction costs. There is little that is specific to option pricing theory here: similar assumptions are pervasive in financial economics. Matters of mathematical convenience of course feature in the choice of assumptions, but wider issues are involved too. 'Is' and 'ought' are here tightly linked (Taleb 1998). These assumptions were not (and were not intended to be) an empirical description of the markets at the time when Black, Scholes and Merton published their work in 1973. Nor do they describe the markets of 2010. But note that they are *more* accurate in 2010 than in 1973. In part, this is because technological changes have speeded up transactions and lowered their cost. In part, though, it is because these assumptions embody key aspects of what has been, above all in the US, an influential vision of how markets *should* be. In 1973, for example, a major transaction cost (at least for an individual or firm that was not a member of a stock exchange) was the high, fixed commissions charged on stock purchases and sales. Fixed commissions were outlawed in the US in 1975, and in the UK in Margaret Thatcher's 'big bang' of 1986, and commissions have since declined to close to zero – indeed actually to zero for major players' knowledge of whose trades is valuable to brokers.

The overlap of 'ought' and 'is' means that technical issues of financial economics are also political. Most obvious is the Tobin tax (a proposed small international tax on foreign-exchange transactions and perhaps other financial trading as well), which if implemented would be a transaction cost. Even if Tobin taxes were very small, a world in which such taxes were universal would, according to the logic of the Black-Scholes-Merton model, have to price options differently (see Leland 1985). Other political issues are less obvious. An implicit assumption (so obvious it did not need spelled out explicitly) of all option pricing theory is that share prices are known. In the US, at least after fast price feeds from the New York Stock Exchange to derivatives[18] exchanges were installed, that assumption was reasonably valid, at least for derivatives for which the underlying assets were shares traded in New York. In the UK, in contrast, it was often the case that disclosure of large stock transactions could be delayed for 90 minutes, which is an eternity in a fast-moving market (Gemmill 1996). The issue is, in a broad sense, a political one: delayed disclosure helped the London Stock Exchange retain the business of large players. It allowed market makers to enter into large block trades while reducing the risk of prices moving against them as a result of the transaction. But delayed disclosure also seems to have been one factor hindering the emergence in Britain of an options market with anything like the vitality of the US options exchanges. British option traders could never be sure that quoted share prices were 'real': that a large undisclosed transaction had not taken place. Hedging one's option position (that is, constructing a replicating portfolio) was thus more problematic in the UK. It was perhaps one reason why option trading never developed on the same scale in the UK as in the US. It is also an indicator that, although it is commonplace to talk of an 'Anglo-American' view of the financial markets, once one starts to open black boxes consequential differences become apparent (see also MacKenzie 2007).

More generally, it is worth noting that Black-Scholes-Merton option pricing theory did more than teach practitioners how to price options. It was rapidly extended to cover a wide variety of contingent claims (that is, claims that will be exercised only if certain states of the world prevail). The methodology of constructing a replicating portfolio and using it to determine prices and to hedge risks was widely adopted not just for options but for derivatives of many kinds. One of the most striking features of the transformation of the global financial system since the early 1970s has been the explosion of the derivatives market. In 1970, the market for options was small; financial futures would have been illegal in the US and in many other countries; swaps had yet to be invented. By December 2008, the total notional amount of these and other derivative contracts outstanding worldwide was $650 trillion (around $97,000 for every human being on earth).[19]

The developments in asset pricing theory initiated by Black, Scholes and Merton were central to this growth of derivatives. It is hard to imagine trading $650 trillion of derivatives without a reasonably credible theoretical guide to their pricing (for all the overall size of the derivatives market, many individual derivatives are illiquid and recent market prices can be hard to obtain) and to controlling the risks they entail. Option pricing and cognate theories matter here not just technically but in providing legitimacy. A major reason for the small size of the derivatives markets in 1970 was the loss of legitimacy derivatives suffered from 1929 onwards. They were widely suspected, most consequentially by market regulators such as the US Securities and Exchange Commission (SEC), of being inherently instruments of speculation, even of gambling; and in 1970 hostility to speculation, and a desire for a clear boundary between investing and gambling, remained a strong impulse. The economics of options (first some of the earlier work and then, as the decisive capstone, Black-Scholes-Merton theory) helped break these connections between derivatives and disreputability.[20]

Of option pricing theory, the first black box to be opened here, this can therefore be said: it was performative, albeit not simply so – see MacKenzie (2006) for the deteriorating fit of the Black-Scholes-Merton model to empirical prices after 1987. Inscribed in the theory, as in financial economics more generally, was a vision of a market: not of how markets actually were, but of an 'ideal' market, where the ideal was not just a matter of eliminating mathematical complexities but became hitched to how markets were, historically, being transformed. And, in its turn, the black box altered its context: it helped to make more real the vision of the market inscribed within it.

Arbitrage

As noted above, arbitrage is trading that exploits price discrepancies. If two similar assets 'should' have the same price, and temporarily don't, then arbitrage profits can be made by short selling the dearer and buying the cheaper. In standard theoretical portrayals, arbitrage requires no capital (the proceeds from the short sale provide the cash for the purchase), and, because the price discrepancies are knowably temporary, it involves no risk. The capacity of arbitrage to close price discrepancies is thus unlimited.

Arbitrage is the key theoretical mechanism in financial economics. A whole set of central propositions have been demonstrated by 'arbitrage proof' – the demonstration that if the proposition did *not* hold, then an arbitrage opportunity would open up. Arbitrage proof was introduced in now-classic work by economists Franco Modigliani and Merton Miller in 1958 (Modigliani and Miller 1958; see also Miller and Modigliani 1961); as we have seen, arbitrage proof was central to the Black-Scholes-Merton work on option pricing. The significance of arbitrage goes beyond the importance of the specific propositions demonstrated in this way. Consideration of arbitrage makes it possible to posit that financial markets are efficient (that is, to speak loosely, that prices in them reflect all known information) even if many, or most, investors are irrational. In the words of finance theorist Steve Ross:

> I, for one, never thought that people – myself included – were all that rational in their behavior. To the contrary, I am always amazed at what people do. But, that was never the point of financial theory. The absence of arbitrage requires that there be enough well financed and smart investors to close arbitrage opportunities when they appear. ... Neoclassical finance is a theory of sharks [i.e. arbitrageurs] and not a theory of rational homo economicus, and that is the principal distinction between finance and traditional economics. In most economic models aggregate demand depends on average demand and for that reason, traditional economic theories require the average individual to be rational. In liquid securities markets, though, profit opportunities bring about infinite discrepancies between demand and supply. Well financed arbitrageurs spot these opportunities, pile on and by their actions they close aberrant price differentials. ... Rational finance has stripped the assumptions [about the behaviour of investors] down to only those required to support efficient markets and the absence of arbitrage, and has worked very hard to rid the field of its sensitivity to the psychological vagaries of investors.
>
> (Ross 2001: 4)

Arbitrageurs can therefore be seen as doing a particular form of 'boundary work': they keep 'the economic' (matters of pricing) separate from 'the sociological' or 'the psychological' (for example, investors' irrational enthusiasms or fears). The above quotation from Ross, for example, comes from a talk designed to rebut 'behavioural finance', which, as its name implies, posits psychological processes as affecting economic matters.

This pivotal role of arbitrage makes it an especially interesting black box to open, and the growing feasibility of arbitrage has been one of the most marked changes in the financial markets since the 1970s (the lower transaction costs referred to in the previous section have been one major factor; close-to-instantaneous dissemination of prices via technological systems is another). Unfortunately there is little empirical work by social scientists on the actual practice of arbitrage and only a modest amount by economists.[21] The case in which I have focused most centrally on arbitrage is that of the hedge fund Long-Term Capital Management (LTCM), which, famously, nearly became bankrupt in September 1998 (it was recapitalized by a consortium of the world's leading banks coordinated by the Federal Reserve Bank of New York).[22] Much of the commentary on LTCM (e.g. see the books by Dunbar 2000 and Lowenstein 2000) has focused on the fund's use of mathematical models: among its partners were Merton and Scholes. This use, however, was less central than the commentary has implied, and LTCM certainly did not place blind faith in the models it used. Instead, what undid LTCM was, paradoxically, its success. It and its predecessor group, headed by LTCM's founder John W. Meriwether at the investment bank Salomon Brothers, were strikingly profitable. In 1994, LTCM's first part-year of trading, its returns before fees were 28.1 per cent (unannualized). After management and incentive fees were deducted, investors received 19.9 per cent (unannualized). Gross returns in 1995 were 59.0 per cent, and returns after fees 42.8 per cent; in 1996, the corresponding figures were 61.5 per cent and 40.8 per cent.[23]

This success attracted imitation by investment banks and other hedge funds, including at least one fund founded deliberately to attract clients unable to invest in LTCM (which quickly became closed to new investment). In some cases, there seems to have been deliberate imitation of LTCM's positions: the fund tried as hard as it could not to let these become known, but the very act of implementing an arbitrage would make one leg of the arbitrage known to the counterparty, and with one leg known it was not in general too hard to work out what the other leg must be. But even those entirely ignorant of LTCM's specific positions would often have been led to take similar positions themselves: precisely because what LTCM did was *not* 'rocket science', *not* highly dependent on the specifics of particular models.

The consequence of conscious or unconscious imitation of LTCM was the building up of what one might call a 'superportfolio' of large, partially overlapping arbitrage positions held by a substantial number of banks and hedge funds. The trigger of the 1998 crisis was the decision of the Russian government on 17 August 1998 to default on its ruble-denominated bonds and to devalue the ruble; the subsequent ruling by Russian courts that cash-settled currency forwards were unenforceable wagers meant that Russian banks were able, perfectly legally, not to honour those contracts (see Milyaeva 2009). The precise form of Russia's decision caused significant losses to arbitrageurs: they used forward contracts to hedge the foreign-exchange risk of holding ruble-denominated bonds, and some had short sold Russian hard currency bonds as a hedge against defaults. For these latter investors, even the good news of 17 August, Russia's avoidance of a hard-currency default, was damaging, because it meant their hedge failed to protect them adequately.

LTCM itself had only limited exposure to Russia. However other holders of the 'superportfolio' had greater exposure, and they had to begin to liquidate other holdings to meet their losses in Russia. This caused the adverse movement of prices of those assets, more liquidations, further adverse price movements and so on in a catastrophic cascade: an unravelling of the superportfolio that led to LTCM's near-bankruptcy.

What is the bearing of these events on our understanding of arbitrage? First, real-world arbitrage almost always involves some capital outlay. Short-sale proceeds, for example, are not in general available in their entirety: lenders retain some or all of such proceeds as collateral. Similarly those who lend money to permit the purchase of securities typically insist on 'haircuts': the borrower must put up at least some of their own capital. Even more consequentially, the world in which arbitrageurs now move is almost always a world that 'marks to market', normally daily: as the market price of a derivatives contract moves in favour of one party or the other, collateral has to be transferred.[24]

Second, the capital needed for arbitrage seldom belongs to the arbitrageur. Although the managers of a hedge fund are often expected to have more than half of their personal wealth in the fund, most of the capital they manage comes from outside investors, and these investors can often withdraw their funds at short notice. (LTCM was unusual in imposing on its investors a three-year capital 'lock-up': this feature was signalled by the 'Long-Term' in the fund's title.) An investment bank is usually a unitary legal entity; but there is, nevertheless, a sense in which its arbitrageurs are 'lent' capital by the bank's senior managers (and ultimately, of course, by the bank's creditors, shareholders and bond holders). Managers and investors may well react to substantial losses by withdrawing capital. So if the two prices that arbitrageurs expect to convergence instead diverge, capital withdrawals may force arbitrageurs to liquidate positions – even if the arbitrageurs themselves know that the divergence is temporary and indeed that it has made the arbitrage opportunity *more* attractive![25]

That is precisely what took place in 1998. There was nothing generally wrong with the choice of arbitrage positions by LTCM or its imitators. Many positions have subsequently gone on to converge just as anticipated, often quite quickly: for example, the consortium that recapitalized LTCM earned a perfectly satisfactory return on its investment, and an interviewee later told me that much of LTCM's portfolio of positions was taken over from the consortium by the Chicago-based hedge fund, the Citadel Investment Group, which made healthy profits on it. En route to eventual convergence, however, prices diverged to an extent that temporarily threatened the stability of the global financial system, and a good part of that divergence was caused by the flight of arbitrage capital. (It is possible at least crudely to test quantitatively for the presence of arbitrage capital flight rather than more general mechanisms of financial crisis: see MacKenzie 2003 for details and data.)

The possibility that arbitrage capital may flee, even as arbitrage opportunities become more attractive, limits arbitrage's capacity to insulate 'the economic' from 'the social'. Even this formulation, however, is inadequate – for the third feature of 1998, emphasized above, is the presence of an elementary social process: imitation. Among the consequences of imitation was a failure of the classic means of controlling financial risk: diversification. LTCM's positions were well spread geographically and across asset classes. At the level of economic 'fundamentals', little or nothing connected its various arbitrage positions (obvious common factors such as interest-rate changes or fluctuations in global stock markets were neutralized by the twinned 'long' and 'short' positions characteristic of arbitrage), and the observed correlations between positions were very low: typically 0.1 or lower. In the crisis, however, these correlations jumped, an interviewee told me, to typical levels of around 0.7, so that diversification was of little avail: almost all LTCM's positions moved against the fund, including those that, by normal economic reasoning, should have moved in its favour in a crisis.

Ethnoaccountancy

The final two black boxes to be discussed are ones that I would like to see opened but have worked on myself only in limited ways. The first is accounting, where I renew an appeal made many years ago for 'ethnoaccountancy' (MacKenzie 1992). I intended the term to be analogous, for example, to 'ethnobotany', which is the study of how different cultures classify plants, and which typically sets aside 'our' botanic classifications. 'Ethnoaccountancy' is the study of how people actually do their financial reckoning, setting aside preconceptions of how that reckoning should be done. It is a notion fully compatible with the 'social turn' taken by many scholars in accounting in the 1980s and 1990s (e.g. see Hopwood and Miller 1994; and for a useful survey Vollmer 2003).

As MacKenzie (1992) pointed out, a key issue for ethnoaccountancy is profit. Profit is of course a key goal of firms in a capitalist economy, yet they can know their profits only through accounting procedures. An ethnoaccountancy of profit need not start from scratch. There is an interesting tradition in accountancy research of statistical analysis of corporations' reported profits and losses, in which statistical anomalies suggest active 'earnings management'. Thus Hayn (1995: 132) reports that 'there is a point of discontinuity around zero. Specifically, there is a concentration of cases just above zero [i.e. small positive profits], while there are fewer than expected cases ... of small losses (i.e. just below zero). ... These results suggest that firms whose earnings are expected to fall just below the zero earnings point engage in earnings manipulations to help them cross the "red line" for the year'. Burgstahler and Dichev (1997: 101), analysing a very large sample of US corporations' reported earnings, estimate that '8–12% of firms with small pre-managed earnings decreases manipulate earnings to achieve earnings increases, and 30–44% of firms with small pre-managed losses manage earnings to create positive earnings'. The data underlying these conclusions stretch back some way in time (Burgstahler and Dichev analyse earnings figures from 1976 to 1994), and they suggest, though do not prove,[26] that 'earnings management' is not a phenomenon just of the Enron era.

What does seem newer, however, is the phenomenon discovered by Zorn (n.d.): the growing tendency in the 1990s of US corporations to meet or exceed securities analysts' consensus forecasts of their earnings. From the mid-1970s to the end of the 1980s, around 50 per cent of firms did so, which is of course what one would expect if those forecasts were unbiased estimations of earnings. During the 1990s, however, the proportion rose to nearly 70 per cent. Possibly firms were succeeding in persuading analysts to lower their forecasts so as to increase the chance of exceeding them, but perhaps firms were massaging their profit figures so as to exceed forecasts. That the latter is a real possibility is suggested by a survey of a meeting of chief financial officers reported by Valdmanis (1998: 18): 'About 12% of CFOs admitted they had "misrepresented corporate financial results" at the request of senior company executives; 55% said that they had been asked to do so but "fought off" the demand.'

Findings such as these, and the Enron and WorldCom debacles, strengthen the case for ethnoaccountancy of profit, but we should beware easy assumptions about the correctable misrepresentation of 'real' profits or losses. The point is that all measurement of profits rests on accounting conventions, and the nature of those conventions, and how they are applied in practice, may have profound effects in shaping corporate behaviour. Consider the analogy of the behaviour of British university departments. They are, no doubt, oriented to the advancement and transmission of knowledge, just as firms are oriented to profit. Yet the details of their behaviour have been affected profoundly by the *particular* forms of research and teaching quality assessment prevalent in recent years. To focus only on Enron-style misrepresentations in university settings would be to miss the *overall* shaping processes. So with earnings: focusing only on scandals would miss the overall way corporate behaviour has been shaped by the ethnoaccountancy of profit. The analysis of these shaping processes can build upon quantitative studies like those outlined above (especially Zorn's fine study), but the quantitative work typically rests on figures produced by the black box of the accountancy of profit. Fully understanding the processes involved will ultimately require ethnographic black-box opening, inquiring into matters such as the nature of accountants' and auditors' discretion, the pattern of incentives they face, their responses to those incentives and any effects of the greatly enhanced prospect of penalties after the scandals. There is certainly existing work to build on here. Yet – because 'One of the disappointing characteristics of field studies in organizations is how few have examined how accounting and audit decisions are made' (Cooper and Robson 2006: 435) – there is still much to be done.[27]

Regulation

The study of the regulation of financial markets is also certainly not virgin territory, with scholars in the 'law and economics' tradition and in international political economy having played particularly important roles. The task in regard to regulation, therefore, is not to open an unopened black box but to go deeper into it: to encourage more fine-grained studies, and to examine connections between the apparent 'detail' of regulation and larger issues in the construction of financial markets.

Let me give an example: single-stock futures.[28] The relevant regulatory feature here is that the US has not one but several financial regulators, notably the Federal Reserve, the SEC and the Commodity Futures Trading Commission (CFTC). These regulators are not always at one, and in particular there has been periodic bitter rivalry between the SEC and CFTC. The products that the markets have traded, and critically the products they have *not* been able to trade, have been affected strongly by the efforts at structural resolution of regulatory conflict. The US markets, for example, have traded, for nearly three decades or more, options on single stocks, options on indices, and futures on indices – but, until November 2002, did not trade futures on single stocks, even though such stock futures were traded in 'regulated' Sweden since the 1980s. Nothing intrinsic to futures on stocks explains their absence in the US. Instead, the single-stock future was for decades an impossible commodity because it spanned regulatory domains: stocks were the heartland domain of the SEC; futures of the CFTC. For either to have ceded regulation of single-stock futures to its rival would have been a huge concession, so it was easiest not to permit such futures to exist. In terms of Mary Douglas's anthropology, the single-stock future was an abomination, an anomaly in a painstakingly negotiated classification system that was also a negotiation of political 'turf'.[29]

Is the regulatory history of single-stock futures more than detail? It bears upon a pervasive asymmetry in the US and many other stock markets. Those who have access to the necessarily capital can readily express a 'positive' opinion or 'positive' information about the prospect for stocks by buying them. Expressing a 'negative' opinion or acting upon 'negative' information is much harder. Imagine, for example, that some time before the bankruptcies of Enron and Worldcom a market participant knew or suspected that their financial situation was a lot less solid than it appeared? How could the participant act on this knowledge? The obvious way to do this is to short sell stock, since a short seller will benefit from a price decline. However short selling encounters practical problems (can the stock in question be borrowed, and is there a risk it may have to be repurchased and returned at a disadvantageous price?) and also regulatory barriers. In the US and many other jurisdictions, many large institutional investors are prohibited from short selling, and in the US short sales could legally be made only after a rise in stock prices (the latter regulation is called the 'uptick' rule, and was in place from 1938 to 2007). 'Voting' for a company by purchasing its stock is easy. Voting against it is harder, and many of those with negative opinions or information therefore 'abstain'.[30]

Stock futures offered an alternative and potentially an attractive way of expressing a negative opinion. The seller of a stock future benefits from a price decline, just as a short seller of the underlying stock does, but free from the 'uptick' rule and many of the other barriers encountered by the short seller.[31] The issue matters because – despite the fact that short sellers are often blamed for price declines – there is reason to think that markets in which it is hard effectively to act on negative information or to express a negative opinion may be prone to instability. The disproportionate ease of acting on positive opinions or information may cause asset prices to become unjustifiably high, and the process of 'correction' in which previously latent negative opinions or information express themselves may correspondingly be dangerously precipitous. The asymmetry in the ease of expressing positive and negative opinion and information may thus lead to an asymmetry in market behaviour, with the speed of decline (when it eventually happens) being far faster than the speed of rising. Hong and Stein (2003) provide a formal model of this process and argue that it may explain the tendency of markets such as the US stock market to succumb to precipitous crashes in the absence of commensurate negative news.

It is tempting to think of states and markets as somehow opposed,[32] and to conceive of the changes in the global financial system since the early 1970s as 'deregulation', the withdrawal of the state. This is a view that cannot survive serious study of the regulation of financial markets. The modern American financial markets are almost certainly the most highly regulated markets in history, if regulation is measured by volume (number of pages) of rules, probably also if measured by extent of surveillance, and possibly even by vigour of enforcement. (The title of Vogel's fine 1996 study, *Freer Markets, More Rules*, captures the point beautifully.)[33] Popular involvement, emotional as well as financial, in markets has typically been deeper in the US than elsewhere, but, possibly in part because of this, outbreaks of popular hostility have been sharper. The European Left has often opposed capitalism in general rather than financial markets in particular, while American populism has often wanted to preserve capitalism while eliminating 'speculation' and other financial abuses. Surprisingly large boosts to the political careers even of Republicans can come from exposing such abuses, even if to those involved at least some of these were mere 'technical infringements'. Republican former mayor of New York Rudolph Giuliani has been the highest placed such beneficiary (I know one arbitrageur who keeps a dartboard adorned with Giuliani's face) but New York's more recent Attorney General, Eliot Spitzer, a rising star of the Democratic Party until damaged by a sexual scandal, was also buoyed by the 'name recognition' that flowed from a high-profile campaign against Wall Street abuses.

Epilogue: The black boxes of the credit crisis

As noted earlier, an intellectual strategy that focuses on opening black boxes sometimes arouses the suspicion that it involves undue focus on 'detail'. However the credit crisis that began in the summer of 2007 shows that scales aren't stable, as actor-network theory would put it. Detailed matters *are* involved in the credit crisis, and they have not remained small; the black boxes of global finance have become very leaky indeed; the 30-year hegemony of 'deregulated' Anglo-American perspectives on finance has been undermined; and problems in the financial system have helped spark sharp recession in the wider economy.[34]

Let me end this chapter by sketching briefly the role in the crisis of the four kinds of black box discussed here, beginning with mathematical models. While the Black-Scholes model is not itself implicated in the crisis, a family of models that owes much to the Black-Scholes-Merton approach does: the Gaussian copula family. The main role of these models is in the evaluation of collateralized debt obligations (CDOs), a category of product at the heart of the crisis. A CDO involves the creation of a trust or special-purpose corporation that buys – or 'synthetically' takes on the credit risk of – a pool of debt instruments, such as loans, bonds, securities based on pools of mortgages and so on. The trust or corporation generates the capital needed to buy the debt instruments by selling to investors (almost always institutional investors, not private investors) a set of securities structured into a hierarchy of tranches. The lowest tranche (the 'equity' tranche) offers the highest rate of return, but bears the first losses should any of the debt instruments default. Higher tranches offer lower returns, but are safer because they are cushioned from default by the tranches below them.

Salmon (2009) describes the Gaussian copula as 'the formula that killed Wall Street'. The claim is exaggerated, but the belief that CDOs, complex as they are, could nevertheless be modelled adequately was a vital part of the process that generated the crisis, in particular by making it possible for the credit rating agencies to award CDOs high ratings (including the highest rating, AAA) even when their asset pools started to include not just securities based on subprime mortgages but even the mezzanine – next-to-lowest – tranches of such securities.

The second black box discussed here, arbitrage, is relevant to the credit crisis in less obvious ways. One of these ways may be through an absence: the role of arbitrage in tying the prices of derivatives to their underlying assets (as, for example, in the arbitrage underpinning the Black-Scholes model) was significantly less in some 'credit derivatives', such as CDOs, than in other derivatives. That, however, is a complex issue that must be left for further elaboration elsewhere.

Two further roles of arbitrage are more clear-cut. The first is that although the initial CDOs were generally set up for the 'balance sheet' reasons discussed below, from the late 1990s onwards they were primarily arbitrage vehicles: those setting them up captured the difference between the total cash flow generated from the assets in the CDO's pool and the total payments to investors, while passing on to the latter the losses caused by default on the assets. It was thus close to riskless profit.[35] The second was a variant of a widely practised arbitrage known as a 'negative basis' trade. In this variant, traders – especially at leading investment banks such as UBS (see UBS AG 2008) – would buy the safest, 'super-senior' tranches of mortgage-backed CDOs (or retain those tranches of CDOs they had themselves structured), and insure them against loss via a 'credit default swap' with a monoline (a specialist bond insurer). They would thus capture the apparently almost riskless difference between their cost of funding (approximately LIBOR, London interbank offered rate) and the 'spread' (that is, rate of return, normally quoted as an increment over LIBOR) offered by the tranche, minus the premium paid to the monoline. There are echoes here of the 'superportfolio' surrounding LTCM. A small number of these trades would indeed have involved only limited risk, but they were entered into on a huge scale by traders in several large banks, leaving the monolines' capacity to honour the insurance they provided in doubt. Negative-basis trades were a significant contributor to one of the most distinctive aspects of the credit crisis: the way in which risk accumulated at the apex of the financial system (see MacKenzie 2009).

The third black box discussed here, accounting, is also intimately involved in the crisis. Crucial to many of the trading strategies that led to the crisis was the capacity to 'book' the present value of the anticipated profits of trades at their inception ('day one P&L' is how participants refer to this). This boosted traders' bonuses and banks' profits considerably. Controversy over accounting has also been very prominent in the crisis. Modern 'fair value' accounting standards require many of the assets at the core of the crisis to be marked to market (revalued as market prices fluctuate). As markets seized up, such prices as were available plunged precipitously, and – vitally – accountants and auditors nevertheless insisted in many cases that assets should be marked to those low prices. (Here the effect of the Enron and WorldCom scandals may well have been at work, with the fear of jail or other legal penalties motivating those accountants and auditors to resist strong pressures to mark more generously.) While 'fair value' accounting and marking are often blamed by banks' senior managers as exacerbating the crisis, another view is possible: that they forced banks' difficulties – indeed, their possible insolvency – into the public domain, thus triggering necessary policy action to recapitalize banks.

The final black box, regulation, offers the most difficult challenges of all. Clearly, the crisis revealed deficiencies in regulation, but not the *absence* of regulation. It was, for example, not the lightly regulated hedge funds but the much more closely regulated banks that were at the heart of the crisis, and the category of instrument at its core – the CDO – owed much of its popularity, at least in the late 1990s and the very early years of the new decade, to the way in which it could be used to shift credit risk off banks' balance sheets and thus to reduce the capital reserves that regulators insisted banks hold. More generally, the crisis has revealed the extent to which the behaviour of banks and their traders was shaped, in detailed ways that largely escaped academic attention at the time, by the pattern of penalties and incentives (often unintended) that regulatory systems presented to them. Reshaping those systems so that they constrain risk-taking while not stifling financial innovation is one of today's toughest policy challenges – and one in which the intellectual strategy advocated here, opening the black boxes of global finance, will be utterly necessary.

Notes

1. This chapter is a revised and updated version of an article that first appeared in the *Review of Political Economy* in 2005. The research on the credit crisis that fed into the revision is being supported by a grant from the UK Economic and Social Research Council (RES-062-23-1958). I am grateful to Taylor & Francis for their permission to reuse the material from the original article.
2. The introduction to the field that best captures this diversity is still Biagioli's reader (Biagioli 1999).
3. For a collection of articles covering 'social studies of finance' in both a science-studies and a broader social-science sense, see Knorr Cetina and Preda (2005); another useful collection is Kalthoff et al. (2000). Other noteworthy science-studies work on contributions to finance include Beunza and

Stark (2004); Knorr Cetina and Bruegger (2002a, b); Lépinay (2007a, b); Millo (2003); Millo et al. (2005); Muniesa (2003, 2005); Preda (2006, 2009). For a review and further references, see Preda (2007a).

4. See Godechot (2000, 2001: 218–30) and Preda (2007b). My own fieldwork among Chicago derivatives traders also suggests a prevalence of chartist beliefs and practices that would be surprising to the financial economist.
5. A high proportion of the written records of ancient civilizations is comprised of records of ownership and taxation: 'The earliest known written documents – marks baked in clay – are tallies of livestock, grain, and oil' writes McMillan (2002: 4).
6. I think I owe this formulation to a remark by Sheila Jasanoff, although the heuristic itself is widely shared.
7. See, for example, Latour (1987), but again the heuristic is pervasive.
8. See, for example, Rosenberg (1982), although from the perspective of more recent science and technology studies Rosenberg lifts the box's lid only partially. Market microstructure theory is another form of 'black box opening' (see Madhavan and Panchapagesan 2000). For its relations to science-studies approaches see Muniesa (2003).
9. This is, in a sense, simply the Weberian account of bureaucracy: see Weber (1970).
10. See, for example, Giddens (1990).
11. This critique is, of course, the basis of the infamous 'science wars'. My thoughts on these will be found in MacKenzie (2002).
12. Perhaps most vocal in this critique has been Langdon Winner: for example Winner (1993).
13. See MacKenzie (1990: 209–14) for a discussion of the design of accelerometers and of the bearings upon which their gyroscope wheels spin.
14. For more details, see MacKenzie (2006).
15. There was also much earlier work by, among others, the French mathematician Louis Bachelier (1900).
16. To short sell an asset is to sell an asset one does not own, for example by borrowing it, selling it and later repurchasing and returning it. A short seller profits from a price decline because the asset can be repurchased for less than the proceeds of the initial sale.
17. See the remarks of a trader quoted by Godechot (2001: 227–8).
18. A 'derivative' is a security or contract, the price of which depends upon the price of another more 'basic' asset (or index level, interest rate, or other quantity): an option is one example of a derivative in that its price depends upon that of the block of shares or other underlying asset.
19. Data from Bank for International Settlements, www.bis.org, accessed 8 June 2009.
20. For details, see MacKenzie (2006).
21. See Beunza and Stark (2004) and Beunza et al. (2006).
22. See MacKenzie (2003).
23. The figures for total returns are calculated from the data in Perold (1999: A19); the figures for returns net of fees are taken from Perold (1999: A2).
24. The consequent demands for capital would lead most economists to argue that what LTCM did was therefore not 'really' arbitrage. The response is simple (see Shleifer and Vishny 1997): much real-world arbitrage, including the

real-world counterparts of some of the classic arbitrages of finance theory, demands capital and involves at least some risk. See MacKenzie and Millo (2003) on options arbitrage.

25. This is the key insight of Shleifer and Vishny (1997), a prescient piece of work in that it models one key feature of 1998: the flight of arbitrage capital in the face of improving arbitrage opportunities. It does not, however, model the other key feature: the imitative superportfolio.
26. The problem is that anticipated small earnings decreases can be turned into small increases by 'real' intervention, such as cuts in expenditure on maintenance or on research and development.
27. For an example of the kind of ethnographic work being called for here, see Leung (2008); a much more modest study is MacKenzie (2008a).
28. Since completing the first draft of this section, I discovered an excellent study in the 'law and economics' tradition of the regulatory background to single-stock futures: Partnoy (2001).
29. On this see Douglas (1970). Millo (2003) discusses the key outcome of SEC–CFTC negotiation: the Shad–Johnson Accord. It is telling that regulatory bodies should have needed this 'peace treaty'.
30. See Partnoy (2003) on the barriers to short selling. Of course one should not exaggerate these barriers. Thus Harvard University's endowment fund took a large short position on Enron via the hedge fund Highfields Capital Management (Bryce 2002: 268) and must have profited handsomely from doing so.
31. Some futures contracts can be settled by delivery of the underlying asset at the contract's maturity. In practice, delivery is seldom or never required, and economically equivalent gains or losses are achieved by futures exchanges requiring daily payment or refund of balances held by the exchange clearing house.
32. Underhill argues that most scholars in international political economy 'despite their protestations, still see the state and the market as separate and indeed antagonistic dynamics' (Underhill 2000: 808).
33. That does not imply that American investment banks, hedge funds and so on are necessarily highly regulated because such entities have a considerable degree of discretion as to the jurisdictions within which they operate.
34. The most insightful study of the crisis, to date, is Tett (2009). Some of the discussion in this section can be found in detail in MacKenzie (2008b, 2009).
35. The main risk – one that caused banks serious losses in the credit crisis – arose from 'warehousing' assets while the CDOs for which they were destined were being constructed and sold.

Bibliography

Austin, J. L. (1962), *How to Do Things With Words*, Oxford: Clarendon Press.

Bachelier, L. (1900), 'Théorie de la Spéculation', *Annales Scientifiques de l'Ecole Normale Supérieure* third series 17: 22–86.

Barnes, B. (1983), 'Social Life as Bootstrapped Induction', *Sociology*, 17: 524–45.

Beunza, D. Hardie, I. and MacKenzie, D. (2006), 'A Price is a Social Thing: Towards a Material Sociology of Arbitrage', *Organization Studies*, 27: 721–45.

Beunza, D. and Stark, D. (2004), 'Tools of the Trade: The Socio-Technology of Arbitrage in a Wall Street Trading Room', *Industrial and Corporate Change*, 13: 369–400.

Biagioli, M. (ed.) (1999), *The Science Studies Reader*, New York: Routledge.

Black, F. and Scholes, M. (1972), 'The Valuation of Option Contracts and a Test of Market Efficiency', *Journal of Finance*, 27: 399–417.

Black, F. and Scholes, M. (1973), 'The Pricing of Options and Corporate Liabilities', *Journal of Political Economy*, 81: 637–54.

Bryce, R. (2002), *Pipe Dreams: Greed, Ego, and the Death of Enron*, New York: PublicAffairs.

Burgstahler, D. and Dichev, I. (1997), 'Earnings Management to Avoid Earnings Decreases and Losses', *Journal of Accounting and Economics*, 24: 99–126.

Callon, M. and Latour, B. (1981), 'Unscrewing the Big Leviathan: How Actors Macro-Structure Reality and How Sociologists Help Them to do So', in K. Knorr Cetina and A. V. Cicourel (eds), *Advances in Social Theory and Methodology: Toward an Integration of Micro- and Macro-Sociologies*, Boston, MA: Routledge and Kegan Paul: 277–303.

Cooper, D. J. and Robson, K. (2006), 'Accounting, Professions and Regulation: Locating the Sites of Professionalization', *Accounting, Organizations and Society*, 31: 415–44.

Douglas, M. (1970), *Purity and Danger: An Analysis of Concepts of Pollution and Taboo*, Harmondsworth: Penguin.

Dunbar, N. (2000), *Inventing Money: The Story of Long-Term Capital Management and the Legends Behind it*, Chichester: Wiley.

Galai, D. (1977), 'Tests of Market Efficiency of the Chicago Board Options Exchange', *Journal of Business*, 50: 167–97.

Gemmill, G. (1996), 'Transparency and Liquidity: A Study of Block Trades on the London Stock Exchange under different Publication Rules', *Journal of Finance*, 51: 1765–90.

Giddens, A. (1990), *The Consequences of Modernity*, Cambridge: Polity.

Gieryn, T. (1999), *Cultural Boundaries of Science: Credibility on the Line*, Chicago, IL: Chicago University Press.

Godechot, O. (2000), 'Le Bazar de la Rationalité: Vers une Sociologie des Formes Concrètes de Raisonnement', *Politix*, 13(52): 17–56.

Godechot, O. (2001), *Les Traders: Essai de Sociologie des Marchés Financiers*, Paris: La Découverte.

Godechot, O. (2007), *Working Rich: Salaires, Bonus et Appropriation du Profit dans l'Industrie Financière*, Paris: La Découverte.

Hayn, C. (1995), 'The Information Content of Losses', *Journal of Accounting and Economics*, 20: 125–53.

Hong, H. and Stein, J. C. (2003), 'Differences of Opinion, Short-Sales Constraints, and Market Crashes', *Review of Financial Studies*, 16: 487–525.

Hopwood, A. and Miller, P. (eds) (1994), *Accounting as Social and Institutional Practice*, Cambridge: Cambridge University Press.

Hume, N. (2002), 'Hocus-Pocus Saves the Day', *The Guardian*, 6 September.

Hume, N., Treanor, J. and Milner, M. (2002), 'FTSE Closes Below 4,000 as Bush Intervention Fails', *The Guardian*, 16 July.

Kalthoff, H., Rottenburg, R. and Wagener, H. -J. (2000), *Ökonomie und Gesellschaft, Jahrbuch 16. Facts and Figures: Economic Representations and Practices*, Marburg: Metropolis.
Knorr Cetina, K. and Bruegger, U. (2002a), 'Global Microstructures: The Virtual Societies of Financial Markets', *American Journal of Sociology*, 107: 905–51.
Knorr Cetina, K. and Bruegger, U. (2002b), 'Inhabiting Technology: The Global Lifeform of Financial Markets', *Current Sociology*, 50: 389–405.
Knorr Cetina, K. and Preda, A. (eds) (2005), *The Sociology of Financial Markets*, Oxford: Oxford University Press.
Latour, B. (1987), *Science in Action*, Cambridge, MA: Harvard University Press.
Leland, H. E. (1985), 'Option Pricing and Replication with Transaction Costs', *Journal of Finance*, 40: 1283–301.
Lépinay, V-. A. (2007a), 'Decoding Finance: Articulation and Liquidity Around a Trading Room', in D. MacKenzie, F. Muniesa and L. Siu (eds), *Do Economists Make Markets? On the Performativity of Economics*, Princeton, NJ: Princeton University Press: 87–127.
Lépinay, V-. A. (2007b), 'Parasitic Formulae: The Case of Capital Guarantee Products', in M. Callon, Y. Millo, and F. Muniesa (eds), *Market Devices*, Oxford: Blackwell: 261–83.
Leung, D. (2008), 'Accounting in the Wild: An Adventure in Ethnoaccountancy', Ph.D. thesis: University of Edinburgh.
Leyshon, A. and Thrift, N. (1997), *Money/Space*, London: Routledge.
Lowenstein, R. (2000), *When Genius Failed: The Rise and Fall of Long-Term Capital Management*, New York: Random House.
MacKenzie, D. (1990), *Inventing Accuracy: A Historical Sociology of Nuclear Missile Guidance*, Cambridge, MA: The MIT Press.
MacKenzie, D. (1992), 'Economic and Sociological Explanation of Technical Change', in R. Rod Coombs, P. Saviotti, and V. Walsh (eds), *Technological Change and Company Strategies: Economic and Sociological Perspectives*, London: Academic Press: 25–48.
MacKenzie, D. (2002), 'What's in the Bottle?', *The London Review of Books*, 24(9): 21–2.
MacKenzie, D. (2003), 'Long-Term Capital Management and the Sociology of Arbitrage', *Economy and Society*, 32: 349–80.
MacKenzie, D. (2004), 'Social Connectivities in Global Financial Markets', *Society and Space (Environment and Planning D)* 22: 83–101.
MacKenzie, D. (2006), *An Engine, not a Camera: How Financial Models Shape Markets*, Cambridge, MA: The MIT Press.
MacKenzie, D. (2007), 'The Material Production of Virtuality: Innovation, Cultural Geography and Facticity in Derivatives Markets', *Economy and Society*, 36: 355–76.
MacKenzie, D. (2008a), 'Producing Accounts: Finitism, Technology and Rule Following', in M. Mazzotti (ed.), *Knowledge as Social Order: Rethinking the Sociology of Barry Barnes*, Aldershot: Ashgate: 99–117.
MacKenzie, D. (2008b), 'End-of-the-World Trade', *London Review of Books*, 30(9) (8 May): 24–6.
MacKenzie, D. (2009), 'All Those Arrows', *London Review of Books*, 31(12) (25 June): 20–2.

MacKenzie, D. and Millo, Y. (2003), 'Constructing a Market, Performing Theory: The Historical Sociology of a Financial Derivatives Exchange', *American Journal of Sociology*, 109: 107–45.
Madhavan, A. and Panchapagesan, V. (2000), 'Price Discovery in an Auction Market: A Look Inside the Black Box', *Review of Financial Studies*, 13: 627–58.
McMillan, J. (2002), *Reinventing the Bazaar: A Natural History of Markets*, New York: Norton.
Merton, R. C. (1973), 'Theory of Rational Option Pricing', *Bell Journal of Economics and Management Science*, 4: 141–83.
Miller, M. H. and Modigliani, F. (1961), 'Dividend Policy, Growth, and the Valuation of Shares', *Journal of Business*, 34: 411–33.
Millo, Y. (2003), 'Where do Financial Markets Come From? Historical Sociology of Financial Derivatives Markets', Ph.D. thesis: University of Edinburgh.
Millo, Y., Muniesa, F. Panourgias, N. S. and Scott, S. V. (2005), 'Organized Detachment: Clearinghouse Mechanisms in Financial Markets', *Information and Organization*, 15: 229–46.
Milyaeva, S. (2009), 'Making Markets, Making Laws: Non-Deliverable Currency Forwards and the Amendment to Article 1062 of the Russian Civil Code', Ph.D. thesis: University of Edinburgh.
Modigliani, F. and Miller, M. H. (1958), 'The Cost of Capital, Corporation Finance and the Theory of Investment', *American Economic Review*, 48: 261–97.
Mosley, L. (2003), *Global Capital and National Governments*, Cambridge: Cambridge University Press.
Muniesa, F. (2003), 'Des Marchés Comme Algorithmes: Sociologie de la Cotation électronique à la Bourse de Paris', Ph.D. thesis: École Nationale Supérieure des Mines.
Muniesa, F. (2005), 'Contenir le Marché: La Transition de la Criée à la Cotation électronique à la Bourse de Paris', *Sociologie du Travail*, 47: 485–501.
Partnoy, F. (2001), 'Multinational Regulatory Competition and Single-Stock Futures', *Northwestern Journal of International Law and Business*, 21: 641–55.
Partnoy, F. (2003), *Infectious Greed: How Deceit and Risk Corrupted the Financial Markets*, London: Profile.
Perold, A. (1999), *Long-Term Capital Management, L.P.*, Boston, MA: Harvard Business School Publishing.
Preda, A. (2006), 'Socio-Technical Agency in Financial Markets: The Case of the Stock Ticker', *Social Studies of Science*, 36: 753–82.
Preda, A. (2007a), 'STS and Social Studies of Finance', in E. Hackett, O. Amsterdamska, M. Lynch and J. Wajcman (eds) (2007), *Handbook of Science and Technology Studies*, Cambridge, MA: The MIT Press: 901–21.
Preda, A. (2007b). 'Where do Analysts come from? The Case of Financial Chartism', in M. Callon, Y. Millo and F. Muniesa (eds) *Market Devices*, Oxford: Blackwell, 40–64.
Preda, A. (2009), *Framing Finance: The Boundaries of Markets and Modern Capitalism*, Chicago, IL: University of Chicago Press.
Rosenberg, N. (1982), *Inside the Black Box: Technology and Economics*, Cambridge: Cambridge University Press.
Ross, S. A. (2001), 'Neoclassical and Alternative Finance', Keynote Address to EFMA Annual Meeting.

Rubinstein, M. (1985), 'Nonparametric Tests of Alternative Option Pricing Models Using all Reported Trades and Quotes on the 30 Most Active CBOE Option Classes from August 23, 1976 through August 31, 1978', *Journal of Finance*, 40: 455–80.

Salmon, F. (2009), 'Recipe for Disaster: The Formula that Killed Wall Street', *Wired Magazine*, 23 February.

Shleifer, A. and Summers, L. H. (1990), 'The Noise Trader Approach to Finance', *Journal of Economic Perspectives*, 4: 19–33.

Shleifer, A. and Vishny, R. W. (1997), 'The Limits of Arbitrage', *Journal of Finance*, 52: 35–55.

Taleb, N. (1998), 'How the *Ought* Became the *Is*', *Futures & OTC World*, Black-Scholes-Merton Supplement: 35–6.

Tett, G. (2009), *Fool's Gold: How Unrestrained Greed Corrupted a Dream, Shattered Global Markets and Unleashed a Catastrophe*, London: Little Brown.

UBS AG (2008), 'Shareholder Report on UBS's Write-Downs', Zurich: UBS AG, 18 April, available at www.ubs.com.

Underhill, G. R. D. (2000), 'State, Markets, and Global Political Economy: Genealogy of an (inter-?) Discipline', *International Affairs*, 76: 805–24.

Valdmanis, T. (1998), 'Accounting Abracadabra: Cooking the Books Proves Common Trick of the Trade', *USA Today*, 11 August.

Vogel, S. K. (1996), *Freer Markets, More Rules: Regulatory Reform in Advanced Industrial Countries*, Ithaca, NY: Cornell University Press.

Vollmer, H. (2003), 'Bookkeeping, Accounting, Calculative Practice: The Sociological Suspense of Calculation', *Critical Perspectives on Accounting*, 3: 353–81.

Weber, M. (1970), 'Bureaucracy', in H. H. Gerth and C. W. Mills (eds), *From Max Weber: Essays in Sociology*, London: Routledge & Kegan Paul: 196–244.

Winner, L. (1993), 'Upon Opening the Black Box and Finding it Empty: Social Constructivism and the Philosophy of Technology', *Science, Technology, & Human Values*, 18: 362–78.

Zaloom, C. (2006), *Out of the Pits: Trading and Technology from Chicago to London*, Chicago, IL: Chicago University Press.

Zorn, D. M. (no date), 'No Surprise Anymore: Securities Analysts' Forecasts and Corporate Profit Reporting, 1981–2000', Cambridge, MA: Department of Sociology, Harvard University.

5

Data Banking: Computing and Flexibility in Swiss Banks 1960–90

David Gugerli

Shaky foundations

Daniel Bell's study 'The Coming of Post-Industrial Society', published in 1973, claimed to be 'a venture in social forecasting' (Bell 1973). Coming as it did on the eve of the most severe crisis of the global economy since World War II, Bell's book was certainly apropos. By the same token, Harvard's eminent sociologist could hardly have imagined how many global events would coincide with its appearance. 1973 was not only the year of the first oil price shock. It would also see the opening of the Chicago Securities Exchange and the end of the Bretton Woods system (Helleiner 1994; MacKenzie 2006).

If Bell had the temerity to peer into the future, few others did. Complicating matters was a breath in the air simultaneously of youthful spring and arctic winter, the precise effects of which were hard to foresee. For many industrial sites with their furnaces and assembly lines, the future had come to an untimely end, just as the adolescent financial 'industry' was revving up, backed by an unprecedented array of information technologies. Metaphorically speaking, the rules were about to change from the *modus operandi* of the industrial assembly line to the *ars combinatoria* of the computerized database. The western hemisphere had entered an era that could only be described as 'postindustrial' or, indeed, 'postmodern'.

It is not surprising then that, in1973, dealing with the future looked to be more of a challenge than in other years. In fact, the year was marked by more claims about imminent threats than had been seen during the preceding decades; and both confidence in existing rules and trust in established procedures were at an all-time low (Siegenthaler 1993). Arguing itself was ineffective, nobody trusted in arguments independently of what they looked like – confirming that the future was nebulous, to say the least, and would in any event be different to what anyone expected. Moreover there was no ground of common understanding on which to plant projections of the future (Luhmann 1976). Consequently people with little taste for escapism were left, like Denis Meadows and the Club of Rome, to calculate the obvious limits of growth – which amounted to contemplating the end of the world (Meadows 1972). Apart from heroic attempts like these at seeing clearly, the situation remained generally messy. For analytical minds like Jürgen Habermas', it could only be explained in terms of the legitimacy problems of late capitalism (Habermas 1973).

Indeed, 'legitimizing the system' turned out to be a substantial challenge, as much in philosophical seminars as in the realm of finance – where neither the previously inconceivable idea of trading options nor the introduction of floating exchange rates meant that everything solid was melting into air (MacDonald 1988). 1973 also saw the foundation of the Society for Worldwide Interbank Financial Telecommunication (SWIFT), which provided a fast and stable way to electronically transmit funds to any member bank and its respective customers (Scott et al. 2008).

Another apparent source of stability was identified by the *Harvard Business Review* in its September–October edition of 1973. In his boldly titled 'Computer Databases: The Future is Now', Richard L. Nolan, then an associate professor of business administration, addressed the 'confused and highly sceptical' top management whose members did not yet understand that the concept of databases was 'real, viable, and beneficial' (Nolan 1973; Kilgus 1971). As such, his article constituted not just a clarion call but also a comforting and reassuring gesture toward 'the system'.

In addition to this institutional and conceptual confidence building in the year of the big crisis (both economic and sociopolitical), two strands of technological development deserve mention. 1973 marked the start of Bob Kahn and Vinton Cerf's fruitful collaboration on a protocol for packet network interconnection (also known as TCP/IP), a robust piece of code that made it possible to connect computers with the highest degree of independence from local hardware and software specifications (Cerf and Kahn 1974). Around the same time, engineers at IBM's Research Laboratory in San Jose, California, began serious work on System R, a very early relational database system with an unprecedentedly flexible and powerful architecture (Astrahan et al. 1976; Chamberlin et al. 1981; Gugerli 2007).

At first blush, the aforementioned cluster of '1973 events' seems to be nothing more than an arbitrary selection of remarkable things that happened to occur that year. In the discussion that follows, I will assert that this cluster actually comprises a set of interdependent developments strongly related to the transformation of the financial sector in the last third of the twentieth century. To understand this transformation, we must consider together such ostensibly disparate factors as the limits of growth, the changes in regulatory regimes, the emergence of new markets, the role of prognostic tools, the arms race in information technology (IT), the shifts in corporate governance and finally the implementation of new enterprise planning and controlling instruments. Furthermore we must relate global developments to the ruptures and adjustments that occurred under very local conditions. Indeed, changes in the global financial system might be better understood as the consequence of local events, rather than the other way around.

Despite the extreme difficulty of accessing archival material, I wish to illustrate my claim with a set of observations concerning three major banks in Switzerland: Credit Suisse, the Union Bank of Switzerland (UBS) and the Swiss Bank Corporation (SBC). All three institutions were embedded in a national or even local economy, while each of them can also be considered to be a multinational or even global player. Based on published material primarily originating from Credit Suisse and, where necessary, supplemented with reports from UBS and SBC, I will argue that the changes these banks underwent in the wake of the 1970s were much more linked to their own structural developments than to the end of the Bretton Woods system. The forces that drove the increased flexibility in governance of these banks are to be found more in the growth-inhibiting shortcomings of their corporate surveillance techniques than in the new flexibilities required (and offered) by the international financial markets after 1973.

Introducing the computer

The buzzword 'flexibility' certainly played an important role in the last third of the twentieth century. It stands for a kind of orientation that permeated all fields of practice and thinking. The 'redesign' of social relations led to new modes of communication. Similarly, the programmes that enterprises and societies had hitherto developed for themselves were changing. The organization of production, supply, retail, work and financing in the corporate world underwent a deep transformation. On the structural level of industrial enterprises, increased flexibility is evident in the decision of vertically integrated companies to exploit the outsourcing strategies of the new 'project capitalism', and in the replacement of planning and control by change management (Boltanski and Chiapello 2007).

The trend away from serial fabrication to lean production and from factory discipline to flexible working hours went hand in hand with a departure from a world of workers and employees to the realm of human capital that could be invested in, methodologically analysed and freely allocated according to the actual needs of the enterprise. Consequently professional vocation gave way to lifelong learning and self-management (Becker 1964; Piore and Sabel 1984; Neitzert 1996; Bröckling et al. 2007).

The society of the era of flexibility gradually replaced social norms with normal range, while its mode of communication toggled from hierarchical to distributed networks, from continuous flow to packet switching, from the strong coupling of synchronicity to the loose coupling of asynchronous communication. Even databases became more flexible when relational ones replaced procedural architectures. Instead of subscribing to planning, command and production, the era of flexibility followed a programme of recombination, heterogeneity and patchwork.

A traditional Swiss bank used to operate under strong political protection in a highly cartelistic environment. It could profit from stable agreements between competitors on fees and interests, and it offered a limited set of services either to a community of wealthy private customers, or a class of modest customers who tended to have one savings account and a small and homogeneous bond account. The conventional Swiss bank was one that could easily deal with its very tame community of shareholders (Swary and Topf 1992: 11–50). For such a bank, dominated by routine, the postmodern programme of recombination, heterogeneity and patchwork presented a rather hostile environment and a substantial challenge. How and why did the banks embrace a more flexible form of resource allocation? How did they manage to not only increase the number of their products and customers but also the possibilities of combining them? (Regini 1999: 3; Baethge et al. 1999: 7). How, even in retail banking, did they develop relatively flexible portfolio management for every single customer? How did they find and adopt new forms of governance and corporate structures that could handle this strategy of combinatorial growth?

The obvious, immediate, and yet misleading answer to this question is: banks introduced computers. Though empirically watertight (see Beccalli 2007: 195–202), this answer carries three caveats. First, a bank is not a bank. It is not precisely clear which type of banks introduced computers. Were they the formerly powerful credit factories that needed to speed up operation of their assembly lines? Were they the product-oriented, centralized banks of the 1960s? Or were they the banks with a variety of profit centres and customer-oriented governance? Second, the meaning of 'introduction of computers' is elusive. Could it be that banks were introduced to computing and not the other way around? Simply buying a machine could not have been the end of the story. Many procedures had to be adapted to the technology to make the technology adoptable (Winter 1974: 205). Which leads to the third caveat: computers are not computers. The advantages they promised, the possibilities they offered, the problems they caused and the surprises they engendered probably changed and multiplied far more rapidly than anybody could have predicted.

That was only the beginning of uncertainty, especially for early adopters of computers. Back in the 1960s, the machine that might have been recommended to a company was not the computer it would actually order; and the one that eventually showed up on the doorstep was already intended to serve a somewhat different purpose – maybe a task that not even the 'next-generation' hardware or software replacement would be able to achieve. Furthermore a computer was always pointing simultaneously towards its provider's and its user's goals (i.e. most probably in different directions). If these goals had anything in common, it was most likely their near-term outlook.

To round out these caveats, one might add a paradox: the time-consuming acceleration effect of computers. To be sure, computers were always linked with speed, change and the new possibilities of the imminent future (Luhmann 1966; Hausammann 2008). But no computer ever arrived as a ready-to-go machine, even if its processor was airborne (see Figure 5.1).

The paradox of time-consuming acceleration does not imply that it was a mistake to associate computers with unprecedented speed and calculating power. Computers were cutting-edge technology, and they did promise to magically transform any kind of administrative task. Yet they also stood for a technology that never quite did what it promised, was unbelievably expensive and required scores of additional personnel and well-trained specialists. For a bank, a computer was a bit of a gamble (Zetti 2009).

Banks were generally secure places for storing and transferring money, and banking was about mediating risks and keeping track of every single transaction that happened within a bank's fortified walls.

Figure 5.1 Labour pains in delivering a Bull Gamma 30 digital processor for the 'Swiss Credit Bank' in 1962
Source: Credit Suisse, Historical Archives.

Consequently the computer's dynamic culture and the mixed menu it offered of powerful calculation, new ways of doing things and tiresome implementation represented quite a challenge, if not a threat. In other words there were good reasons for banks to be technologically and organizationally conservative. Back in the 1960s bankers took pains to ensure that their computers were almost exclusively associated – both semantically and pragmatically – with the values of power and speed. Computers would apply industrial strength to bureaucracy, eventually setting up an assembly line for transposing data, calculating numbers and processing preliminary steps for decisions (UBS 1965: 16–17; Bonhage 2007: 102; Gugerli 2009). It was, for instance, a 'modern and powerful data processing facility' that was purchased from Bull to process Credit Suisse's routine administrative jobs: 'For several months now (i.e. 1963, DG), among other tasks, the Bull Gamma 30 has assumed the daily processing of customer accounts and also regularly handles closing operations and the various reports associated with that' (CS quoted in Bonhage 2007: 98).

Banks were buying computers around the same time as large retail business firms, the post office and some branches of public administration. Yet they were no technological risk takers. On the contrary: the idea was that computers would simply fill in for conventional calculators and tabulating machines, not that they would take aim at the structure of a bank's governance. As a matter of fact, however, there was a widespread suspicion already in the 1960s that introducing computers would bring about fundamental changes to the administration and governance of any enterprise. Some business administration journals trumpeted that computer-based 'management information systems' with hitherto unknown analytical possibilities would be available in the very near future (Haigh 2006). This was disturbing news for a business whose main assets were stability and security rather than change and flexibility. At the very least, the technology bore careful watching (Kilgus 1971).

It is therefore revealing to read three to four decades' worth of the banks' annual reports, paying special attention to the changing manner in which computers are presented. Annual reports are routine self-descriptions; they justify what *has* been done and they try to explain to their readers (mostly competitors, shareholders and clients) what *should* be done in the next few months. In other words, annual reports are a bank's highly ritualized public promise either to continue or to improve last year's performance. They form a communicative space into which new technologies such as computers must be integrated. As such, they constitute a category of text that helped to usher computers into their bank-specific role. The annual report had to endow a computer with the qualities it would need to serve a bank's purposes.

Growing pains

The discursive setting into which computers were introduced in the 1960s was still a 'context' in which marginal costs of growth were skyrocketing and limits of growth could only be ignored thanks to the overall economic boom. Banks were still extending their networks of branches, and restructuring was hardly fodder for discussion. 'Do more of the same, even if you don't earn more' was the operating mantra. It fell to the annual reports of all major Swiss banks to point out the steep growth of branches. These reports invariably complained about the increased costs – one of the consequences of the banks' dogged hunt for more customer funds up to 1974, when Credit Suisse, UBS and SBC agreed to coordinate openings of new branches to reduce operative costs CS (1974: 35). Because employees' wages were soaring and qualified personnel were difficult to find, additional customer funds could only be captured through new branches, with concomitant infrastructural costs (see Figures 5.2 and 5.3). It was not hard to conclude from the annual reports that there was ample room and need for rationalization.

One of the most prominent advisers of the Swiss banking sector, Ernst Kilgus, noted an aggregated growth in total assets of Swiss banks from 105 to 170 billion Swiss francs between 1966 and 1969 without any structural changes and under strong pressure from the labour markets (Kilgus 1971). Given this context it was important to present computers as machines that could enhance administrative procedures and to justify them as an investment in greater productivity. During the 1960s,

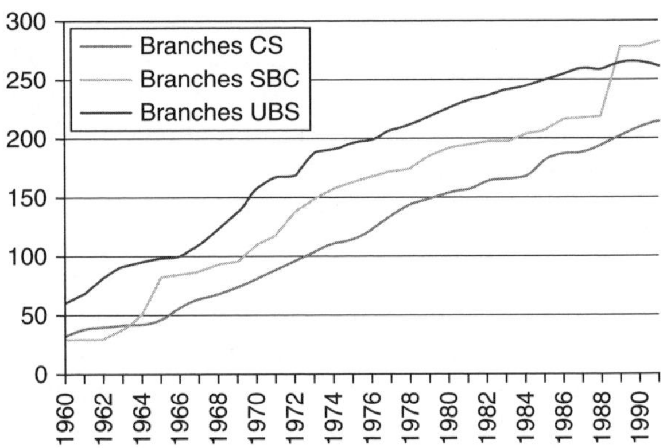

Figure 5.2 Growth of branches 1960–91: Credit Suisse, Union Bank of Switzerland (UBS), Swiss Bank Corporation (SBC)

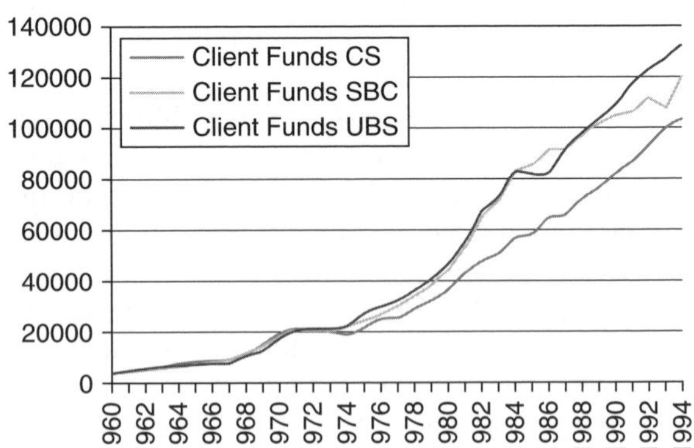

Figure 5.3 Growth of client funds 1960–94: Credit Suisse, UBS, SBC

the banks mainly subscribed to this view of the computer. In the realm of Swiss banking, as in public administration and retail business in Switzerland, the computer was perceived as the most important means of rationalization and an excellent instrument for coping with growth (Girschik 2002, 2005, 2006, 2009; Gugerli 2002, 2009; Zetti 2006b; Hausammann 2008; Illi 2008).

In the years after the first processor was transported by air to Credit Suisse, the bank again reported the opening of 'a new calculating centre'. Every word of this text was carefully chosen. The new installation was said to be located 'at headquarters' in Zurich and equipped with a 'state-of-the-art' computer. After having closely linked power, control, and advanced instrumentation of both, the report went on to tell its readers that the new calculating centre was launched at the end of the 1967. In other words, it had opened just before the critical year-end and thus in time to be featured in the annual report's text and graphic design, adorning the inside cover as the very latest on the technological frontier (CS 1967: 24).

The new machine was described as having a 'large, extended memory' and a 'powerful magnetic tape station', which, the bank was proud to declare, made the centre 'unique among its kind for banking in Switzerland'. Shifting the focus to the familiar, the text then described the computer as being used to 'automate accounting of stocks and bonds', and to 'improve services for a broad range of private banking customers'. Immediately after announcing that other parts of the bank had successfully streamlined, the annual report made the point that it was still extremely difficult to find qualified employees. Thus the report's readers could not doubt that the computer was very much needed by the bank (CS 1967: 24; CS 1969: 24).

The discursive juxtaposition of rationalization, computing, power, control, personnel and growth remained stable over the next few years. Although existing equipment usually fell short of expectations and often choked on the massive chunks of data fed it by banks, the goal of rationalization remained the North Star, a more or less reliable policy a bank could pursue by acquiring computers, tweaking procedures and adapting conventional transactions to data processing and to the available calculating power (and vice versa) (Neukom 2004: 57). Indeed, in 1972, Credit Suisse invoked its 'strategy to fight against shortage of personnel through the extension of the calculating infrastructure' to justify the purchase and installation (in Zurich) of two brand new IBM 370 mainframes in addition to its existing Bull and IBM computers (CS 1972: 34; Zetti 2006a).

At this point, alert readers of the annual reports might have noticed a change in the narrative. It was probably the first time that machines were given names in such a publication. This is especially noteworthy considering that, back in 1967, the annual report totally ignored the switch from Bull to IBM as the bank's main hardware provider. In 1972, however, computers simultaneously acquired monikers and lost their previous, clearly identified raison d'être. The new mainframes were no longer intended to perform specific automation tasks (like accounting of stocks and bonds) nor simply to replace personnel. The purpose or primary role of this additional calculating power was now presented and defined in very general terms. The machines would serve as 'a platform for very complex database systems' that were 'currently being built up' at the bank and whose entries should become 'electronically readable' on 'terminals' residing on desktops. Computers would become 'the basis for the complete automation of large areas of our bank'.[1]

This was obviously a new and far more radical approach. It was also the first time the bank used the term 'database system' in an annual report, although it dropped the subject immediately after mentioning the vision of computer-based automation for the whole bank. There was certainly more comfort in explaining the familiar topics of the professional training programme for employees and the bank's improved infrastructure for sports (CS 1973: 31; Jung 2000: 343–4). No doubt the qualifying epithet 'very complex' was appropriate and necessary for such an important milestone. However 'very complex' might also have been meant to foreshadow the next year's report, when 'floating exchange rates, measures against foreign capital, governmental interventions to curb the boom, and a bearish stock market' showed that the only thing the bank could actually count on was its programme for computerizing the entire enterprise, 'including all branches'. The first step of this programme consisted of introducing cost-centre accounting (CS 1973: 31; Jung 2000: 343–4). The application of massive computing power was presented as a way to find certain stability amid the alarming signs of a deep economic crisis. After all, very complex systems should be able to cope with very complex situations!

Database culture and restructuring

Until the middle of the 1970s, centralized mainframe computers served the ends of automation and rationalization. Now they began to take over the accounting of entire banks, spurring them to migrate online.[2] Simultaneously the bank-specific version of a database culture gradually suffused the thinking and planning of top management (CS 1977: 47; SKA 1978). With the extensive growth of the branch network and the number of clients, the managers at headquarters had the increased burden and challenge of controlling branch activities. Computer-based data management seemed a promising way of analysing the enterprise across its primary organizational boundaries and therefore realigning the branches' centripetal activities.

In 1975 Credit Suisse launched a major survey of its customers (CS 1975: 40) and simultaneously produced a 'white book' presenting various scenarios of the bank's future organizational development in a kind of free association.[3] What we can derive from the annual reports and the bank's carefully controlled historiography is that this marked the dawn of computer-based flexibility, both in analytical and in organizational terms. Credit Suisse started to develop tools that gave the bank greater insight into its own operations and also enabled it to develop a new sensitivity to its clients (Jung 2000: 343–4). These words have a nice ring to them. But replacing 'insights in operations' with 'control' and 'client sensitivity' with 'wealth and income-dependent classification of clients' might give one a more adequate impression of the bank's reorganization strategies in the late 1970s and early 1980s. In any case, both strategies required a lot of computing power. The goals and achievements in terms of automation and rationalization in the late 1960s and early 1970s were now supplemented by a set of sophisticated controlling tools and survey techniques.

The trend toward increased self-awareness on the part of the bank was clearly accelerated in 1977 when the criminal capital acquisition strategy of a single Credit Suisse branch caused a speculative loss of more than 2 billion Swiss francs, with severe consequences for the bank's leadership. It is noteworthy that attempts at restructuring the bank with the help of additional computing power for cutting-edge database technology had started before the 'Chiasso case' became a widely discussed scandal in the press and in the federal parliament (Mabillard and Weck 1977). It is also clear that 'Chiasso' underscored the necessity of improving management procedures and developing a culture of controls consistent with the accounting and governance rules of contemporary business administration (Kilgus 1968, 1971, 1982).

Back in 1972 when the term 'database' cropped up for the first time in the bank's annual report, it was still quite difficult to figure out how to introduce a database system in a way that made any sense. 'Database' could mean many things, especially 'very complex' ones. Furthermore, 'Building a Base for a Data Base,' as the title of an article in *Datamation* ran, probably reflected a 'management perspective' more than a feasible engineering scenario (Cuozzo and Kurtz 1973; Balderston et al. 1977). Nevertheless the IT specialists at Credit Suisse must have known that the field of database technology was on the move, and not only for its advocates in the schools for business administration. By 1973 the first-generation, brute-force approach to searching and batch-processing hierarchically structured data was reaching its limits.[4] Managers and IT specialists were mulling over the possibilities for enhancing the programmer's freedom to navigate in a given data set (Bachman 1973).

One attractive solution to these problems, at least conceptually, was proposed by a British mathematician working at the IBM Research Laboratory in San Jose. Edgar F. Codd's pathbreaking design for a new database architecture received widespread attention and galvanized the community of database technicians (Codd 1970). Sometime around 1973 the first reports of the development of System R, IBM's attempt to develop a working relational database, must have reached the well-informed circles of the IT community dealing with data management in banks, especially in view of close collaborations like the one between Credit Suisse and IBM engineers. Even sceptics among the bank's and the provider's programmers would have been acquainted with current debates on database management systems and data recombination (Date and Codd 1975).

Why was the new database concept interesting for bankers? First, Codd and his followers aimed to put the relational database on a mathematically sound footing. In addition they were adamant that future database management systems should be characterized by a series of crucial elements chief among which were 'simplicity, symmetry, data independence, and semantic completeness' (Astrahan and Chamberlin 1975: 580). Above all, in order to guarantee both user and data independence, 'future users of large data banks must be protected from having to know how the data is organized in the machine (the internal representation)' (Codd 1970: 377).

A generalized 'search and query language' would ensure that queries run on a specific database wouldn't require the service of a professional programmer. Codd believed that databases should be set up in such a way that normal users (e.g. managers and housewives) could search them easily: 'The relational model is a particularly suitable structure for the truly casual user (i.e. a non-technical person who merely wishes to interrogate the database, for example a housewife who wants to make enquiries about this week's best buys at the supermarket).' The claim was immediately turned to radical prophecy: 'In the not too distant future the majority of computer users will probably be at this level.' (Date and Codd 1975: 95). Casual users, especially if they were managers, might want to ask a database questions that had never been asked before and had not been foreseen by any programmer (Gugerli 2007).

The possibility of recombining datasets using a unique primary key enabled the combination of properly formatted data. What had previously been separate blocks of data – gathered in different formats, organized in different files, managed by different departments and sometimes even stored on different media – would now become accessible simply by dint of the user's questions and analytical intentions. One hypothetical task that developers employed to illustrate the combinatorial power of a relational database management system was, 'Fire everybody on the first floor!' (Stonebraker et al. 1976).

Actually, this kind of managerial task can only be solved if there is a way to combine human resource department data with that from buildings and grounds. What permitted the ad hoc crossing of organizational limits was the relational database's formal consistency and data independence. Asking new questions of existing chunks of information made possible new analytical opportunities, no matter what the original purpose of the data. Such a scenario was clearly heaven on earth to any manager in search of information. It was also the axis on which consulting activity would eventually turn.

In the early 1970s, when System R and other relational databank systems were developed, this potential was still fairly distant. And it remained so until the early 1980s, when the first commercial applications of relational database management systems (such as Oracle and DB2) became available on the software market (Symonds and Ellison 2003; Date 1984).[5] The informational crossing of an organization's divisions, though, was one of the most promising strategies since the 1970s and was applied more and more in Swiss banks in the 1980s. In 1982 – under the close guidance of McKinsey & Company – Credit Suisse introduced a programme of cost-centre accounting, and a year later developed a new cost control strategy for the entire bank. Between 1983 and 1986, an overhead-value analysis that was also suggested by McKinsey offered an unprecedented, deep insight into the bank's economy. It revealed, for instance, substantial, systematic losses in the bank's retail business (CS 1983: 27; SBC 1984: 62). Simultaneously, a programme running between 1983 and 1987 analysed customer relations and profitability (Jung 2000: 345–6).

By the middle of the 1980s the overhead-value analysis, and the customer relations and profitability analysis, had paved the way for a veritable management information system called FISKA. Set up in 1987, it provided the kind of computer-based administration of the bank's transactions that most business administrators had been dreaming of for two decades (Winter 1974: 207). The manager's power to recombine existing data along with the crossing of organizational boundaries had become a major management tool and principle. What's more, the technological implementation of the relational database, that is, its programmes and procedures, could be presented in the bank's annual report.

Customizing the computer

In 1988, more than a quarter of a century after the first Bull 30 processor was delivered, Credit Suisse's annual report contained a fairly extensive section titled 'Production and Informatics'. The goal of an annual report is generally to maintain order; this particular report simply celebrated it. 1988 turned out to be the year in which the computer 'program' followed a clearly structured narrative. First of all, computers were not just computers anymore. They served different purposes and therefore could be distinguished. For example 'mainframe computers with database systems' served 'the efficient processing of transactions', whereas so-called information and management systems mainly ran on 'personal computers'. By the end of 1988, the bank had well over 11,000, that is, 80 per cent of its individual work spaces equipped either with terminals to mainframe systems or with one of Credit Suisse's 2500 personal computers. Conventional postal services were concentrated in a single factory that allowed 'rational and flexible' compilation and distribution of customer reports, while half of the personnel were using electronic mail for internal communications. Roughly ten per cent of all employees had informatics-related jobs; many of them had even been trained at the bank's own school for informatics (CS 1988: 43).

The following year, there was not much to add to this clear-cut picture, except for an obvious emphasis on 'networks'. These had been linking the different systems and led to a 'high level of integration' of the entire bank's IT. Of course many projects were still ongoing,[6] but the document clearly intended to report 'business as usual': the development of a foreign-exchange trade system, the further diffusion of electronic office applications, the management and control of credit limits and support for 'production', that is, interactions with customers. Was this (again) a hint to the attentive reader? The report noted, without elaboration, that the bank was going to re-conceptualize 'the basic systems' and the 'customer master data files' (CS 1989: 35).

As a matter of fact, developing IT-based interactions with customers was one of the most dynamic areas of computing at the bank in the late 1980s (Swary and Topf 1992; Rogge 1997: 267–302). It went hand in hand with an enterprise structure commonly referred to as 'customer-oriented' or 'customer-segmentation strategy' (Baethge et al. 1999: 8). This was actually a restructuring programme: small branches at the periphery with reduced autonomy under close computer-based controlling, a few big and efficient production centres and finally a general adjusting of all services to the customers' demands. Credit Suisse reported in 1989: 'We believe clear customer segmentation will result in a better cost-benefit ratio of our banking services, both for our customers and for the bank' (CS 1989: 22).

The services and the tariff policies introduced by the bank in the second half of the 1980s were actually designed to get rid of the 70 per cent of customers who were administratively costly and produced no returns for the bank. The idea was somehow to make them go away without losing their funds. Extending the ATM network[7] and introducing an early form of telebanking called Videotex in 1986 that used the customer's TV set and telephone line (Campbell and Hilary 1981; Freiburghaus 1983; Knecht 1984; Gfeller 1993; Kyrish 1996; Lütolf 2002), as well as a 24-hour telephone service in 1993, helped to discourage walk-in customers – with concomitant savings in terms of employees' attention and work time. It was much more attractive to have clients either telephone a specialized, massively equipped call centre or fill in all the necessary forms for a transaction on their own screen without bothering anybody (SBC 1983: 64).

Conclusion

All these services were based on reliable database systems and advanced network connections operating in real time. The customer-oriented bank of the late twentieth century was a flexible, database-oriented enterprise structured according to the requirements and possibilities of computing. In the words of Baethge: 'The development of databases of customer's relationships with the bank permitted the banks to develop cross-selling strategies and to expand their business activities. Banks offered a wider range of products and services following deregulation, and technology helped them handle the growing volume of transactions more efficiently' (Baethge et al. 1999: 7). However it took almost three decades to introduce computers into a form of business that is best described as 'data banking'. During this period Swiss banks not only replaced their transaction-based organizational model with a technology-supported sales and service system but they also abandoned their traditional growth strategy. Instead of continuing to build up a network of branches that acted as local delegates for headquarters and offered a full palette of services, Swiss banks opted for a customer-segmentation strategy that, on the one hand, permitted group-specific, computer-based economies of scale and, on the other, flexible portfolio management.

It is worth noting that, owing to their implementation only in the late 1980s, changes in the domestic regulatory regimes of the financial sector at large had little influence on banks. Nevertheless, beginning in the 1960s, structural changes did take place that gradually transformed the banking business. The early but slow adoption of the computer as a means for automated and streamlined data processing in the 1960s gave way to a more fundamental role of computers in banking. Around 1973, that is, just before the big economic crisis hit, computers and the tools beloved of business-administration-oriented consultants (cost analysis, profitability studies) became the most important instruments in restructuring the banking business overall, and indeed every bank's organizational mode.

This led to a veritable arms race in IT. Databank technology, as well as online and even real-time banking joined with early attempts at using IT to enable retail banking customers' access to their assets. Simultaneously, the implementation of new enterprise planning and controlling instruments led to profound shifts in corporate governance and paved the way for the big mergers in banking of the roaring 1990s.

Notes

The author wishes to thank Lea Haller, Daniela Zetti, Patrick Halbeisen, Simone Roggenbuck, Spiros Arvanitis and Alexandros Kyrtsis for their critical remarks and Patricia Hongler for her support. A first draft of this chapter was written at the Max Planck Institute for the History of Science, Berlin. Responsibility for errors and omissions remains, of course, with the author.

1. CS (1972: 34): 'Die auf diesen Anlagen im Aufbau begriffenen sehr komplexen Datenbanksysteme, die bis an die einzelnen Arbeitsplätze über Bildschirme elektronisch lesbar sein werden, bilden die Basis für eine umfassende Automation weiter Bereiche unseres Bankbetriebes.' SBC bought its IBM 370/165 roughly at the same time and planned to change its 'program' from a data factory to a more complex information system SBC (1971: 28), while the UBS dreamed of an integrated 'Union Bank Information System Concept': see UBS (1973: 25).

2. CS (1977: 46). In 1983 the bank reported that 'almost all bank-specific transactions are now carried out "on-line in real time"' (CS 1983: 28). On 'the terminal' as a symbol and an instrument of real-time banking, see SBC (1976: 46); see also SBC (1977: 54).
3. Unfortunately, to date, the book belongs to the confidential archives of Credit Suisse and cannot be consulted, allegedly to protect individual rights of the contributors.
4. This is also the case for computer centres at universities. See Gugerli et al. (2005: 347–61).
5. In 1990 the relational database model was mentioned for the first time in SBC (1990: 29).
6. In 1987, Credit Suisse reported 317 ongoing projects in informatics.
7. Between 1980 and 1984 the number of machines grew from 211 to 1397 (Swary and Topf 1992: 12).

Bibliography

Note: Annual reports by Credit Suisse (CS), the Swiss Bank Corporation (SBC), and the Union Bank of Switzerland (UBS) are quoted in the following formats: CS (Year), SBC (Year), UBS (Year).

Astrahan, M. M., Blasgen, M. W., Chamberlin, D. D., Eswaran, K. P., Gray, J. N., Griffiths, P. P., King, W. F., Lorie, R. A., Mcjones, P. R., Mehl, J. W., Putzolu, G. R., Traiger, I. L., Wade, B. and Watson, V. (1976), 'System R: A Relational Approach to Database Management', *ACM Transactions on Database Systems*, 1: 97–137.

Astrahan, M. M. and Chamberlin, D. D. (1975), 'Implementation of a Structured English Query Language', *Communications of the ACM*, 18: 580–8.

Bachman, C. W. (1973), 'The Programmer as Navigator', *Communications of the ACM*, 16: 653–8.

Baethge, M., Kitay, J. and Regalia, I. (1999), 'Managerial Strategies, Human Resource Practices, and Labor Relations in Banks: A Comparative View', in M. Regini, J. Kitay and M. Baethge (eds), *From Tellers to Sellers Changing Employment Relations in Banks*, Cambridge, MA: The MIT Press: 3–30.

Balderston, F. E., Carman, J. M. andHoggatt, A. C. (1977), 'Computers in Banking and Marketing: The Technology is Here, with Promises and Problems for Both Consumers and Corporations', *Science*, 195: 1115–19.

Beccalli, E. (2007), *IT and European Bank Performance*, Basingstoke: Palgrave Macmillan.

Becker, G. S. (1964), *Human Capital: A Theoretical and Empirical Analysis, with Special Reference to Education*, Chicago, IL: University of Chicago Press.

Bell, D. (1973), *The Coming of Post-Industrial Society: A Venture in Social Forecasting*, New York: Basic Books.

Boltanski, L. and Chiapello, E. (2007), *The New Spirit of Capitalism*, London: Verso.

Bonhage, B. (2007), 'Befreit im Netz: Bankdienstleistungen im Spannungsfeld zwischen Kunden und Computern', in S. Kaufmann (ed.), *Vernetzte Steuerung: Soziale Prozesse im Zeitalter technischer Netzwerke*, Zurich: Chronos.

Bröckling, U., Masschelein, J., Simons, M. and Pongratz, L. (eds) (2007), *The Learning Society from the Perspective of Governmentality*, Oxford: Blackwell.

Campbell, J. A. and Hilary, T. B. (1981), 'The Videotex Marketplace: A Theory of Evolution', *Telecommunications Policy*, 5(2): 111–20.

Cerf, V. G. and Kahn, R. E. (1974), 'A Protocol for Packet Network Intercommunication', *IEEE Trans. Comm. Tech.*, 22(5): 627–41.

Chamberlin, D. D., Astrahan, M. M., Blasgen, M. W., Gray, J. N., King, W. F., Lindsay, B. G., Lorie, R., Mehl, J. W., Price, T. G., Putzolu, G., Selinger, P. G., Schkolnick, M., Slutz, D. R., Traiger, I. L., Wade, B. W. and Yost, R. A. (1981), 'A History and Evaluation of System R', *Communications of the ACM*, 24: 632–46.

Codd, E. F. (1970), 'A Relational Model of Data for Large Shared Data Banks', *Communications of the ACM*, 13: 377–87.

Cuozzo, D. E. and Kurtz, J. F. (1973), 'Building a Base for Data Base: A Management Perspective', *Datamation*, 19: 71–6.

Date, C. J. (1984), *A Guide to DB2 a User's Guide to the IBM Product IBM Database 2 (a Relational Database Management System for the MVS Environment) and its Companion Products QMF and DXT*, Reading, MA: Addison-Wesley.

Date, C. J. and Codd, E. F. (1975), 'The Relational and Network Approaches: Comparison of the Application Programming Interfaces', *Proceedings of the 1974 ACM SIGFIDET (now SIGMOD) Workshop on Data Description, Access and Control: Data Models: Data-Structure-Set versus Relational*, Ann Arbor, MI, 1 May 2001: 83–113.

Freiburghaus, K. (1983), 'Der Videotex-Betriebsversuch', *Technische Mitteilungen PTT*, 61: 229–33.

Gfeller, P. A. (1993), 'Videotex in der Schweiz', in R. Trachsel (ed.), *Ein halbes Jahrhundert Telekommunikation in der Schweiz*, Aarau: Sauerländer: 257–68.

Girschik, K. (2005), 'Als die Kassen lesen lernten: Die Anfänge der rechnergestützten Warenwirtschaft bei der Migros', *Traverse. Zeitschrift für Geschichte*, 3: 110–24.

Girschik, K. (2006), 'Machine Readable Codes: The Swiss Retailer Migros and the Quest for Flow Velocity since the mid 1960s', *Entreprise et Histoire*, 44: 55–65.

Girschik, K. (2009) 'Als die Kassen lesen lernten: "Eine Technikgeschichte des Schweizer Einzelhandels", 1950–1975', *DGES*, Zurich: Federal Institute of Technology (ETH).

Gugerli, D. (2002), 'Die Entwicklung der digitalen Telefonie (1960–1985): Die Kosten soziotechnischer Flexibilisierungen', in K. Stadelmann, T. Hengartner and M. F. K. Bern (eds), *Telemagie: 150 Jahre Telekommunikation in der Schweiz*, Zurich: Chronos: 37–52.

Gugerli, D. (2007), 'Die Welt als Datenbank. Zur Relation von Softwareentwicklung, Abfragetechnik und Deutungsautonomie', in D. Gugerli, M. Hanger, M. Hampe, B. Orland, P. Sarasin and J. Tanner (eds), *Daten*, Zurich, Berlin: Diaphanes: 11–36.

Gugerli, D. (2009), 'Das Monster und die Schablone: Zur Logistik von Daten um 1950', *Traverse: Zeitschrift für Geschichte*, 3: 66–76.

Gugerli, D., Kupper, P. and Speich, D. (2005), *Die Zukunftsmaschine: Konjunkturen der Eidgenössischen Technischen Hochschule Zürich 1855–2005*, Zurich: Chronos.

Habermas, J. (1973) *Legitimationsprobleme im Spätkapitalismus*, Frankfurt, a.M: Suhrkamp.

Haigh, T. (2006), '"A Veritable Bucket of Facts": Origins of the Data Base Management System', *SIGMOD Record*, 35: 33–49.

Hausammann, L. (2008), 'Der Beginn der Informatisierung im Kanton Zürich: Von der Lochkartenanlage im Strassenverkehrsamt zur kantonalen EDV-Stelle (1957–1970)', Ph.D. Thesis, *Philosophische Fakultät*, Zurich: University of Zurich.

Helleiner, E. (1994), *States and the Reemergence of Global Finance: From Bretton Woods to the 1990s*, Ithaca, NY: Cornell University Press.

Illi, M. (2008), *Von der Kameralistik zum New Public Management*, Zurich: Chronos.

Jung, J. (2000), *Von der Schweizerischen Kreditanstalt zur Credit Suisse Group: Eine Bankengeschichte*, Zurich: Verlag Neue Zürcher Zeitung.

Kilgus, E. (1968), *Das Rechnungswesen im Dienste der Unternehmungsführung Antrittsrede an der Universität Zürich, gehalten am 20. Januar 1968*, Zurich: Schulthess.

Kilgus, E. (1971), *Betriebswirtschaftliche Probleme des Bankbetriebes*, Bern: Haupt.

Kilgus, E. (1982), *Bank-Management in Theorie und Praxis*, Bern: Haupt.

Knecht, W. (1984), *Videotex: Das neue Medium*, Zurich: IBO-Verlag.

Kobelt, C. (1987), 'Informatik bei einer Grossbank – SKA liess Fachpresse hinter die Kulissen gucken', *Technische Mitteilungen PTT*, 65: 211–36.

Kyrish, S. (1996), *From Videotex to the Internet: Lessons form Online Services 1981–1996*, La Trobe: La Trobe University.

Luhmann, N. (1966), *Recht und Automation in der öffentlichen Verwaltung: Eine verwaltungswissenschaftliche Untersuchung*, Berlin: Drucker & Humblot.

Luhmann, N. (1976), 'The Future Cannot Begin: Temporal Structures in Modern Society', *Social Research*, 43(1): 130–52.

Lütolf, R. (2002), Die Einführung von Videotex in der Schweiz (1979–1987) im Vergleich mit derjenigen in Deutschland und Frankreich. Eine Analyse der Fehler, Thesis, Zurich: University of Zurich.

Mabillard, M. and R. d. Weck (1977), *Der Fall Chiasso*, Genève: Tribune Editions.

Macdonald, R. (1988), *Floating Exchange Rates: Theories and Evidence*, London: Unwin Hyman.

MacKenzie, D. (2006), *An Engine, Not a Camera. How Financial Models Shape Markets*, Cambridge, MA: The MIT Press.

Meadows, D. H. (1972), *The Limits to Growth: A Report for the Club of Rome's Project on the Predicament of Mankind*, London: Earth Island.

Neitzert, M. (1996), 'Human Capital in the Hot Sun', *Economic Development and Cultural Change*, 45: 69–87.

Neukom, H. (2004), 'Early Use of Computers in Swiss Banks', *IEEE Annals of the History of Computing*, 26(3): 50–9.

Nolan, R. L. (1973), 'Computer Databases: The Future is Now', *Harvard Business Review*, 51: 98–114.

Piore, M. J. and Sabel, C. (1984), *The Second Industrial Divide*, New York: Basic Books.

Regini, M., Kitay, J. and Baethge, M. (eds) (1999), *From Tellers to Sellers: Changing Employment Relations in Banks*, Cambridge, MA: The MIT Press.

Rogge, P. G. (1997), *Die Dynamik des Wandels. Schweizerischer Bankverein 1862–1997. Das fünfte Vierteljahrhundert*, Basel: F. Reinhardt.

Scott, S. V., Van Reenen, J. and Zachariadis, M. (2008), 'The Impact on Bank Performance of the Diffusion of a Financial Innovation: An Analysis of SWIFT Adoption', *WISE Conference*, Paris.

Siegenthaler, H. -J. (1993), *Regelvertrauen, Prosperität und Krisen: Die Ungleichmässigkeit wirtschaftlicher und sozialer Entwicklung als Ergebnis individuellen Handelns und sozialen Lernens*, Tübingen: Mohr.

SKA (1978), *Automation of Bank Operations in the Eighties Report of Zurich Conference; November 1977*, Zurich.

Stonebraker, M., Wong, E., Kreps, P. and Held, G. (1976), 'The Design and Implementation of INGRES', *ACM Transactions on Database Systems (TODS)*, 1: 189–222.

Swary, I. and Topf, B. (1992), *Gobal Financial Deregulation: Commercial Banking at the Crossroads*, Cambridge, MA: Blackwell Publishers.

Symonds, M. and Ellison, L. (2003), *Software: An Intimate Portrait of Larry Ellison and Oracle*, New York: Simon & Schuster.

Winter, J. B. (1974), 'Wertschriften-Abrechnung, -Disposition und -Verwahrung mittels EDV in Mittel- und Grossbanken', *Historisches Seminar*, Zurich: University of Zurich.

Zetti, D. (2006), 'Personal und Computer: Automation des Postcheckdienstes mit Computer, ein Projekt der PTT 1963–1975', *Historisches Seminar*, Zurich: University of Zurich.

Zetti, D. (2009), 'Die Erschliessung der Rechenanlage: Computer im Postcheckdienst, 1964–1974', *Traverse: Zeitschrift für Geschichte*, 3: 88–101.

6
Is the Future of the ATM Past?

Bernardo Bátiz-Lazo and Claudia Reese

Introduction

Greater use of credit and debit card payments as well as the mirage of the 'cashless society', led some North American and British observers to consider automated teller machines (ATMs) a 'passing technology'.[1] Not so (or at least not in the foreseeable future) is the unanimous conclusion of 20 British managers in financial and non-financial intermediaries with direct responsibilities in self-service technology (and management of ATM fleets), who were asked to opine on that sentiment between March and January 2008. Although the use of cash has decreased to 'historical' low levels, its use remains steady while the ATM remains the undisputed vehicle for people to acquire cash (as opposed to transactions at the bank retail branch or 'cash back' at food retailers).[2] One interviewee opined:

> When I joined the bank [in 1973], I was against ATMs. We didn't know that ATMs were the future. I thought the technology was a little early and thought we could use retail establishments as the vehicle to provide cash to customers. Supermarkets in the United States at that time used to have excess cash as they used to cash checks for people. The question was how to provide on-line, real-time support.
>
> (Interview, 8 September 2009)

Today, self-service vendors have successfully deployed machines with dual cash distribution and deposit functionality. In some cases these are responsible for more than half of all the cash deposit transactions.[3] Hence ATMs play and will continue to play an important role in the future of retail bank markets.

With the end of cheque clearing in 2018 looming in the horizon, how were the 20 managers that took part in the survey selected? Responses from British managers were elicited following archival research into the history of cash dispensing technology and ten in-depth interviews with engineers closely linked with either the development of the first cash dispensers in the UK or responsible for introducing important changes to that technology. These ten interviews took place between January and March 2008. Recollections of the testimonials were contrasted with a host of archival records. These included surviving documents of banks, savings banks and building societies, annual reports of banks and computer manufacturers, industry magazines (e.g. the *Banker*), newspapers (e.g. *Financial Times* and the *Times*) and in-house magazines of financial institutions and manufacturers. The combination of in-depth interviews and archival research thus helped to frame the basic agenda for a questionnaire about issues around self-service practices in retail bank markets. Triangulation with several sources helped to avoid reliance on a single informant or source in ascertaining the areas of greatest concern for self-service in British retail financial services. At the same time, our approach enabled us to portray these issues in their long-term context.

The participants worked up a total of 22 questions on the broad areas of cash dispensing and self-service banking. Responses were not limited to these questions as participants were encouraged to elaborate views and concerns that seemed relevant to the overall agenda. What follows is not a systematic analysis of the responses by British managers. Instead this article provides a summary of the key points emerging from our survey. These key points were drafted as the interviews with managers progressed, and when finished, the draft was circulated among participants as well as a handful of managers with similar responsibilities in other counties (namely the US, Germany and Mexico). In other words, rather than presenting survey results as a tabulation of the 20 semi-structured interviews, what follows tells of the main business and technological concerns for self-service in banking today while presenting them in their historical context.

But why look at self-service or even ATMs in Britain? What makes the UK cash dispensing market interesting? After all for almost half a decade, ATMs have not gone far beyond 'cash and dash' in most countries. Besides, there might be more interesting examples like Portugal and Spain where ATMs offer a wider range of services and functionality than in Britain. We deemed the British market interesting because the first successful cash dispensers were deployed in England in 1967. Access to surviving records in business archives, patent filings as well as interviews with engineers and bankers, allowed us look at the development of this technology from its inception through to its diffusion and 'maturity' – and all of these stages taking place within the same market. Through archival research we learnt how Britain was often a first mover in ATM technology. For instance interviewees reminisced about the relative success of early experiments with new functionality. Other examples of early/first mover advantage were also found when looking at the development of the hardware. For instance, National Cash Registers (NCR) grew to dominate the manufacturing of ATMs during the late 1980s and most of the 1990s, while locating production and R&D facilities in its plant at Dundee, Scotland. Of course, although the British self-service market has been innovative and highly successful in many respects, it has also experienced inertia and ossification in others.

Another aspect that makes the British market interesting is the creation of a single, jointly owned platform for interoperability of proprietary ATM fleets, namely LINK. A single shared national network stands out when compared to a peak of some 200 different national networks in the US in 1986. Since achieving full interoperability in 1998 LINK grew to be the world's most active network, dealing with up to 226 million transactions per month, and at its busiest processing over 1 million transactions an hour in 2007. LINK has 50 members and there are over 130 million LINK cards in circulation from 38 issuers. Related to LINK is the fact that in the UK network few customers pay directly to have access to their cash balances through ATMs. This feature dominates the interaction between participants and being fairly unusual in the international scene further distinguishes the workings of cash dispensers in the UK.

Of particular interest to the unifying theme of this book is the role of regulators and regulations with regard to the developments of self-service technology in retail banking. Britain's 'hands off' approach contrasts with experiences in other countries. For instance in the US the Comptroller of the Currency, the Federal Insurance Deposit Corporation and the Federal Reserve Board actively collaborated in the development of an automated electronic payments clearing house in the mid 1970s (Walker 1975, 2). Regulatory change during the 1980s is also important as it helps to explain the 'tipping point' in the adoption of cash dispensers in many countries. But these changes relate to the diversification and geographical location of financial intermediaries rather than to cash machines themselves. Hence ATMs in Britain are interesting for this book as an example of 'laissez-faire' while acknowledging that in other geographies (and particularly the US), technology might have been used to overcome regulatory barriers.

Given the longstanding use and unique features of ATMs in Britain, it seemed appropriate to ask for respondents' thoughts concerning the current and future challenges for cash dispensing technology.

The remainder of this chapter proceeds as follows. The next section discusses the perception of electronic cash distribution within the internal management of financial intermediaries. These oscillated between a view of this technology as, on balance, a requirement for effective competition in retail finance markers (i.e. a threshold capability) and a view of it as part of a 'loss-leader' marketing strategy (i.e. an instrument to articulate customer relationship management initiatives). This section also encompasses a discussion of issues relating to on-branch and off-branch location of ATMs. The third section considers sources of inertia and ossification of the technology, while the fourth presents the opposite argument by discussing sources of instability, change and dynamism in the market. The final section summarizes and presents the main conclusions from this study.

Cost centre or marketing tool? (The 'choosing the right appropriation' method)

As portrayed in Table 6.1, various business models (i.e. corporate strategies) combined with the jointly owned platform result in distinct approaches to the ownership and location of ATMs. Many providers have developed systems for detailed profit and loss analysis of individual locations. These were introduced to give transparency to investments made by providers, in maintaining and running their infrastructure to manage cash in-branch and non-branch locations. However lack of agreement on which appropriation method to use results in a wide variety of cost accounting approaches and opens up the possibility of some systems looking more efficient than they really are.

There is also variation in how the ATM is integrated with the retail branch. Since the 1970s some participants have given individual branches 'ownership' of the machine at their branch. Branch staff are expected to replenish, and provide some basic maintenance as well as being alert to faults and malfunctions. Others run the ATM fleet as a standalone business. Having a distinct profit centre has often resulted in only the most profitable (or 'essential') branch locations being retained.

However in-branch is only 'unprofitable' if the location is considered on a standalone interchange basis. On a distribution strategy basis, the in-branch ATM is generally a lower cost way of serving customer requirements than over the counter. Therefore, it represents

Table 6.1 Business models in the UK market for cash dispensing services (Number of machines in operation with reference to location – 2007)

Types of operators	**Number of operators**	**Branch ATMs**	**Non-branch free ATMs**	**Non-branch pay to use ATMs**	**Sum**	**%**
Bank	11	10.811	8.684	—	19.495	*30%*
Building societies turned bank	5	4.047	1.636	952	6.635	*10%*
Mutuals (Co-op Bank & building societies)	7	1.491	3.53	—	5.021	*8%*
Independent ATM Deployers (IAD)	13	2.589	4.05	25.184	31.823	*50%*
Retailers* and others	3	13	11	926	950	*1%*
Sum	39**	18.951	17.911	27.062	63.924	
Per cent of total		*30%*	*28%*	*42%*		*100%*

Note: * excludes Tesco Personal Finance
** 11 of LINK's 50 members do not own any ATM.
Source: LINK statistic on member's ATM networks, December 2007.

an efficiency gain. Relocation and closure of individual in-branch ATM locations are thus more likely to be responses to strategic than financial considerations.

Some participants with a long history in managing ATM fleets also described 'cycles' or oscillations in the strategic priority of controlling the costs of cash dispensing. One participant described this as follows:

> [This business stream manages] two of our channels, one of the channels is the branch agency network, and the other channel is the ATM network. We have 2500 ATMs, give or take one or two. They historically were part of IT division and they were viewed as an IT piece and what we've done is we've thought actually 'no, this isn't right, they are a channel, a distribution channel', so we've brought it into retail [banking business stream] and hence for the last 6 months I've been running ATMs, along with other things as well, but the ATM stream. (Interview, 25 July 2008)

This cycle thus describes how ATMs are sometimes seen as part of the infrastructure and sometimes more as a distribution or marketing channel: an emphasis on cost containment has often resulted in a loss of functionality and the closure of 'non-essential' locations. Continued downsizing often led to a perception of lost growth opportunities. As a response, strategy makers appointed marketing people with the responsibilities of managing remote channels (with a specific mandate to expand the ATM network). The pursuit of customer relationship management initiatives was often associated with increased functionality (while looking to find ways to engage non-customers using own ATMs) and an expansion of the fleet into off-branch sites. The perception of a failure to achieve targets then led to a new cost containment phase.

It is interesting to note that in Table 6.1 there are 11 medium sized or small asset sized intermediaries; members of LINK who offer current accounts but own no cash dispensers at all. Their customer base was too small to justify the capital investment while a single, nationwide interconnected network offered their customers the possibility to access their liquid balances at different locations without a major loss of 'convenience'. One interviewee whose organization did not own any ATM but was part of LINK recalled:

> Cash infrastructure is expensive and handling cash is expensive. Cash handling is a low margin business. If you are doing it, it is on the basis that if you do enough of it you will make a profit. But we probably couldn't do enough of it to make anything that was meaningful so we would rather focus our efforts on making money some other ways. ... [I]t sounds very elitist, it's not. As far as we are concerned it's very pragmatic. Like many people in the country our credits, our salaries, our direct debits, outstanding orders, etc. are paid into and out of bank accounts. I don't know anyone who finds that a real problem.
>
> (Interview, 2 June 2008)

Having customers accessing 'free withdrawal' cash points owned by others implies paying the multilateral interchange fee (MIF) through LINK.[4] The value of MIF reflects the average cost of acquiring members making their machines available to the card issuer. The MIF emerges from the combination of transaction volume plus actions to make LINK more cost effective, secure and reliable.

Most financial intermediaries compete for non-branch locations with independent ATM deployers (IADs). Since their emergence in

1998, their business model has been to install machines at non-branch locations to offer greater 'convenience' (e.g. pubs, corner shops and small or medium sized train stations), in remote or otherwise unattractive places. Of course customers of financial intermediaries also expect convenience and to have a safe environment. This has meant that some banks have significantly reduced the number of 'outdoor' ATMs and replaced them with machines in the hall of the retail bank branch.[5] This does not only help to reduce the damage to the machine itself (e.g. due to weather conditions) but also opens the possibility for bank staff to engage in sales of other (higher margin) services. Other financial intermediaries have taken the opposite strategy and deployed a large number of standalone kiosks where cash dispensing is often combined with other 'client capture' facilities (such as a public telephone or Internet access point). Figure 6.1 illustrates one of these kiosks.

The IAD model is driven by a lowest cost operator mentality, allowing them to plug the geographic and opportunity gaps in distribution. The founder of one of the largest IAD explained:

Figure 6.1 Standalone self-service kiosk (Milton Keynes, May 2008)

> [T]he first corporate sector [we aimed for] was the pub market, because each big pub change owns some 5000 outlets. They've all got 'machine departments' who look after the fruit machines, the pool tables, etc. So here we had people that we could go and talk about machines with and more importantly, they've got a budget. We would say: 'Look we'll put this cash machine into your venue, it's got a number of benefits, the first benefit is that say, four people got out for a night drinking right, three of them have got enough money, it comes to the fourth person's round right and they don't have enough cash, what does he/she does? They are going walk out the door and find a cash machine. The cash machine is probably down the road and his/her mates are probably going to go with him/her because they are not going to let that last round go. But once they go they will all find another pub, they are not going stay here, waiting for the other to come back. So not only have you lost that customer, you've lost all his/her friends.' If you put a cash machine in the pub, we worked out that some 20 percent of the money taken out goes straight back into the business in drinking and in gaming.
>
> (Interview, 4 December 2007)

Some IAD generates income through MIF in high 'foot traffic' locations. In others, machines usually levy a surcharge.[6] The typical IAD prefers to work with 'easy to use' hardware and some of them actually sell the machine to their landlord (in order to focus on operational issues). Figure 6.2 illustrates this strategy, through a machine that requires little space (i.e. easy to fit), low distribution capacity (i.e. less risk of fraud or theft) and is easily replenished by staff. Locating a cash dispenser within the bar area was 'convenient' for customers at this particular pub. This outlet combined restaurant and on-premises drinking and was part of an out of town hotel chain.

Some IAD models find viable locations with as little as half a dozen transactions per day. Transaction volume is much lower than dispensers at branches of financial intermediaries and food retailers: IADs now control half the number of machines in operation but are responsible for about four per cent of total annual transactions.

Interestingly, some financial intermediaries have responded by locating 'free withdrawal' machines nearby those of IADs and even successfully deployed surcharging machines. An example of the latter has been Alliance & Leicester (which since July 2004 is part of Grupo Santander). This former building society deployed surcharging machines under its

Figure 6.2 Machine installed at the end of the bar in a pub (Llandudno, March 2008)

own brand name while escaping vilification by the popular press.[7] One interviewee opined:

> I guess the number of charging ATMs increased quite rapidly and then there was this little worry really fuelled by the HBOS decision to sell its remote ATMs to CardPoint, suddenly there was this public concern that free ATMs would disappear. Indeed the number of free ATMs did not decline but it did level off and basically [since 2005] remained static.
>
> (Interview, 5 February 2008)

On balance, IADs are not considered serious competitive threats to established financial intermediaries. This is because frequent transactions at an IAD's machine do not result in the migration of liquid balances. In other words, individuals remain loyal to their financial intermediary. IADs have thus failed to develop their own independent relationship with frequent users. However competition for non-branch locations since circa 2007 sparked a rise in rental fees that has had significant impact on everyone's margins. IADs and financial intermediaries now question the financial viability of many locations while increased competition has led to a drop in the number of independent IADs.

The threat of food retailers

Peter Welch and Steve Worthington are among those who have reflected on the threats to banks in the UK of cash provision and other financial services by food retailers. Their work identifies distinctive actions in the process of product diversification to offer finance and financial 'products', a move that has also been called 'financialization'.[8] In this regard, joint ventures between banks and retailers (namely Tesco and the Royal Bank of Scotland Group in Tesco Personal Finance, and J. Sainsbury's and HBOS in Sainsbury's Bank) as well as unique models (the collaboration of the Co-operative Bank with stores owned by its parent, the Co-operative Group) brought about shared ownership of ATM locations with the highest 'foot traffic'. It comes as no surprise these three shared locations are the largest net 'acquirers'[9] within LINK and have effectively neutralized the competitive threat of retailers (as far as the cash dispensing services market is concerned).[10] As stated by our interviewees:

> [Food retailers] will not be a source of anxiety as long as they continue to sell financial services as if they were baked beans.
>
> (Interviews, 3 March 2008, 28 March 2008, 9 May 2008).

The success of food retailers has been to change the mentality and perception of customers about when, where and how some financial services can be acquired. It is exactly the 'baked bean' mentality that enables the supermarket to act as a channel for mass market financial 'commodity products' like unsecured loans, general insurance and cash distribution. If this should change, the more astute financial intermediaries have positioned themselves to make sure that they have a part in future developments of financial products by non-financial players.

So with a single national shared network and major competitive threats either co-opted or thwarted, can there be any realistic expectation of 'new and improved' cash dispensing technology in the UK? As detailed in the next two sections, there are incentives and disincentives for the evolution of business models and technology in the cash dispensing services market.

Sources of inertia and ossification

David (1985) defined a *path-dependent* sequence of economic change as one in which eventual outcomes are influenced by remote events, including developments shaped by circumstances rather than systematic planning. History matters. Where you have been in the past determines where you are now and where you can go in future. When faced with alternative technologies, random developments can give advantage to one that then becomes the norm as it is further adopted and further improved. Indeed even small, apparently trivial differences in the chosen technological path can have huge consequences for where participants are and where they can go.

There is disagreement as to whether path dependence is a form of market failure. For those who do consider it a sign of sub-optimal solutions, the 'best' technology does not prevail but a 'lower quality' configuration. This is so not because of strategy or prescience but as a result of an early lead combined with chance events may eventually 'corner the market' as other technologies are 'locked-out'. For instance, Campbell-Kelly claims that the legacy software written in FORTRAN and COBOL during the 1960s and 1970s and the ever-increasing number of programmers trained to use them, caused them to become ever more securely entrenched; this being the first example of a 'lock-in' in the history of software.

Path dependence thus refers to the way in which apparently insignificant events and choices can have huge consequences for the development of a market or an economy. It suggests there is strong inertia once initial technological choices are made. In turn, this inertia limits possibilities for the adoption of innovations in the future. For instance, the deployment of ATM networks requires important capital investments (with the asking price of individual machines in the thousands of dollars). Adopting alternative technologies such as payments made through bar code images in mobile phones seems less likely in geographies with dense networks per capita (such as Spain, Belgium or even the UK) than countries that have high mobile phone usage and have yet to make a significant investment in ATMs (such as Mexico or Nigeria).

But although the ideas of path dependence and lock-in imply that alternative layouts and applications fail to prosper for long periods of time, they do not necessarily associate them with a fatalistic view of technological change. For instance, there are examples of *path breaking applications* in the history of software such as real-time reservation bookings (i.e. the SABRE system) and relational databases (Campbell-Kelly 2003, ix, 186).

The ideas of path dependence and lock-in within the history of self-service in Britain would see the ATM embedded in the long term process of automation and mechanization, that is, the 'robotization' of both the internal processes of financial intermediaries, and individual transactions in retail financial markets. This technological trajectory spanned the twentieth century and saw the introduction of typewriters, steel filing cabinets, telephones, punch card tabulators, mechanical and electro-mechanical accounting machines. After De La Rue committed to supplying its cash dispensers exclusively to Barclays in 1967, Chubb's MD2 was basically the only available technology and consequently became the leading cash dispenser in the UK during the 1970s (see further Bátiz-Lazo 2009). The likes of International Business Machines (IBM), NCR, Burroughs and Diebold then had to adapt and comply with the four digit personal identification number (PIN), dimensions for external facia and many other decisions made by Chubb in the UK, Omron Tateishi in Japan, Asea-Metior in Sweden and Docutel in the US, rather than by designing from first principles.

The creation of a single, jointly owned platform for interoperability of proprietary ATM fleets through LINK in the UK is clearly an example of lock-in as a standard interconnection has dominated the cash dispensing market since 1998 and pre-empts the development of any alternative platform. LINK was formed in 1985 – as an independent company that housed a mainframe computer – by a group of building societies, the Co-operative Bank, Girobank and American Express (see further Bátiz-Lazo 2009, 17). All of them were characterized by having too small a volume of business to justify the cost of deploying a proprietary fleet. At the time there were other competing offerings emerging from the interoperability of other building societies (i.e. Matrix) and some of the banks (i.e. NatWest, Midland and TSB Group). LINK's success was much more a result of 'positive feedback' than precognition of how new opportunities were 'looming in the technological fog' (Campbell-Kelly 2003, 242–3). LINK became the dominant platform as it was designed to reflect the average fully burdened cost of serving the transaction while acting as a clearing house and facilitator of the movement of fees. Interoperability developed through connections to the central computer. Each new participating organization associated with greater business volume and this, in turn, led to lower average cost per transaction (i.e. downward pressure on interchange fees) while, at the same time, the network became more attractive to ultimate users (i.e. retail consumers) as it offered an increasing number of cash dispensing points. Financial reasons as well as reasons of convenience eventually became a high barrier for others to imitate.

The advantage of LINK technological configuration strengthened as the technological choices made by other networks (such as that by NatWest, Midland and TSB Group) proved to be poor as far as increasing interoperability and scalability were concerned. LINK emerged as the successful network as it was able to attract greater business volume than alternatives (either proprietary fleets or interlinked). As a result today there is a highly standardized software product. There is lock-in because innovation (in the form of new services) is hard to incorporate. This results from the combination of the service innovation with regulatory and compliance costs that often distort the picture, with mandated upgrades significantly impacting the cost base. As noted by one participant:

> We have seen in the industry a number of companies over time come to us and say 'we've got a new and better solution to a PIN number'. For instance, we've seen a sort of rolling numbers. There is now biometrics around as a complimentary to a PIN or indeed to replace it. We are seeing that in Arabic states and perhaps newer banking environments where they can just jump technology steps. I guess one of the things about having a very mature and large ATM [fleet] in the UK, is that you need a 'LINK recommendation' and an agreed rule to change things. If that were the case, it would probably require a five year migration path and not everyone is ready to buy into such commitment.
>
> (Interview, 1 May 2008)

Another interesting example of lock-in and one that has perhaps had global consequences relates to IBM's Customer Information and Control System or CICS. IBM's early expertise with remote, real-time systems led it to develop the first real-time cash machine (i.e. the first ATM)[11] in partnership with Lloyds Bank in 1971 (see further Bátiz-Lazo 2009). At the same time in the US, it developed a piece of software that connected a user's application programme to an operating system and a database. This programme was called CICS and was developed in 1967–8 as a request of utility companies in New York (Campbell-Kelly 2003, 149–51). Initially there were 50 licences issued in the first year. By 1971 there were only 111 users. The programme was not very large but had a complex logic that freed programmers from many difficulties of handling simultaneous transactions (a key feature of a large proprietary ATM fleet). This together with the emergence of visual applications, greater interest in real-time systems and IBM's success in encouraging third-party CICS application developers and consultants, positioned it as the dominant application for real-time teleprocessing by 1974 (just in time for the take-off of a new generation of ATMs by the likes of IBM, NCR, Diebold and Burroughs). CICS was not without competitors. But IBM marketed it so aggressively that by the mid-1980s (when the tip-off point in the adoption of ATMs was taking place in Britain and elsewhere) teleprocessing monitors[12] from independent providers had been 'blown away'. Hence CICS became an early example of lock-in in the history of self-service banking; independent providers were 'locked out' and CICS helped the ATM to become the dominant path in self-service banking, as alternative technologies to 'brick and mortar' distribution such as drive-in, mobile branches and postal deposits were either completely abandoned or sidelined.

But automation of banking did not happen for its own sake – it occurred because intermediaries sought to achieve greater efficiency (specifically of cheque clearing, cash distribution and the accounting function). Automation and computer technology also facilitated the diversification of financial and non-financial intermediaries within retail financial markets. This process took place in tandem with large pools of individuals becoming active in these markets; after having been marginalized or excluded throughout the contemporary history of Western style capitalism. This trend accelerated in the UK with the digitalization of customer accounts on the back of the decimalization of sterling in 1971 and the payment of wages directly into current accounts (replacing payment by cash). In the late 1970s and early 1980s, cash dispensers were seen as a critical device for competition in retail finance, as a way to ease congestion at retail branches (especially by banks) and also as a way to be a credible competitor in the High Street (by building societies).

More recently, the success of cash dispensing technology in moving customers out of the retail bank branch has been superseded with a view that considers the effective deployment of self-service technology in branch as creating a clean and welcoming high service environment, where staff are on hand to assist with transactions, but more importantly to advise and sell. This move has been reinforced by the introduction (in the UK and elsewhere) of automated cash counting machines. The new devices sit alongside or are bundled with cash dispensing technology and have overcome customer resistance to envelope deposits (a feature of cash machines since the 1970s that did not find customer acceptance in Britain while it did in the US). The new cash depositing facilities offer online, real-time crediting of customer accounts and voice recognition of the amount deposited as well as photographic evidence of cheque deposits.[13]

But in this success lies a paradox: more automation is desirable as it can help to reduce cost structures; but operational considerations have bred a new challenge: how to engage the customer (who is no longer coming into the branch) in a sales pitch? Opportunities for advertising are limited but could be made more effective. Time and again market reports tell of consumer distaste for general advertising at the cash terminal, and printing information on the back of receipts has had little success in raising awareness (as well as being environmentally unfriendly).

Solutions suggested by manufacturers, such as NCR's tailored software screen behind 'My @TM', have been largely unsuccessful (Anonymous 2000). Meanwhile, pitching for regular non-customers is attractive as in their everyday life consumers tend to use the same three to five locations on a regular basis. Net acquirers of transactions could be tempted to develop targeted advertising for users banking at other financial intermediaries. Certainly, non-clients who occasionally use own-ATMs are one of the most interesting (but difficult to engage) audiences worth thinking about for customer relationship (CRM) purposes. But retrieving the information to make this possible could be contrary to the British data protection legislation. In any case, it is an area where managers of banks will welcome new marketing ideas. One participant stated:

> I know there were some experiments with it. We're not that convinced. We've put internal adverts on our ATMs ... but it's usually on the introductory screen. What we haven't really done is to try and layer in things in the dead time. Instead of saying please wait while we count your cash, it would be much better to have an intelligent thing for that customer but it has to be tailored. If it's not tailored its wallpaper and they will pay no attention to it whatsoever. But I think there is scope for us to make offers or even maybe to get information from the customers say 'we've tried to call you but your number seems to be out of date can you call us?' You know we could do things, there's no doubt we could definitely do things. We've tried in the past with offers printed on the back of balance enquiry slips and stuff like that. It doesn't work.
>
> (Interviewee, 23 May 2008)

Could greater automation in the form of ATMs be used to attract new customers? Today's customers expect the transaction at the ATM to last no more than 30 seconds (i.e. 'cash and dash'). 'Cash and dash' has resulted in a reduced functionality of the ATM in 2008 when compared with that offered in the dawn of the technology: already in 1975, IBM and NCR promised British customers the possibility of not only withdrawing bank notes but also making deposits, dealing with account enquiries, placing chequebook or account statement requests, obtaining foreign currency exchange rates and making account transfers. In 1984 the NCR 5070 was considered the first fully functional machine while offering transfers, payments, printing of detailed statements and envelope deposits. Today most 'through the wall' machines in Britain are limited to cash dispensing different denominations, balance enquiry and, at some machines, mobile phone top up.

One has to acknowledge that since the 1980s the cash dispenser has been mechanically reliable. After forty years of successful operation and increasing technical sophistication, there is a direct link in the evolution of cash dispensers into ATMs and from the latter to platforms for self-service technology in airports and food retailers. Yet participants in our survey were unanimous on the point that automatic cash dispensing was, is, and will be the raison d'être of the ATM. This serves to explain why through their history alternative banking related functions have been tried and tested while manufacturers have always had innovations in the pipeline that never found broad acceptance.

Some participants opined that any innovation in the foreseeable future is more likely to emerge in association with software and in a way that can be shared through the network. The case of 'La Caixa', the largest Spanish savings bank, was noted as it transformed its ATMs by increasing their functionality: from updating passbooks and performing a host of banking services, to acting as point of sale for entrance to entertainment venues (such as cinemas, theatres and pop music concerts). This increased functionality developed into a very profitable opportunity to attract non-customers to its proprietary ATM network.

But on reflection the case for similar innovations in the UK was not straightforward: on the one hand, there is limited action (and indeed incentive) for individual organizations to depart from the established norm to the extent that innovations within proprietary networks fail to achieve 'critical scale'. On the other hand, the challenge for any proposed innovations around the LINK platform (such as the Oyster card in London) is to make a business case that is acceptable to all members.

Legacy information technology platforms partially explain the inertia and reluctance that prevent the widespread adoption of innovative software-related applications. Some platforms can take up to ten years between updates and these come at non-trivial costs.

Finally it is worth mentioning the success story of Wincor. By 2002 the Paderborn-based German company was very much on the way to mounting a successful challenge to the leadership (and, for some, the complacency and arrogance) of NCR as the leading global hardware and software provider of ATMs (O'Brien 2002). Today managers of middle-sized and even some large participants in cash dispensing find Wincor hardware and software a solution they are happy to embrace wholeheartedly. Many feel Wincor 'has listened to the customer'. Some of its application software has indeed become the standard as it has been successfully adopted, and replaced in-house programming solutions. Other providers, however, prefer not to outsource their software since they see the development of technology platforms as a core capability.

Sources of dynamism

Path dependence has been mainly used by economists of neoclassical orientation to explain exceptional cases where 'history matters'; under the general assumption that history does not matter. For economists, path dependence relates to sub-optimal solutions, to things that ought not to have happened. However and as mentioned, there is no consensus that path dependence reflects market failure. For one, having invested in learning to make and use a particular technological application, it makes no economic sense to switch to an alternative that is no better than the original (*Economist* 2009). There is also increasing evidence from the historical record that has shed a different light on market errors and lock-in to technological trajectories (Liebowitz and Margolis 1990, 1995). The ATM fleet is part of a wider network of electronic payment systems and as such it influences and is influenced by developments around the greater use of credit debit cards, replacement of cheques and cash payment by debit cards, as well as technology supporting electronic funds transfer at point of sale (EFTPOS). These are increasingly global networks and so developments in large 'virgin' markets such as India and China could well influence the developments and/or practices in Europe and North America.

The idea of the ATM configuration being a sub-optimal solution and emerging from fortuitous circumstances or chance developments is also debatable. Cash dispensers did not materialize from the ether. Nor as claimed by Shepherd-Barron, did they emerge from his inspiration in a bathtub. There is a strong case to be made for managers of deposit accepting intermediaries (such as Barclays Bank and Midland Bank in the UK, and the savings banks in Sweden) actively participating in the process of developing cash dispenser technology (Bátiz-Lazo and Reid 2008; Bátiz-Lazo et al. 2009). But the role of bankers was from a position of 'technology clients': they provided engineers at Chubb, Speytec and De La Rue access 'to the field', as bankers supplied domain expertise that was essential to the success of the endeavour but left the assembling of the device as well as the design of critical components to engineers (such as the dispensing mechanism itself and the personal identification number that assured the right person was debiting the account). This episode from the 1960s is one more example of 'users' shaping the nature and functionality of the original technology – because the device came together only at the requirement of the banks and not as a result of the foresight of the engineers.

Later on, in the early 1980s, NCR's success in achieving the position of world's manufacturer was due to the close attention that the team at Dundee paid to 'intermediate users' (i.e. staff at retail branches) and 'ultimate consumers' (i.e. the public at large) in the development of an easy to use interface supported by easy to maintain machinery (Kotter 1990). This view was in direct opposition to that which prevailed in the market at the time and which envisioned the ATMs as remote terminals of a mainframe or working solely to attend banks' concerns with security and interoperability.

As for things to come, it is possible to think (although unlikely in the foreseeable future) that a further drop in cash transactions will bring about the decline or indeed the elimination of ATM technology. This would open the possibility for the dominance of cash distribution through alternative means like payback at the point of sale. One interviewee gave an opinion along these lines:

> But I think we are also reaching the stage where there are players in the UK who are seeing the decline of cash, they're seeing the decline of ATM transactions and they're seeing the decline of income and you will probably see a number of people really start to question whether or not the ATM type estate, particularly in the remote estate [i.e. non-branch], is worth the overhead of keeping internally, so I think there will be a large amount of consolidation over the next few years.
>
> (Interview, 2 May 2008)

There are thus reasons to believe in the 'mutual shaping' or 'co-evolution' of technology and society (e.g. Coombs et al. 1992; Pinch 2001). From this perspective the stability of technology is fragile. Social change, for one, can introduce alternative 'needs'. There is a vast literature on co-evolution between technology and society in financial services (e.g. Yates 2005; Nagurney et al. 2007), which for space considerations will not be reviewed in detail. The purpose of this research agenda is the study of technology and corporate strategy in their social and historical context, that is, the dynamics of the design, construction, development, implementation and use of retail financial services.

An example of alternative 'needs' relates to vulnerable consumers.[14] For instance, strict guidelines to assure accessibility of cash points to the physically disabled in the UK. In spite of costly adjustments to layouts and screens to increase usage, many 'vulnerable customers' still avoid ATMs for fear of being exposed to assaults while conducting cash transactions in the open. They prefer to use telephone banking, Internet banking or tellers at retail branches. The question of how to engage with vulnerable consumers is very much on today's and tomorrow's agenda for the providers of cash dispensing services. Particularly as government population forecasts suggest that the group of people aged over 75 years (i.e. another group of potentially vulnerable customers) will grow by 76 per cent in the next 25 years.

Interaction with the larger public should thus be seen as a source of potential innovation, organizational learning and necessary adjustments to changing policies. Another notable situation in the history of ATMs in Britain, along the lines of social change, relates to 'phantom withdrawals', that is, debit transactions that the customer has disputed. Few of today's managers of ATM fleets remember having dealt with a 'phantom withdrawal' but between 1981 and 1993 problems associated with them dominated public attention as mirrored in tabloid newspapers (i.e. *Daily Mail*) and annual reports of both the Banking and the Building Societies' Ombudsmen. The Jack Committee estimated that there was on average one disputed ATM transaction per hour across the country. While it was not known how many breaches of ATM security involved a dispute at all, since only small sums were involved, it seemed reasonable to assume that there was widespread dissatisfaction (Jack 1989, 79, 83).

Phantom withdrawals are part of a larger debate about the security and integrity of the cash withdrawal system and have to be understood in the context of whether customer or card issuer would take responsibility for the consequences of fraud. Banks had traditionally assumed the consequences of fraud when cashing a cheque with a false signature. But when confronted with the possibility of phantom withdrawals, financial providers claimed that the transaction had to be correct because the withdrawal had been activated by card and PIN. Financial intermediaries rejected the possibility of technical failure while downplaying the risk of fraud (or trying to pass its consequences to retail customers). This was important from the standpoint of the service provider in order to maintain confidence and overall consumer trust in electronic payment systems. However some 'ill feeling' permeated the previously unspoilt record of the ATM, since clients felt their honesty and integrity was being challenged – specifically since it turned out that fraud and to a lesser extent technical and clerical error had indeed taken place. Integrating mini-cameras within the ATMs helped to sort out fraud from 'abuse' (namely, a family member other than the account holder using the card and PIN versus a stranger having effectively cloned the card and PIN).

In our view, the moral of the story is that the episode gave LINK the incentive to find a quick solution to the parliamentary enquiry of 2005 into cash machine charges.[15] Under the leadership of John Hardy, LINK responded proactively and instead of letting public sentiment about financial exclusion soar, LINK was expedient in producing a survey of low income areas that identified locations where no 'free withdrawal' machines were available. Results suggested 83 per cent of the 10,000 lowest income areas had access to free of charge cash machines but deploying 700 machines would raise the coverage to 90 per cent. In order to reach that target, individual members were to be compensated for deploying machines in otherwise unprofitable sites through the payment of a 'financial inclusion premium' (one well above the usual MIF for any transaction made at free withdrawal machines). By April 2008 more than 400 free to use cash machines had been installed.

LINK's social action is unique to the UK among the world's ATM deployers. For its supporters, the move is evidence of the organizational learning that helps to explain why 'first movers' are better able to cope with technological and social change. For sceptics, it is a move that aims to pre-empt regulatory action that would otherwise have forced members of LINK to service unattractive locations at higher costs than the 'financial inclusion premium'. But regardless of which side you support, it is evident that members of LINK have been persuaded to act in unison. At the same time, LINK's staff do not sit idle. They continuously explore possibilities for alternative services, new locations and innovative functionality for its members. Some of these innovations are specifically designed to address changes in social trends and circumstances of vulnerable consumers. In other words, there is evidence of ongoing developments that could disrupt inertia and open unforeseen paths in an otherwise stable 'technological trajectory'.

Conclusion and future challenges

Whether it is within the corner shop, the hole-in-the-wall of the food store or the automatic kiosk in an unstaffed retail branch, in the next five to 15 years the ATM technology is here to stay; but how? It is unrealistic to think that their evolution will be solely dominated by inertia or by disruption. There is clearly an interaction between the future of the machine, its functionality and the potential for shared networks. Ultimately, technological trajectories are neither accidental nor predetermined but responsive to their users. In the case of self-service banking, this 'user' is, on the one hand, the bank or IAD as supplier of cash dispensing services and, on the other hand, the ultimate consumer. As one interviewee opined:

> Convenience is the driving force behind ATMs and I have yet to see something, [ultimate] consumers want, disappearing.
>
> (Feedback letter, 15 January 2009)

However when interacting with technology retail customers no longer constitute a homogenous group. Our research suggests that the young consider automation (in the form of cash dispensing equipment) a fact of life and are confident to interact with it in their daily lives. Young people expect more 'convenience', that is, freedom to assemble financial services according to individual preferences, income and lifestyle. For example, they expect availability of cash dispensers at leisure facilities. They are also willing to experiment with new functionalities like mobile phone top-ups or prepayment of entertainment. In tandem, there is a growing proportion of elderly people making active use of self-service technology. Indeed cash dispensers have sat in the High Street for most of the adult life of today's 65-year-olds. But this group is less willing to experiment with new applications. Another aspect to be considered is that vulnerable consumers such as pensioners and the physically disabled have special requirements for 'safe environments'. They generally do not object to self-service, but they want to use it while they are in control of who is approaching, in well-lit spaces, with help readily available.[16]

Other sources for innovation relate to changes in business models, ATM hardware and software. These can be solutions that combine greater convenience for customers and cost effectiveness for financial intermediaries. Some of these are already on the horizon. Most notably automatic counting technology, which can be expected to be more widespread as it will help reduce transactions at the retail bank branch teller as well as articulate the idea that branch staff should focus on selling rather than dealing with low-value-added transactions.

Security concerns have permeated the history of this technology and will most likely continue to do so, the recurrent themes being vandalism of fascias, protecting the store of money and ascertaining that the person has the right to debit the account. But a balance must be found between the cost of upgrading the stock, financial economies of increased security and the impact that such technology might have on customer convenience. For instance one could expect software applications that provide on-screen alternatives to replace the ten button keyboard to feed a PIN.

Biometrics is another alternative to replace the keypad or to be used along with a PIN as increased security. In Britain, this was pioneered in 1998 by Nationwide Building Society, who tested people's reaction to the use of biometric iris recognition technology at ATMs and branch counters. The technology was developed by Sensar and the trials included other kinds of biometrics being tested, namely face and voice verification. The success of the trials gave Nationwide Building Society confidence enough to roll out a biometric-supported system as additional security to check signatures across its network of 681 UK branches between 2002 and early 2003. However, at the time of writing, there had been no other major attempt to deploy biometrics-based technology in the UK cash dispensing market.

Security upgrades such as iris and fingerprint recognition will remain 'mothballed' until the cost of fraud versus cost of deployment effectiveness increases – and, more important – until customers are ready to accept intrusive applications such as iris and fingerprint recognition and biometrics in chips. But one is often enthusiastic in believing change will come about some time in the future by virtue of recent developments. Since 2006 some 20,000 ATMs with hand vein scanners had been successfully deployed in Japan.[17] Their success had encouraged real-life pilot tests in Germany (although with a slightly different hardware). Some participants thus considered that the use of biometrics in banking was still in its infancy. The author of a report on biometrics in Japan stated:

> If [Japanese] banks get significant consumer adoption of the new technology, it will be a valuable case study for banks around the world on how to successfully implement a biometric strategy in retail banking.
>
> (Celnet 2006)

As has often been the case in the history of the ATM, increased cost effectiveness takes place either by developments elsewhere (that make such technology more affordable) or increased fraud. Since the latter has been pretty stable for the last five years, it is more likely that other applications making use of iris and fingerprint recognition (say in airports) make this sort of technology a better proposition for ultimate consumers and in turn provide incentives for users to upgrade their stock. Yet there is greater potential for the interface with ultimate consumers to change by replacing the plastic card inserted into the card reader – this through contactless, mobile phone (mCommerce) and new 'form factors' applications providing highly convenient recognition, validation and authorization solutions.

Cash transactions via ATMs still lack a purposely designed statutory framework in the UK. The banking code of conduct has settled some of the most burning questions concerning liability. But overall the new risk profile that has emerged from electronic payments and their provision by non-bank payment providers has not been tackled head on by the law – or by regulatory authorities. Identity theft, operational breakdown and malicious attacks have taken unprecedented forms. In response to these, self-regulation of the industry has lead to real-time controls over payment authentication and improved payment processing. However the possibility of public involvement in risk management is looming on the horizon. For example, responsibility and control in matters of data protection and operational security may increasingly be aligned (Sullivan 2007).

In financial markets one must always keep an eye on the future actions of regulators, competition and monetary authorities. For instance it is worthwhile having a closer look at the impact of developments around the Single Euro Payments Area (SEPA) on current business models. SEPA rules already clearly define how a transaction should be treated across borders. In this respect the biggest barrier relates to IADs; specifically it relates to whether or not surcharging will be allowed, and if not, what the sustainable level of interchange fees will be in a pan-European market. At the same time, global banks could sidestep developments around SEPA by developing an advantage through the creation of an internal platform for international payment clearing that offers customers lower charges than those of clearing through VISA, Mastercard or a possible pan-European network.

However any potential income generation must be balanced with the low percentage of retail clients who are indeed internationally mobile. At the same time, the costs of developing such interconnection can be dear and risky. Since the late 1960s the majority of big users in the commercial sector (such as banks) have chosen to develop in-house programming capabilities rather than rely on package software or software contractors (Campbell-Kelly 2003, 72). Moreover by 1990 it was evident that integrated software packages for major banking operations were not viable. The combination of legacy systems with increased capacity through mergers and acquisitions results in large banks today having a dozen or so incompatible ATM and credit card platforms. These cost some £15 million to run individually each year. The cost of integrating into a single platform (say that of the biggest or most important market for the bank) while customizing for organizational and legal idiosyncrasies could escalate to between £50 and £100 million, which is a big expenditure even for a large, global bank. But would this expenditure to reduce costs be justifiable for potential results that are two to three years down the line? This provided that standardization goes according to schedule, the software works as planned, people remain motivated and there are no delays. Regional platforms as suggested above might be a more attractive and less risky solution than integrating into a single platform. This could emerge as aging platforms are 'starved' and integration grows organically. But while profitability (and thus bonuses) remain strongly divided by geography (rather than product line), country managers have few incentives to cooperate.

But perhaps the most important future innovation will be the use of ATMs to articulate customer relationship management initiatives. As mentioned, from its beginning as standalone cash dispensers to modern ATMs, this technology has been very successful in helping to move customers away from the retail bank branch. This view has evolved as ATMs are now seen as key in the deployment of self-service initiatives. The apparent success of pilot projects involving automated cash deposits will intensify that trend and reduce foot traffic. How then will financial intermediaries engage customers in a sales pitch? Clearly, the aim being to discuss offerings with consumers the intermediaries are interested in pushing out the door rather than to pitch for 'commoditized' products (that can be sought and ascertained by customers through the post, Internet, or telephone). The ever-crucial 30 seconds that customers are willing to spent in front of an ATM screen could be filled with targeted adverts, information or features while cash is being dispensed, provided these other activities are lawful, fast, intuitive and easy to understand as well as simple to operate. This is a challenge one would like to think would be more likely met by the ingenuity of managers at financial intermediaries than by directors of food retailers, or engineers at Dundee and Paderborn.

Notes

This research proceeded with the financial support of the British Academy (LRG-41806). We are grateful to the many participants in our discussions – all of whom remain anonymous. Research assistance from Robert Reid and Leonidas Efthymiou is gratefully acknowledged. We are also indebted to Paul Stanley, John Hardy, Bhaskar Dasgupta, Simon Lilley, Susan Scott, Gustavo del Angel, Hermann-Josef Lamberti and Matthias Bueger for their detailed comments as well as those from participants of the one-day conference 'Global Change and Information Technology for Financial Institutions: The Turn of the Seventies' Athens, 29 November 2008. We are grateful for the hospitality, during the conference, of the National Bank of Greece and particularly for the generosity of the chairman of the Bank, Takis Arpaglou, the conference organizer Alexandros-Andreas Kyrtsis and the co-organizer and Head of the Historical Archives of the National Bank of Greece, Gerasimos Notaras. The usual caveats apply.

1. For the UK see for instance Coopey (2004) and Harrington (1997). For the US see for example Haber (1996).
2. Throughout this article we make an important distinction between cash dispensers and ATMs. Their raison d'etrê is to offer cash distribution but with the caveat that the cash dispenser requires human intervention to ultimately debit the customer account while the ATM updates the bank's ledger online (either through batch processing or in real-time). See further Bátiz-Lazo and Reid (2008) and Bátiz-Lazo (2009).
3. Feedback letter, 12 January 2009.
4. Note the MIF is not paid to LINK but by the issuer to the acquirer. LINK only acts as a clearing house and facilitates the movement of the fees. Moreover it is set differently for branch and off-premise locations and also differently for cash withdrawals and balance enquiries. It is designed to reflect the average fully burdened cost of serving the transaction. As such, it rewards the efficient (with profit) and punishes the inefficient (with losses). This should theoretically result in a downward pressure on interchange fees. However regulatory and compliance costs often distort the picture, with mandated upgrades significantly impacting the cost base from time to time.
5. Feedback letter, 12 January 2009.
6. Under LINK rules, owners of machines providing 'free' withdrawals receive the MIF. 'Surcharging' machines will not receive MIF as the customer is paying for the service directly. Surcharges can be seen as a payment by ultimate consumers for convenience while 'disloyalty charges' can be seen as a levy to discourage own customers using machines from others.
7. In October 1998, as part of its incorporation into LINK, Barclays attempted to introduce a £1.50 'disloyalty charge'. The 'disloyalty charge' was to be paid to the customer's bank while the acquirer received the MIF. As late as November 2005, the *Daily Mail*'s Sean Poulter continued to report on the 'cash machine rip off'.
8. 'Financialization' has been coined to describe greater involvement of countries, business and people with financial markets and in particular increasing levels of debt (i.e. leverage). On growth of leverage among consumers see for

example Manning. However, the essential nature of financialization is highly contested. For instance, in their path breaking study, Froud et al. document how large, non-financial, multinational organizations come to rely on financial services rather than their core business for sustained profitability. They document a pattern of accumulation in which profit making occurs increasingly through financial channels rather than through trade and commodity production. Instead, in the preface of his edited book, Epstein uses 'financialization' to denote the prevalence of Anglo-Saxon capitalism and the ascendancy of 'shareholder value' as a mode of corporate governance. In other words, growing dominance of capital market financial systems over bank-based financial systems. In our text we have noted an alternative view and one that follows American writer and commentator Kevin Phillips, who gives a sociological and political interpretation of financialization, referring to it as 'a process whereby financial services, broadly construed, take over the dominant economic, cultural, and political role in a national economy'. This as we are of the view that applications of computer technology (such as ATM and EFTPOS) have been instrumental in the overall process of financialization of consumers: by giving ready and immediate access to liquid balances technology, they have helped to increase opportunities for impulse buying (raising the opportunity cost of searching among price/quality alternatives and reducing budgetary discipline). There are also possibilities for technology to have an impact at a more aggregate level; in the text we note how the lack of proprietary hold on ATMs and interoperability through shared networks have resulted in food retailers being the largest income (MIF) generators in the UK. This is thus an example in which technology successfully helped firms to overcome 'core rigidities', cross over a business sector and become dominant in that sector. The digitalization of international financial markets (i.e. the pricing of risk through real-time computer networks rather than through banks' internal processes) is ubiquitous and yet another example of bank disintermediation. The rather narrow point we are making here, and which we fail to elaborate due to space concerns, is that the role of technology as part of financialization is in need of attention.

9. In credit card transactions an 'acquirer' is said to refer to the bank representing the merchant. The merchant is where the retail transaction takes place. The merchant then takes the draft to be credited to its account at its bank. The bank cashing the draft may be different to the bank issuing the card. In cash dispensing transactions, 'acquirer' refers either to the actual owner of the machine or the company representing the owner. Again, either of these may differ depending on the issuer of the card.
10. All retailed locations are publicly tendered each year. Locations of other large food retailers are primarily served by HSBC on either rental space (Asda and Morrison) or outsourcing agreement contracts (Marks & Spencer).
11. On the role of human intervention in distinguishing between cash machine and ATM see note 3.
12. Teleprocessing dates to the early 1960s and encompasses activities in which computing is supplied to the user by means of public or private telecommunications networks (Campbell-Kelly 2003, 63). For early use in US and Spanish banking see Bátiz-Lazo et al. (2009) and Bátiz-Lazo and Maixé-Altés (2009) respectively.

13. It is interesting to note that Luther Simjian's bankograph first introduced the idea of photographic evidence of deposits in 1959 (see further Anonymous 1961; Bátiz-Lazo and Reid 2008).
14. Vulnerable consumers are said to include young people, old people, members of some ethnic minorities, the unemployed, those with low income, those suffering from long-term illness, or those suffering from a disability (see further Ritters 2003, 5).
15. Increased public discomfort with the growing number of IADs resulted in a parliamentary enquiry into payment of cash machine charges. Interestingly it was an enquiry with a focus on cash machine charges by IADs and their effect on consumers as a whole. Regarding the popular feeling at the time, see Anonymous (2004).
16. This is also a requirement in cities with high crime rates in Latin America (such as Mexico and Bogota), as a result of which the hole-in-the-wall has disappeared (Interview, 19 September 2009).
17. Feedback letter, 12 January 2009.

Bibliography

Anonymous (1961), 'Machine Accepts Bank Deposits', *New York Times*, 4 April.

Anonymous (1975), 'Barclays has Ordered 100 NCR 770', *Financial Times*, 27 May.

Anonymous (1998a), 'Big Four Banks Join the Link', *Sunday Times*, 25 October.

Anonymous (1998b), 'Nationwide to Test Biometrics at ATM', *Financial Technology International Bulletin*, 15(5): 1–3.

Anonymous (2000), 'Personalised ATM', *Spotlight*, 9 September.

Anonymous (2004). 'MPs Probe Cash Machine Charges', *Daily Mail*, 21 December 2004.

Arthur, B. W. (1989), 'Competing Technologies, Increasing Returns, and Lock-In by Historical Events', *The Economic Journal*, 99(394): 116–31.

Bátiz-Lazo, B. (2009), 'Emergence and Evolution of ATM Networks in the UK, 1967–2000', *Business History*, 51(1): 1–27.

Bátiz-Lazo, B., Karlsson, T. and Thodenius, B. (2009), 'Building Bankomat: The Development of On-Line, Real-Time Systems in British and Swedish Savings Banks, c.1965–1985', Association of Business Historians Annual Conference, Liverpool.

Bátiz-Lazo, B. and Maixé-Altés, J. C. (2009), *Managing Technological Change by Committee: Origins and Development of Data Processing Networks in Spanish and British Savings Banks (circa 1960–1988)*, Joint Conference of the EBHA/BHC, Milan, Bocconi University.

Bátiz-Lazo, B. and Reid, R. (2008), *Evidence from the Patent Record on the Development of Cash Dispensers and ATM Technology*, IEEE History of Telecommunications Conference, Paris.

Bátiz-Lazo, B. and Wardley, P. (2007), 'Banking on Change: Information Systems and Technologies in UK High Street Banking, 1919–1969', *Financial History Review*, 14(2): 177–205.

Blair, S. (2007), 'Grid Expectations', *Engineering & Technology*, 2 December: 28–9.

Booth, A. E. (2007), *The Management of Technical Change: Automation in the UK and USA since 1950*, Houndmills: Palgrave Macmillan.

Bridgman, T. and Willmott, H. (2006), 'Institutions and Technology: Frameworks for Understanding Organizational Change – The Case of a Major ICT Outsourcing Contract', *Journal of Applied Behavioural Science*, 42(1): 110–26.

Campbell-Kelly, M. (2003), *From Airline Reservations to Sonic the Hedgehog: A History of the Software Industry*, Cambridge, MA: The MIT Press.

Celnet (2006), 'Biometric ATMs in Japan: Fighting Fraud with Vein Pattern Authentication', Retrieved 10 September 2009 from http://reports.celent.com/PressReleases/20060329(2)/BiometricsJapan.htm.

Chandler, A. (1992), 'Organizational Capabilities and the Economic History of the Industrial Enterprise', *Journal of Economic Perspectives*, 6(3): 79–100.

Coombs, R., Knights, D. and Willmott, H. (1992), 'Culture, Control and Competition: Towards a Conceptual Framework for the Study of Information in Organizations', *Organization Studies*, 13(1): 51–72.

Coopey, R. (2004), 'A Passing Technology: The Automated Teller Machine', in P. Lyth and H. Trischler (eds), *Wiring Prometheus: Globalisation, History and Technology*, Aarhus: Aarhus University Press: 175–92.

Cushing, K. (2002), 'Nationwide will use Biometric Technology to Check Signatures', *Computer Weekly*, 4: 1–4.

David, P. (1985), 'Clio and the Economics of QWERTY', *American Economic Review*, 74(2): 332–7.

David, P. A. (2000), 'Path Dependence, its Critics and the Quest for "historical economics"', in P. Garrouste and S. Ioannides (eds), *Evolution and Path Dependence in Economic Ideas: Past and Present*, Cheltenham: Edward Elgar: 15–40.

Economist (2009), 'Path Dependence', Retrieved 30 August 2009 from http://www.economist.com/research/economics/alphabetic.cfm?term=pathdependence#pathdependence.

Epstein, G. A. (2005), *Financialization and The World Economy*, Cheltenham: Edward Elgar.

Froud, J., Johal, S., Leaver, A. and Williams, K. (2006), *Financialization and Strategy: Narrative and Numbers*, London: Routledge.

Haber, L. (1996), 'Banking on the Future', *LAN (New York then San Francisco)*, 11(7): 119–23.

Harrington, A. (1997), 'The Future lies in On-Line Banking', *CA Magazine (Institute of Chartered Accountants of Scotland)*, 101(1088): 4, 16–20.

House of Commons (2005), Fifth Report of Session 2004–5, Cash Machine Charges (Paper No. 191), Treasury Committee, Her Majesty's Stationary Office, London.

Jack, R. B. (1989), *Banking Services: Law and Practice Report by the Review Committee*, Her Majesty's Stationary Office, London.

Kotter, J. P. (1990), *A Force for Change: How Leadership Differs from Management*, London: The Free Press.

Liebowitz, S. J. and Margolis, S. E. (1990), 'The Fable of the Keys', *Journal of Law and Economics*, 33(1): 1–25.

Liebowitz, S. J. and Margolis, S. E. (1995), 'Path Dependence, Lock-In, and History', *Journal of Law, Economics & Organization*, 11(1): 205–26.

LINK (2008), 'Welcome to LINK', Retrieved 25 May 2008 from http://www.link.co.uk/mn_homepage.html.

LINK Press Centre (2008), 'Link Reports Continued Progress in Installing Free-To-Use Cash Machines in Lower Income Areas', Retrieved 2 June 2008 from http://www.link.co.uk/press/2008/mn_press_release_20080410.html.

Manning, R. D. (2000), *Credit Card Nation*, New York: Basic Books.

Milligan, B. (2007), 'The Man Who Invented the Cash Machine', Retrieved 25 June 2007 from http://news.bbc.co.uk/1/low/business/6230194.stm.

Nagurney, A., Cruz, J. M. and Wakolbinger, T. (2007), 'The Co-Evolution and Emergence of Integrated International Financial Networks and Social Networks: Theory, Analysis, and Computations', in R. Cooper, K. P. Donaghy and G. J. D. Hewings (eds), *Globalization and Regional Economic Modeling*, Berlin: Springer: 183–226.

O'Brien, D. (2002), 'Danny's Talk', *Spotlight*, July/August: 6.

Orlikowski, W. and Barley, S. (2001), 'Technology and Institutions: What can Research on Information Technology and Research on Organizations Learn from Each Other?', *MIS Quarterly*, 25(145–65).

Phillips, K. (2006), *American Theocracy: The Peril and Politics of Radical Religion, Oil, and Borrowed Money in the 21st Century*, London: Penguin.

Pinch, T. (2001), 'Why You go to a Music Store to Buy a Synthesizer', in R. Garud and P. Karnøe (eds), *Path Dependence and Creation*, Mahwa, NJ: Lawrence Erlbaum: 381–400.

Poulter, S. (2005), 'Why More of Us Have to Pay to Draw out our Cash', *Daily Mail*, 12 November.

Ritters, K. (2003), *Consumer Education in the UK*, London: Trading Standards Institute.

Sienkiewicz, S. (2002), 'The Evolution of EFT Networks from ATMs to New On-Line Debit Payment Products', Discussion Paper *Payments Cards Centre*, Philadelphia, PA: Federal Reserve Bank of Philadelphia.

Sullivan, R. (2007), 'Risk Management and Nonbank Participation in the U.S. Retail Payments System', *(Kansas City Federal Reserve Bank) Economic Review*, 2nd quarter: 5–40.

Walker, D. A. (1975), *Characteristics of Retail Electronic Funds Transfer Systems in the United States*, Federal Deposit Insurance Corporation WP 75–5, Washington, DC.

Welch, P. and Worthington, S. (2007), 'Banking at the Check Out', *Journal of Financial Transformation*, 21: 77–84.

Yates, J. (2005), *Structuring the Information Age*, Baltimore, MD: The Johns Hopkins University Press.

7

Understanding the Characteristics of Techno-Innovation in an Era of Self-Regulated Financial Services

Susan V. Scott

Introduction

Can we identify the key characteristics of techno-innovation in the era of deregulated financial services? This is an important question particularly now when many are laying the blame for the emergence of a 'credit crunch' in 2008 on ill-managed innovations that fuelled growth in contemporary financial services (see Tett 2009). This chapter draws together findings from a programme of research examining the role of technology in the transformation of work practices in the financial sector, and their entanglement with risk and regulation. Examples from multiple longitudinal field studies are used to explore the following questions: What inspires innovation in financial services? How are processes of techno-innovation managed? What are the expected and unexpected consequences of techno-innovation?

The study of innovation and financial services

Academia has produced a range of theories on innovation reflecting a spectrum of disciplinary engagement. The field of innovation studies has largely discredited the previously dominant deterministic view in which innovation was thought to proceed in a sequential manner with one superior technological design prevailing over all others. The notion of technological superiority itself is frequently equivocal. For example, in the 1970s, JVC won dominant market share with their Video Home System (VHS) videocassette tape recording format despite competition from a rival product from Sony called Betamax which, while offering technically superior picture quality, did not offer a long play facility (Cowan 1991; Cusumano et al. 1992;

Liebowitz 1995; Pitt 1996). Scholars now generally recognize that innovation takes a precarious, uncertain direction and focus their attention on explicating aspects that relate most closely to their particular disciplinary interest.

For example Schumpeterian economists regard innovation as a major driver of the economy, closely linked to productivity. Innovation economists[1] are producing a growing body of literature on innovation, market structure and productivity (see Romer 1990; David and Olsen 1992; Aghion et al. 2005; Aghion et al. 2006; Aghion and Howitt 2007). In management science, attention has been focused on processes of end-user innovation (see von Hippel 1988); how systems of work are enacted (see Ciborra 1993; Suchman 2007); enabling knowledge creation to support innovation (Von Krogh et al. 2000); and, more recently, distributed innovation (Kogut and Metiu 2001; Coombs and Metcalfe 2002; Acha and Cusumano 2007; Lakhani and Panetta 2007).

Moving further afield within the social sciences, scholars in Science and Technology Studies (STS) have developed important insights into processes of innovation by analysing the backstage practices of scientists in laboratories (Latour 1987; Knorr Cetina 1999). The contribution of this academic community is to show how human values affect scientific research and technological innovation, and how these in turn affect society, politics and culture. As a special issue of the journal *Organization* noted, STS literature is achieving increasingly widespread recognition for its contribution to understanding innovation within business schools (Woolgar et al. 2009). This literature has generated three themes that are of significance for thinking about techno-innovation in financial services: firstly, what are referred to as 'trials of strength' (Callon 1986) surrounding controversies and the achievement of order; secondly, analysing what goes forward and what gets left behind in times of change; thirdly, the side effects or unintended consequences that emerge from processes of innovation.

Within the STS community, a group of scholars have specialized in social studies of finance (Callon 1998) and the performance of economic models in markets (MacKenzie 2008). Like mainstream STS, the emphasis of their analyses is on understanding innovations in sociopolitical context but with a distinctive focus on the cultural world and work habits of professionals in financial markets. Key topics of research have been technical and economic phenomena such as pricing and trading (see examples in collected volumes such Knorr Cetina and Preda 2006; Callon et al. 2007; MacKenzie et al. 2008). However it could be argued that the conceptual foundations of such social studies of finance predispose them to frame research questions around relationships within a broadly defined technical field rather than the technology per se, thus diffusing interest in understanding particular projects of techno-innovation.

As one of the original and most extensive sites of computer-based innovation, financial services routinely serves as a source of data for scholars studying the use of technology in organizations (see Scarbrough 1992; Howells and Hine 1993; Fincham et al. 1994). Since the pattern of IT development in financial services reflected mainstream technology movements (transaction processing, office automation, expert systems, networks) these studies helped establish important insights that have served as principles of organization studies; for example the realization that IT services must be integrated with the business function to be effective. Nonetheless, despite providing useful illustrations to support such points, financial services are effectively a backdrop for these discussions of IT in organizations. Domain specific analysis is usually confined to reviewing the current state of IT and its major application areas within financial services with some attention paid to the implications of these for IT development practice (see Fincham et al. 1994: 150).

In sum, despite the many claims that IT and the development of financial services are closely linked, there are few studies of innovation in service sectors within the management literature and opportunities still exist for scholars to make further contributions in this important subject area. This chapter addresses two under-researched areas in management: longitudinal field studies of technology in financial services and processes of distributed innovation.

What inspires techno-innovation in financial services?

Most accounts of IT in financial services recognize that, historically, techno-innovation has been inspired by a push for efficiency. The main focus of this effort was to remove humans from systems of work. For those that have only experienced contemporary financial services organizations, it is perhaps hard to imagine the level of labour intensity that originally characterized financial centres. Below is an extract taken from a book written by one of the forefathers of computing, Charles Babbage, in 1835. It is included to provide historical perspective and highlight the nature of work processes before the implementation of information technology. The passage describes a manual system of interbank clearing that Babbage encountered as part of a research project

> In a large room in Lombard Street, about thirty clerks from the several London bankers take their stations, in alphabetical order, at desks placed round the room; each having a small open box by his side, and the name of the firm to which he belongs in large characters on the wall above his head. From time to time other clerks from every house enter the room, and, passing along, drop into the box the checks due by that firm to the house from which this distributor is sent. The clerk at the table enters the amount of the several checks in a book previously prepared, under the name of the bank to which they are respectively due. Four o'clock in the afternoon is the latest hour to which the boxes are open to receive checks; and at a few minutes before that time, some signs of increased activity begin to appear in this previously quiet and business-like scene. Numerous clerks then arrive anxious to distribute, up to the latest possible moment, the checks that have been paid into the houses of their employers. At four o'clock all the boxes are removed, and each clerk adds up the amount of the checks put into his box and payable by his own to other houses. He also receives another book from his own house, containing the amounts of the checks that their distributing clerk has put into the box of every other banker. Having compared these, he writes out the balances due to or from his own house, opposite the name of each of the other banks; and having verified this statement by a comparison with the similar list made by the clerks of those houses, he sends to his own bank the general balance resulting from this sheet, the amount of which, if it is due from that to other houses, is sent back in bank-notes. At five o'clock the Inspector takes his seat; when each clerk, who has upon the result of all the transactions a balance to pay to various other houses, pays it to the inspector, who gives a ticket for the amount. The clerks of those houses to whom money is due, then receive the several sums from the inspector, who takes from them a ticket for the amount. Thus the whole of these payments are made by a double system of balance, a very small amount of bank-notes passing from hand to hand, and scarcely any coin.
>
> (Babbage, 1835: 173)

undertaken to understand the ways in which technology could best be applied in industry:

Some financial services professionals feel that in contrast to the days when banks were seeking out new technology to render transaction processing more efficient, financial systems are now pitched against each other in pursuit of profit and their work practices are driven by data. A senior representative from a major financial organization attending the conference associated with this volume said that this permeated the whole financial system from retail, risk management, payments, trading, and settlement through to communications about daily organizational processes. For example he remarked that while there was a time in recent memory when email was regarded merely as a supplementary communication medium, whereas now it is an integral part of the business flow: 'I experience it as organizational consciousness. It is not an option, it is unavoidable. Like all our information systems. It drives our professional lives'.

What have been the staging points in the experience of a sector where labour intensity has been replaced by information intensity? As the premise of this book suggests, deregulation inspired some forms of techno-innovation; removing the statutory boundaries between different parts of financial services led to a rapid expansion of business and an intense phase of commercial consolidation. Information and communication technologies were part of the process of change as organizations addressed increases in volume, scale and scope of financial services.

Among the programmes characterizing techno-innovation in the early part of this era were universal banking, electronic payment systems, cheque truncation and decimalization. Alongside this a transformation in management reporting took place. Previously, information on accounts was held in branches subject to examination only by representatives from local head office or a (usually annual) visit by a corporate inspection department. Networking branches enabled centralized computer-based data-processing that presented an opportunity to consolidate data around key categories to produce management reports. This meant not only that head offices were not dependent upon local inspection for all their management information but also that local managers could receive branch level reports providing an overview of their 'book', albeit using relatively basic accounting criteria.

Market events and landmark developments have also inspired techno-innovation. For example the loss of LIFFE's majority share in the liquidity of the German government bund contract was directly related to the widespread adoption of electronic trading in London (Scott and Barrett 2005). The development of new market infrastructure, such as CREST[2] or the Continuous Linked Settlement system (CLS)[3] has prompted major changes in previously manual back-office areas of associated organizations.[4] Finally, compliance regulation has provided an almost constant source of leverage for those attempting to introduce techno-innovation.[5]

At the global level, liberalization of trade restrictions led to a growth of international trade in the post-war period that created increased demand for international banking products and services. Before the 1970s, international banking was the preserve of a small number of banks; work practices were manual, paper-based and often intermediated by correspondent banks. The rapid process of globalization that has taken place is illustrated by the following data: 'In 1960, 9 US banks had a physical presence overseas, consisting of 139 branches and subsidiaries. By 1970, 80 US banks operated abroad through 540 branches and subsidiaries. By 1982, almost every large and medium-sized bank in [the US] engaged in international banking; 162 banks had 900 branches and 758 subsidiaries operating abroad' (Roussakis 1997: 405).

As technology made business processes more efficient it opened up the possibility of competition on both price and service. When price and service are not achieved within a reasonable timeframe, fair trading organizations have taken up the cause of the consumer and pressured the financial community to embrace techno-innovations, as in the review of UK payment systems by the Office of Fair Trading (see OFT 25 March 2009). When these step changes have occurred it has often left financial service organizations facing the realization that their profit centres are shifting, which in turn creates pressure to techno-innovate.

While the interdependency of these phenomena (regulation, events, shifting profit centres) with techno-innovation is apparent there is a scarcity of research that attempts more fine-grained analysis that would help us understand the nature of techno-innovation in financial services – its genesis, practice and consequences. This is the special contribution of Alexandros-Andreas Kyrtsis in the introduction of this volume, presenting us with a thesis that traces the characteristics of innovation during the current era of self-regulation in more detail than before.

To recap the argument in his introductory chapter in this volume, he maintains that two main features characterize the financial services landscape: what he refers to as 'blended tactical solution technologies' and 'architectural concepts'. Solution technologies are short-term and organized around projects that were initiated in response to an immediate problem rather than a long-term strategic vision. Architectural concepts are at the heart of emerging international electronic financial networks and represent a particular kind of development logic moving through specific communities at different times. Kyrtsis maintains that both of these models share a similar constitution: financial services represent an applied area for technology in which innovation is drawn from other fields rather than generated within the sector.

This is a proposition that is taken up here: does techno-innovation arise out of immediate need or are there longer processes of innovation at work? In the next section, case study material is presented to help us consider whether techno-innovation is reactive rather than proactive.

Techno-innovation in the financial services sector: Examining the evidence from longitudinal field studies

The empirical material presented in the next section is from two longitudinal field studies. The first focuses on the introduction of risk management software called Lending Advisor (LA) into corporate lending practice in a major UK retail bank. The data for this study was gathered by the author between 1993 and 1998.[6] The second is a historical study about the adoption and diffusion of SWIFT, the international payment system. This research was initiated by the author in 2004 and subsequently became the focus of doctoral research undertaken by Marcos Zachariadis[7] at the LSE. Although the core SWIFT research project (including all descriptive statistics produced) is the sole work of Zachariadis, the author participated in the interviews, archival work and site visits upon which this analysis is based.[8]

The inspiration for Lending Advisor: Background

Until the period under study, banking was a deeply traditional sector in the UK and had remained virtually unchanged for nearly 200 years. Historically the activities of financial services providers in the UK were bounded and legislation confined retail banks to certain types of business. Cross-sector competition was therefore limited, with retail banks focused on financing industry and providing money transmission facilities, while building societies were restricted to savings and mortgages. From the 1960s until the 1990s, retail banking in the UK was dominated by the 'Big Four': Barclays, Lloyds, Midland and National Westminster.

The origins of the bank in the field study, UK Bank, go back to 1896 when 20 family-owned banks amalgamated. The administration within UK Bank was traditionally organized along scientific management lines into a functional hierarchy by region with customer contact maintained through a local branch network. The local bank and the local bank manager have been important actors in their community, embedded in a powerful local network that included teachers and clergy.

During the 1950s–80s, a career in a major UK retail bank was regarded as a respectable traditional occupation with considerable status that tended to be a 'job for life'.

The stability that had characterized this sector saw its first significant challenge during the 1960s, when the Big Four were referred to the Monopolies Commission. A high level of cooperation had developed between the major retail banks and they found themselves accused of being an oligopoly and of cross-subsidization. Thus began a slow process during which restrictions were loosened in order to encourage greater competition in the banking sector, culminating in landmark legislation in 1986 that brought about deregulation of the UK banking industry.

After deregulation, continuous commitment to a free-market economy by successive UK Conservative governments helped to generate conditions of 'hypercompetition' (Zuboff 1996). Traditional lines of demarcation within the sector were broken down and competition widened to a broader product range (Thwaites 1991). As discussed above, ICTs were essential to increasing volume, scale and scope of financial services; after back-office information systems were rolled out, operations in the branch network came next. However lending, described by bankers as 'part art and part science', was not regarded as a suitable site for techno-innovation because of the 'sticky' (von Hippel 1994) nature of situated, local knowledge required to assess risk.

The origins of LA lie in the last mortgage crises in the UK. In 1992, the bank in the study (referred to as UK Bank) cut its dividend and reported losses of 3.29 billion Euros primarily associated with loan defaults in its mortgage business. Six months before this news was made public, the bank appointed an additional risk management director who subsequently appointed a team to address this problem. They held brainstorming sessions, went to industry conferences and sat through many software sales demonstrations. During this exploratory phase, they were approached by a small company in Palo Alto, California, who offered to partner with them to develop a customized decision support system for corporate lending, based upon oil prospecting software that the company had developed in partnership with ELF, the French petrochemical firm. The decision support system had already been implemented in Canadian banks, but UK Bank would be their first client in Europe. The development partnership would mitigate costs for the bank and produce a customized system that would reassure UK Bank stakeholders.

So what inspired techno-innovation in this case? Where did they look for ideas? There is a direct relationship between LA and the need to address the concerns raised by both regulators and shareholders after the 1992 losses. This would appear to support Kyrtsis' assertion that financial services develop solution technology in response to immediate problems. Moreover the use of oil prospecting probability models as the basis for decision support in lending practices also appears to confirm his suggestion that innovation is drawn from other fields rather than generated within sector.

The inspiration for SWIFT: Background

Next we present material from a study of SWIFT, the Belgium-based international communications platform and messaging service that connects financial institutions worldwide. SWIFT could be regarded as characteristic of an 'architectural concept', the second feature of techno-innovation in financial services according to Kyrtsis' thesis. It forms part of the core infrastructure constituting contemporary financial services. SWIFT is a member-owned cooperative that currently has a membership of over 8300 banking organizations, securities institutions and corporate customers in more than 208 countries. SWIFT's corporate communications describes its role as follows:

> We provide the proprietary communications platform, products and services that allow our customers to connect and exchange financial information securely and reliably ... SWIFT enables its customers to automate and standardize financial transactions, thereby lowering costs, reducing operational risk and eliminating inefficiencies from their operations. SWIFT is solely a carrier of messages. It does not hold funds nor does it manage accounts on behalf of customers, nor does it store financial information on an on-going basis. As a data carrier, SWIFT transports messages between two financial institutions. This activity involves the secure exchange of proprietary data while ensuring its confidentiality and integrity.[9]

Let us consider the inspiration for SWIFT: deregulation had opened up the opportunity to develop international products and services but, as discussed above, the means to transact were still relatively crude and labour intensive. One of our research participants was based in the European headquarters of a major US bank in London during the 1960s. When a payment instruction was received by phone or Telex, the details would be written down by hand and then passed to a secretary who would type them out on a form. This was then folded, put in a canister and sent via a vacuum tube to the authorization/confirmation section on the floor above.

This description of the manual payments process is typical as is the considerable potential that it held for system breakdown and error. For example our research participant told us that after a particularly busy morning, staff in the payment section found themselves without the confirmation necessary to complete transactions. A staff member went to the second floor to investigate, to be met by a bemused confirmation section who had been waiting for payment instructions all morning. The vacuum tube between the two floors had become jammed and remained so until staff enlisted the services of a chimney sweep who cleared the blockage and restored payment processing in Europe that day.

The idea of a secure, common communications platform that would facilitate payments around the world was initiated by representatives from five different banks during the 1960s. SWIFT was founded with a working group of 20 banks who set about recruiting further members for a commitment to support the project. A former board member described the genesis of SWIFT as follows:

> This was about 20 banks getting rid of their problems. I was there. In fact, one of my first jobs was in the money transfer department. I actually joined the bank before we had the computers so I've seen this whole sort of evolutionary process happen. It was literally in English [free text] and then some guy had to interpret that and put all the account numbers on, the debit account, the credit account, and the typists would come along and type out forms ... people realized if we're using this form as an input device with all the instructions and information coming in ... if we got the messaging in the right structure you could cut out all these people. 50% of all transactions ... was one community ... if you took those 20 banks, 60% of their interaction was with each other anyway. So if you put them together you don't have to have a big community to get efficiency, and it was really about how do we get these computers to create efficiency, very simple!

The acronym, SWIFT, stands for the Society for Worldwide Interbank Financial Telecommunication, which gives us considerable insight into the concept behind its founding: whereas today SWIFT is referred to as a network, it was founded as a *society*. The notion of a network effect was not part of the consciousness of those involved in the original SWIFT project during the 1970s. Their focus was solely on creating an entity, a closed society, to bind members together in an organizational form that would enforce standards designed to realize efficiencies in transactions between the member banks. The notion of direct, synchronous connectivity between international banks was alien; for example, there was a brief period of anxiety when SWIFT was first trialled because nothing happened. SWIFT staff gradually realized that they hadn't prepared bank staff for this moment and all the banks were switched to 'receive'. After a few telephone calls, some banks switched to 'send', others remained on 'receive' and SWIFT was in motion.

In 1977, Albert, Prince of Belgium (now King) sent the first message and SWIFT launched with 518 commercial banks in 22 countries. Enrolment increased rapidly: by their tenth anniversary, SWIFT had 2360 customers in 64 countries who sent 222,300,000 messages. In 2008, a total of 1,257,110,454 messages were sent by 8468 live users in 208 countries. Most banks now regard SWIFT as a core infrastructure and it is widely regarded as the most secure, the most 'trusted third party' (Van Auseloos 1996) within the financial services sector.

So what inspired techno-innovation in this case? Where did the originators look for ideas? The data suggests that they were highly focused on a well-defined problem: how to move from manual processing to bring efficiency, reduce errors and increase capacity. Kyrtsis describes technologies in financial services as: 'very traditional ... inspired by analogue systems but with high performance requirements because of transmission and database management issues as well as the need to interface with multiple end-users'. The SWIFT network was, indeed, based around existing analogue systems and many characteristics of the former Telex information system were carried forward in its design. For example SWIFT messages are limited by the need to conform to the four-line 35-character format institutionalized during the Telex era.[10] So it would appear that evidence from the case studies supports the proposal of financial services innovation characterized by solution technologies and architectural concepts.

Further perspectives on the key characteristics of techno-innovation: Drift and intercalated processes of change

In this discussion section, it is suggested that longitudinal data may shift our perspective on the nature and status of techno-innovation in financial services. For example, data gathered at the start of the LA field study indicated that budget was made available because the software could be presented as a solution to an immediate problem. However data gathered on the project in later years showed that once the software was implemented an identifiable process of 'drift' (Ciborra 2001) took place. Drift is a concept used in the study of information systems to evoke the notion of 'technology both as a drifting system and as an organism to be cultivated' (Ciborra 2001, 32).

This extract from an interview with the project manager, three years after the LA launch, illustrates this:

> All Lending Advisor has ever been is a software application. In an ideal world you would develop an information system by identifying a business need – a problem. Then you would gather together your business and technical experts and come up with a solution which you would then design and implement in a series of stages. Lending Advisor was never like that. As soon as the business need had been identified, Lending Advisor raised serious issues. Why was there this gaping hole in their strategy? What was needed to fill it? Lending Advisor brought up issues along the way which made its development very distinctive.
>
> (Project Manager quoted in Scott 1998)

Let us consider some of the issues that contributed to drift on the LA project. At the heart of a decision support system is an inference engine with a model that requires its parameters to be set. As noted earlier, the original software had been developed for oil prospecting and therefore needed to be customized for the banking sector. LA knowledge engineers had to analyse and represent the loans process in order to decide what constituted best practice. Whose work practices would be taken forward and whose would be left behind?

Other choices that the design team had to make focused on linking the way that they weighted the model used by the inference engine to UK Bank's strategic lending priorities. What part of the loans market did the bank regard as important within their portfolio? While it was relatively unproblematic to apply LA to loans in some parts of the portfolio, other specialist areas raised concerns.

For example one of UK Bank's traditional value centres had been small business, and they had developed a reputation for being '*The* small business bank'. Local branch managers had been encouraged to develop expertise in small business lending; the logic behind this was that as small businesses grew, they remained loyal to the bank that helped them and committed to more products or services in line with growth. However small businesses are innovations in themselves, and gain market share by filling a gap in a market or developing in an area that hasn't been exploited before. This presented problems for the LA system that was designed to draw upon standard business codes and a historic data set which many of these businesses overflowed, or in which they didn't feature.

These design challenges emerged side by side with policy issues about how LA would be positioned within the overall practice of lending. What would the relationship be between human expertise and the LA assessment? Could managers override the assessment? What were the consequences for the managers if they did? Now that each manager's lending portfolio could be assessed centrally using the executive information system capability offered by LA, how would this be used in the bank's appraisal and reward structure? LA marked the beginning of performance-related pay for loans managers. Indeed, it represented the end of the use of the title 'branch manager' and the re-grading of jobs. Rather than being regarded as an expert practice undertaken by a professional person of status within the community, small and medium corporate loans became part of a largely administrative process.

Although presented as a solution to an immediate problem, LA became folded into a range of emergent strategies within UK Bank. This is illustrated by the following extract from an interview with the director of the LA design and development team four years after the project launch:

> Lending Advisor emerged out of a functional line, not a corporate line. We didn't know that LA would lead to all these changes. The world was changing around us, we knew that, but a lot of the consequences of LA are a 'chicken and egg' situation. LA enabled the bank to make changes ... but that was not part of the original project. Once the other functional lines began to recognize the potential opportunities presented by LA they began to structure changes around it. I want to emphasize to you that the long term implications and consequences of LA were not really apparent at that point. LA had dropped into my lap by accident. I recognized the profundity of it and the idea that it could lead to strategic changes. However, these were regarded as potential opportunities at that point rather than a deliberate programme of change.
>
> Director LA Design and Development
> Team quoted in Scott 1998

Moving our attention to SWIFT, our field study shows that it was intended to serve as part of the interbank architecture and designed as the solution to a problem at hand. However its membership grew rapidly, creating a wealth of connectivity and a massive economy of scale. Once again, rather than an orderly process of linear development, a wake of innovation followed the launch of SWIFT. Whereas the roll-out of a new computer-based system is now met with anxiety, the introduction of SWIFT in the 1970s was treated as an exciting event, as this extract from the Barclays Bank archive shows:

> The amount of interest shown on the morning of 9th May was considerable. We in inward payments, Poole branch, for instance, were visited by a number of management and staff – not forgetting computer services – keen to see the first message arrive. It was realized by all concerned that, although the system was open to receive from France and Belgium, there were no guarentees that any SWIFT members in those countries would transmit to us. Fortunately, the arrival of a number of payment instructions from Societe Generale de Banque in Belgium prevented 'live' day for us becoming a non-event. As the weeks have gone by, transmissions have increased slowly as more and more members have linked up with SWIFT and gained confidence in this system. Outward transmission from Barclays will soon become available *which will broaden the scope of those departments already involved and enable other areas of work to take advantage of the system. All in all, it is evident that SWIFT will have a very far-reaching effect on banking in the future, particularly for Barclays International whose capacity for extending the system internally is so great.*
>
> (Barclays archive HOC 138–77 3 May 1977, emphasis added)

As the last part of this document suggests, there is evidence that the adoption of SWIFT was not only seen as key to interconnectivity between banks but also regarded as holding considerable potential for internal change within the member organization. However the changes that took place were situated, emergent and plans were worked out in practice rather than as part of a sector-wide master plan. For example in the following quotation a former board member describes retiring the bank's internal standards initiatives in favour of adopting SWIFT on a broader basis to achieve further efficiencies:

> [Our bank] had its own standard ... then we suddenly realized ... that why do we have to have our own internal standard? If you're using one standard externally why don't we use that same standard internally? ... We basically took the SWIFT message and put our internal wrap around

it and used SWIFT standard internally from that point and on. We suddenly realized it's not only good for dealing with everyone else.

Although SWIFT was a significant innovation at its initiation, there have been concerns that over time it has become an inhibitor to further change in the financial community. In academic terms, it has become what Hanseth (2001: 60) refers to as an 'installed base'. SWIFT found itself in the role of monopoly network and standards designer having to prioritize requests for changes. Questions have been raised about whether SWIFT's 'standards development is meeting the requirements of all the constituents in the financial supply chain'.[11] In recent years, major corporations have felt the need to petition SWIFT for more recognition in its membership and governance.[12] SWIFT has attempted to address this issue by developing a special category of membership, the Member-Administered Closed User Group (MA-CUG), in an attempt to accommodate corporate interests. It has also shown a willingness to consult with other standards organizations and formed working groups such as Innotribe[13] at SIBOS.[14]

Founded as a member-owned utility and given responsibility for managing the world's primary financial messaging network, SWIFT developed a substantial repository of best practice, an extensive system of consultation and hosts an annual conference (SIBOS). As time moved on, what started as a focused project group and subsequently grew into a community of practice, began to be regarded as a cartel with control over the possibility for innovation in networks and standards in the sector. Ironically then, in light of the widespread recognition of its ground-breaking role in the realization of globalized financial services and its status as one of the sectors most remarkable 'network innovations', SWIFT came to be accused of stifling techno-innovation.

Discussion

Both of these field studies provide insights into the nature of problem frames and what management scholars have come to recognize as the enactment of 'technology in the context of use' (Orlikowski et al. 1995). Kyrtsis appropriately identifies techno-innovation initiatives within his study of financial services organizations as the exemplification of 'tactical solution technologies'. He found these technologies in a context of use that wrapped them within a problem frame where they fitted; like a 'square peg for a square hole'. This is because just as 'problems are not simply presented to management, problems are constructed by them'

(Boland and Pondy 1983: 223), so solutions are designed to form part of a convincing organizational narrative (Boland 2001). However, as we can see in the LA and SWIFT studies, over time further encounters with technology may inspire different problem formulations. Rather than one problem frame dominating over the other, we see the technology become folded into multiple 'solution' narratives. In other words their meaning and use may drift over time in unpredictable ways.

The multiplicity of technology in its context of use can perhaps also be seen as expressive of a polycultural phenomenon that characterizes the global financial services community. Markets depend upon multiple interpretations and asymmetries of information; financial centres are made up of organizations each of which has a different, distinctive risk appetite. This helps to ensure that, at any one time, a community of willing buyers and sellers can be found. In this regard, there is an interesting parallel with the physics community in Galison's (1997) study, who manages to support the advance of scientific practice in the presence of (despite) multiple threads of discourse, each of which maintains differing ontological and epistemic positions.

Similarly it could be said that each financial services organization has a different long-term tradition of 'image and logic' (Galison 1997) that gives them distinct identities. Regardless of this, financial services manage to find 'common cause between and among them' (Galison 1997: 781), moving markets despite tension between distinctiveness and interconnection. The fragmentation of techno-innovation in financial services has been a source of consternation for both financiers and regulators over the years with numerous initiatives designed to achieve consolidated efficiency. These range from the Business Industry Codes embedded in LA, to the transaction standards associated with SWIFT, as well as global efforts such as the blueprint for a World Clearing House. Such moves appear highly logical at first glance – however it is possible that a degree of disunification reduces systemic risk and supports creativity.

For example it is possible that polyculturalism has been an important ingredient of techno-innovation in financial services. Drawing on concepts developed in Mary Douglas' risk studies, Fiol notes that 'colliding thought worlds ... [can] provide fertile grounds for the seeds of entrepreneurial activities' (1995: 71). Although the financial services professionals engaged in the project studied by Fiol held internally consistent images of their world, there were tensions and contradictions between the organizational groups involved. However she notes that their 'views differed systematically' and as a result they were able to render the project 'operationalizable' (1995: 88) despite these colliding thought worlds.

Building on this, we can suggest that processes of innovation in this sector are intercalated. This is a term coined by Galison to describe situations where:

> Two groups can agree on rules of exchange even if they ascribe utterly different significance to the objects being exchanged; they may even disagree on the meaning of the exchange process itself. Nonetheless, the trading partners can hammer out a local *coordination* despite vast *global* differences. In an even more sophisticated way, cultures in interaction frequently establish contact languages, systems of discourse that can vary from the most function-specific jargons, through semispecific pidgins, to full-fledged creoles rich enough to support activities.
>
> (Galison 1997, 783)

Intercalated processes of change in financial services mean that techno-innovation is loosely coordinated without having a homogenizing effect. Regulators play an important role in this but most financial services professionals will point to other ways in which this occurs. New products and services transform financial services but without specific organizations losing their separate identities and practices.

From this perspective, each project of techno-innovation acts as an engine of change; in other words, communities within financial services innovate at different rates and generate their own path-dependent innovations trajectory. The innovation shifts within and between these communities are not simultaneous: multiple innovations occur at different rates and times around the community and are inserted into the global mix. While many of the basic ingredients may have been imported from other fields, people in the financial services have shown themselves to be adept at incremental, situated practices of innovation: they involve themselves in tinkering and folding, they mash ideas and technologies together and then, drawing on the relationships around them, configure a path to profit.

Conclusion

Inevitably our ways of conceptualizing the key characteristics of techno-innovation in financial services are in a state of ongoing development and evolve side by side with processes of change in the sector. For example the dominant management literature published at the time that the projects of techno-innovations discussed in this chapter were initiated was 'rational, regard[ing] organizations as a unity with everyone working towards one aim [with] strategy formation [portrayed] as a logical, linear process' (Walsham 1993). The focus was on mission statements reflecting a grand plan or what is commonly referred to as top-down strategy.

Organizations were seen to be no more than the planned outcome of rational decisions made by senior management (Knights et al. 1997). For the most part the role ascribed to computer-based information and communication technologies was technologically deterministic. However this is not supported by the field studies presented in this chapter – which focus on strategy in practice and view the whole concept of organization as problematic, with strategy formation as a dynamic sociopolitical process that unfolds over time within multi-level contexts (Ciborra 1991; Orlikowski et al. 1996).

So what do these two case studies tell us about innovation in financial services? The discussion of LA and SWIFT complements the proposition that financial services are a 'blend of tactical solution technologies and architectural concepts'. While they confirm the standing of these categories, they extend and develop them by allowing techno-innovation a biography in the course of which their status as 'solutions' shifts over time. So we see that phenomena that began as the solution to a specific problem become an engine of innovation, folded into multiple strategies. We also find that community initiatives can begin as great innovations but over time sediment into an installed base and have to be reinvented yet again.

It is important to remember that techno-innovation is not always positive, it can be negative and therefore we need to have a capacity to identify toxic innovation. For example the implementation of LA marked a watershed in UK retail banking and other banks soon embarked on similar projects of techno-innovation in lending. However many regarded the lengthy customization processes involved in implementing decision support systems as too costly and therefore opted for computer-based credit scoring systems such as those used in the credit card industry (Poon 2007, 2009). This helped to accelerate an increasingly concerning pattern of bank lending that contributed to the so-called credit crunch in 2008.

What does it mean to attempt techno-innovation in financial services? Those involved in the projects discussed in this chapter are working in a living laboratory. To survive they had to learn how to construct a convincing narrative to win budgets and cope with events.

Part of this included developing a critical understanding of their role in making a market for software solutions (Pollock and William 2007, 2009). Many of them spent considerable periods in their career moving from one project to another (often leaving just as the initiative went online).

While the practitioners that I have encountered have assembled cumulative project knowledge, they may benefit from deepening their awareness of the systemic amplification created by ongoing techno-innovation within the sector. While techno-innovation accumulates in firm-specific financial services products and practices, it also manifests in interconnected processes and path-dependent infrastructure. Those involved may have the impression that they are taking discrete building blocks and stacking them in an orderly way, like the children's toy Lego™. However techno-innovation in financial services is not like Lego™; it is closer in nature to working with a chemistry set. Compounds that have been sourced elsewhere are gathered and added together. As a consequence, there may be discovery but there will also be side effects, and occasionally meltdown.

Notes

1. Academics at The Centre for Economics at LSE have established an important body of work in this area representing what some regard as the most significant research agenda in contemporary economic thinking. http://ideas.repec.org/e/pva45.html.
2. CREST was established in 1996 as the central securities depository for the UK market operating an electronic settlement system which is used to settle international securities.
3. CLS was founded in 1997 to manage settlement risk in the foreign exchange market. http://www.cls-group.com/About/Pages/default.aspx.
4. Interview with market infrastructure manager, SWIFT London Headquarters, 31 March 2009.
5. See special issue of *Information Systems Frontiers* on Governance, Risk and Compliance in Information Systems 2009, 11(5).
6. A full account of the methodology employed and the unabridged case study can be found in Scott (1998).
7. I gratefully acknowledge the support, assistance and feedback of Marcos Zachariadis in the course of writing this chapter. Also see Scott et al. (2008).
8. For details see Scott, Van Reenen, and Zachariadis (2008).
9. See http://www.swift.com/about_swift/company_information/index.page?lang=en.
10. Interview, Head of Standards Initiatives, SWIFT Headquarters, Brussels, 7 May 2009.
11. 'The Evolution of Global Payments', *Dialogue: The Voice of the SWIFT Community*, Q2, 2005, p. 20.

12. 'Triggering transformation *without a crisis*: How can inhibitors to change in the payments business be overcome?' *Dialogue: The Voice of the SWIFT Community*, Q4, 2005, pp. 8–9.
13. Innotribe is a SWIFT initiative for community members to brainstorm about new ideas and their implications for the SWIFT infrastructure https://www.swiftcommunity.net/communities/225/detail.
14. See http://www.swift.com/sibos2009/About/about_index.page?

Bibliography

Acha, V. and Cusmano, L. (2005), 'Governance and Co-Ordination of Distributed Innovation Processes: Patterns of R&D Co-Operation in the Upstream Petroleum Industry', *Economics of Innovation and New Technology*, 14 (1–2): 1–21.

Aghion, P., Bloom, N., Blundell, R., Griffith, R. and Howitt, P. (2005), 'Competition and Innovation: An Inverted-U Relationship', *The Quarterly Journal of Economics*, 120(2): 701–28.

Aghion, P., Griffith, R. and Howitt, P. (2006), 'Vertical Integration and Competition' *American Economic Review*, 96(2): 97–102.

Aghion, P. and Howitt, P. (2007), 'Capital, Innovation, and Growth Accounting', *Oxford Review of Economic Policy*, 23(1): 79–93.

Babbage, C. (1835), *On the Economy of Machinery and Manufactures*, London: Charles Knight.

Barclays archive (1977), HOC 138–77, 3 May.

Bijker, W. E. (1997), *Of Bicycles, Bakelites, and Bulbs: Toward a Theory of Socio-technical Change*, Boston, MA: MIT Press.

Boland, R. J. (2001) 'The Tyranny of Space in Organizational Analysis', *Information and Organization*, 11: 3–23.

Boland, R. J. and Pondy, L. R. (1983), 'Accounting in Organizations: Toward a Union of Rational and Natural Perspectives', *Accounting, Organizations and Society*, 8(2/3): 223–34.

Callon, M. (1986), 'Some Elements of a Sociology of Translation: Domestication of the Scallops and the Fishermen of St Brieuc Bay', in J. Law (ed.), *Power, Action and Belief: A New Sociology of Knowledge?* London: Routledge: 196–223.

Callon, M. (1998), *The Laws of the Markets*, Oxford: Wiley-Blackwell.

Callon, M., Millo, Y. and Muniesa F. (eds) (2007), *Market Devices*, Oxford: Blackwell.

Ciborra, C. (1991), 'From Thinking to Tinkering: The Grassroots of Strategic Information Systems', Proceedings of the 12th International Conference on Information Systems, New York, December, J. I. DeGross (ed.), Association for Computing Machinery, New York. Revised version re-published in *The Information Society*, 1992, 8(4): 297–309.

Ciborra, C. (1993), *Teams, Markets, and Systems: Business Innovation and Information Technology*, Cambridge: Cambridge University Press.

Ciborra, C. (2001), *From Control to Drift: The Dynamics of Corporate Information Infrastructures*, Oxford: Oxford University Press.

Coombs R. and Metcalfe, J. S. (2002), 'Organizing for Innovation: Co-Ordinating Distributed Innovation Capabilities' in N. Foss and V. Mahnke (eds) *Competence, Governance, and Entrepreneurship: Advances in Economic Strategy*, Oxford: Oxford University Press: 209–31.

Cowan, R. (1991), 'Tortoises and Hares: Choice among Technologies of Unknown Merit', *The Economic Journal*, 101: 801–14.

Cusumano, M. A., Mylonadis, Y. and Rosenbloom, R. S. (1992), 'Strategic Maneuvering and Mass-Market Dynamics: The Triumph of VHS over Beta', *The Business History Review*, 66(1): 51–94.

David, P. A. and Olsen, T. E. (1992), 'Technology Adoption, Learning Spillovers, and the Optimal Duration of Patent-Based Monopolies', *International Journal of Industrial Organization*, 10(4): 517–43.

Fiol, C. M. (1995), 'Thought Worlds Colliding: The Role of Contradiction in Corporate Innovation Processes', *Entrepreneurship Theory and Practice*, (Spring): 71–90.

Fincham, R. Fleck, J. Proctor, R. Scarbrough, H. Tierney, M. and Williams, R. (1994), *Expertise and Innovation: Information Technology Strategies in the Financial Services Sector*, Oxford: Oxford University Press.

Galison, P. L. (1997) *Image and Logic: A Material Culture of Microphysics*, Chicago, IL: University of Chicago Press.

Hanseth, O. (2001), 'The Economics of Standards' in C. U. Ciborra *From Control to Drift: The Dynamics of Corporate Information Infrastructures*, Oxford: Oxford University Press: 56–70.

Howells, J. and Hine, J. (1993), *Innovative Banking: Competition and the Management of a New Networks Technology*, London: Routledge.

Knights, D., Noble, F. and Willmott, H. (1997), 'We Should be Total Slaves to the Business: Aligning Information Technology and Strategy: Issues and Evidence' in B. P. Bloomfield, R. Coombs, D. Knights and D. Littler (eds) *Information Technology and Organizations: Strategies, Networks, and Integration*, Oxford: Oxford University Press: 13–31.

Knorr Cetina, K. (1999), *Epistemic Cultures: How the Sciences Make Knowledge*, Boston, MA: Harvard University Press.

Knorr Cetina, K. and Preda, A. (eds) (2006), *The Sociology of Financial Markets*, Oxford: Oxford University Press.

Kogut, B. and Metiu, A. (2001), 'Open-Source Software Development and Distributed Innovation', *Oxford Review of Economic Policy*, 17(2): 248–64.

Kyrtsis, A-. A. (2010), 'Introduction: Financial Deregulation and Technological Change', in this volume.

Lakhani, K. R. and Panetta, J. A. (2007), 'The Principles of Distributed Innovation' *Innovations*, 2(3): 97–112.

Latour, B. (1987), *Science in Action*, Milton Keynes: Open University Press.

Liebowitz, S. J. (1995), 'Path Dependence, Lock-In, and History', *Journal of Law Economics & Organization*, 11: 205–26.

MacKenzie, D. (2008), *An Engine, Not a Camera: How Financial Models Shape Markets*, Boston, MA: MIT Press.

MacKenzie, D., Muniesa, F. and Siu, L. (2008), *Do Economist Make Markets: On the Performativity of Economics*, Princeton, NJ: Princeton University Press.

Office of Fair Trading 'Payment Systems Working Better for Consumers but More to be Done, OFT Finds', 25 March 2009, http://www.oft.gov.uk/news/press/2009/34-09.

Orlikowski, W. J., Yates, J., Okamura, K. and Fujimoto, M. (1995), 'Shaping Electronic Communication: The Metastructuring of Technology in the Context of Use', *Organization Science*, 6(4): 423–44.

Orlikowski, W. J., Walsham, G. and Jones, M. R. (1996), *Information Technology and Changes in Organizational Work*, London: Chapman & Hall.

Pitt, M. (1996), 'JVC: The VHS Success Story', in C. Baden-Fuller and Pitt, M. (eds), *Strategic Innovation: An International Casebook on Strategic Management*, London: Routledge: 302–35.

Pollock, N. and Williams, R. (2007), 'Technology Choice and its Performance: Towards a Sociology of Software Package Procurement', *Information and Organization*, 17: 131–61.

Pollock, N. and Williams, R. (2009), 'The Sociology of a Market Analysis Tool: How Industry Analysts Sort Vendors and Organize Markets', *Information and Organization*, 19: 129–51.

Poon, M. (2007), 'Scorecards as Devices for Consumer Credit: The Case of Fair, Issac & Company Incorporated', in M. Callon, Y. Millo and F. Muniesa (eds) *Market Devices*, Oxford: Blackwell: 284–306.

Poon, M. (2009), 'From New Deal Institutions to Capital Markets: Commercial Consumer Risk Scores and the Making of Subprime Mortgage Finance', *Accounting, Organizations and Society*, 34: 654–74.

Romer, P. M. (1990), 'Endogenous Technological Change', *Journal of Political Economy*, 98(5): 71–102.

Roussakis, E. N. (1997), *Commercial Banking in an Era of Deregulation*, Westport, CT: Greenwood Press.

Scarbrough, H. (1992), *The IT Challenge: IT Strategy in Financial Services*, London: Prentice Hall.

Scott, S. V., Van Reenen, J. and Zachariadis, M. (2008), 'The Impact on Bank Performance of the Diffusion of a Financial Innovation: An Analysis of SWIFT Adoption', WISE Conference, Paris, 14 December.

Scott, S. V. (1998), *Computer-Mediated Interpretation of Risk: The Introduction of Decision Support Systems in a UK Retail Bank*, Unpublished Ph.D. thesis, University of Cambridge.

Scott, S. V. and Barrett, M. I. (2005), 'Strategic Risk Positioning as Sensemaking in Crisis: The Adoption of Electronic Trading at the London International Financial Futures and Options Exchange', *Journal of Strategic Information Systems*, 14(1): 45–68.

Suchman, L. (2007), *Human-Machine Reconfiguration: Plans and Situated Actions* (2nd edn), Cambridge: Cambridge University Press.

Tett, G. (2009), *Fool's Gold: How Unrestrained Greed Corrupted a Dream, Shattered Global Markets and Unleashed a Catastrophe: How a Tribe of Bankers Rewrote the Rules of Finance and Unleashed an Innovation Storm*, London: Little Brown.

Thwaites, D. (1991), 'Forces at Work: The Market for Personal Financial Services', *International Journal of Bank Marketing*, 9(6): 30–6.

Van Auseloos, J. (1996), 'Responsibilities of TTPs in Trusted Networks', *Information Security Technical Report*, 1(1): 52–6.

Von Hippel, E. (1988), *The Sources of Innovation*, Oxford: Oxford University Press.

Von Hippel, E. (1994), '"Sticky Information" and the Locus of Problem Solving: Implications for Innovation', *Management Science*, 40(4): 429–39.

Von Krogh, G., Ichijo, K. and Nonaka, I. (2000), *How to Unlock the Mystery of Tacit Knowledge and Release the Power of Innovation*, Oxford: Oxford University Press.

Waema, T. M. and Walsham, G. (1990), 'Information Systems Strategy Formulation', *Information and Management*, 18(1): 29–39.

Walsham, G. (1993), *Interpreting Information Systems in Organizations*, Chichester: Wiley.

Woolgar, S., Coopmans, C. and Neyland, D. (eds) (2009), 'Does STS Mean Business?', Special Issue of *Organization*, 16(1).

Zuboff, S. (1988), *In the Age of the Smart Machine: The Future of Work and Power*, Oxford: Heinemann.

Zuboff, S. (1996), 'The Emperor's New Information Economy', in W. J. Orlikowski, G. Walsham, M. R. Jones and J. DeGross (eds) *Information Technology and Changes in Organizational Work*, London: Chapman & Hall: 13–17.

8

Techno-Organizational Diversity, Network Topologies and the Manageability of Banks

Alexandros-Andreas Kyrtsis

Bank management and operational risk management without organizational visibility

As the *Economist* wrote (10 October 2009), 'Big banks are as close as businesses can get to being unmanageable.' The same fears have been expressed in a more pejorative tone by Paul Tucker, the Deputy Governor of the Bank of England: 'Complex structures rendering a bank unsupervisable must not be permitted' (House of Commons Treasury Committee 2009). These remarks should draw our attention also to questions concerning the organizational side of managerial uncertainties. Overcoming uncertainties in banking and finance is of course at the heart of managerial practices. The organization of uncertainty, through the use of schematic representations of ideas about prospective outcomes of action, is a crucial aspect of disputes on manageability (Power 2007). Risk models, like the famous Black-Scholes formula, VAR (value-at-risk) models and other tools of financial engineering can be obvious ways to conceive such schematizations. However uncertainty in banking and finance has not solely to do with the valuation of assets. Its causes can be searched for also in the diversity of financial operations and in the complexity of their organizational dynamics. In spite of the rich and vibrant organizational landscapes of the banks, especially since the early 1990s, risk perception remains overwhelmingly bound to accounting-objects. To this category belong also models for the valuation of derivatives and the related assessment of market, credit and liquidity risks (see MacKenzie in this volume).

The focus on accounting representations, as opposed to topological representations of organizational processes, or network representations, should not surprise us if we take a closer look at the way bankers have been educated to understand management issues. In the most widely read textbooks addressed to this public, like the ones by Hempel et al. (1994) and Koch (1995), almost the entirety of the topics are related to accounting. The whole range of managerial functions is reduced to financial management as a way of 'selecting the portfolio and mix of products and services offered to balance expected returns with assumed risk, within the objective of maximizing shareholder value' (Koch 1995: 3). Later editions of these textbooks (Koch 2009; Hempel et al. 2009), apart from certain references to regulatory issues, do not substantially alter the picture. Organizational, and more specifically techno-organizational aspects of banking and finance, remain underrepresented. If we take the two textbooks by Koch and Hempel et al. together, organizational issues are treated in very few paragraphs in Hempel and only marginally in scattered and unconnected remarks in the rest of the pages of both books. In Hempel et al. (1994: 88) there is only one substantial reference to organizational issues. But what we can read there in no way evokes the climate of organizational studies. In a short paragraph managerial action is related predominantly to coping with risks originating in the potential dishonesty of the staff, the inappropriateness of organizational structures and the inconsistency of management's decisions, as well as in compensation plans that do not provide appropriate incentives. Koch's handbook is obviously not attracting much attention to substantial organizational issues. What the reader *can* learn is that 'management quality is assessed in terms of senior officers' awareness and control of bank's policies and performance. Examiners carefully review bank policy statements regarding loans, investments, capital, and general budgeting to determine whether the bank is well run. [...] The lack of concern over policy statements and regulatory guidelines should have been an indicator of future problems. Capital adequacy, earnings strength, and liquidity are determined by formulas based on the composition and size of various bank balance sheet accounts' (Koch 1995: 41). Concerning technology, a hot issue for banking and finance, discussion of pertinent topics is almost non-existent. In Koch (1995) technology appears nowhere in the index, and in Hempel et al. (1994) only once as 'technological risk'. There is no further reference to the connection between operational risks and technological information infrastructures. But what is predominantly missing is a sense of organizational diversity. This omission implies also a lack of feeling for the relation between organization and information and communication technologies.

Bankers cannot complain about a lack of intellectual resources that can help expand the traditional cognitive horizon. It is also true that many of the younger among them have become fairly knowledgeable in organizational studies. Even the Chartered Institute of Bankers of England has recently added a few modules in its training programmes dealing with organizational and technological issues. But the dominant stance of the guild of bankers and financiers has not been seriously challenged by the tradition created by organizational analysts. The origins of this tradition of thought can be found already in the 1940s. Key concepts and approaches for the understanding of both the potential and the limits of the management of complex organizations, which can be found in Drucker's classics (*Concept of the Corporation* 1946 and *The Practice of Management* 1954), continue to influence the intellectual foundations of sophisticated management and the study of the interrelationships between organization and information technologies (Guillén 1994: 85–90). Many of the original ideas have undergone an evolution, often skewed by ephemeral management-consultancy fashions, but the core is still there. Also, more fundamental disputes such as those related to the abandonment of the structural approach to organizational analysis in anthropocentric trends, or those followed in social-theoretic studies on information system development (Hirschheim et al. 1995, 1996; Checkland and Holwell 1998; Ciborra 2000, 2002; Kallinikos 2006), have not diminished the value of the older works that shaped the field.

Here we can pick out two core points, which however simple are thought-provoking: the first is that companies are human organizations rather than economic data; the second is that, for the analysis of organizational processes (not necessarily for the analysis of other social processes), it is important to bear in mind that the 'behaviour of commodities' depends on the behaviour of people (Drucker 1993: 75–6). These ideas have created unique cognitive platforms of creativity. The understanding of the behaviour of real people acting within concrete spatio-temporal frameworks is the foundation we can build on to understand the fluctuations of corporate data and to assess the information needed for production of commodities and their exchange in monetarized markets. There are also further implications of these simple but not always obvious ideas: because action was related to various organizational stakeholders, the dynamic configurations of interactions between these stakeholders – and the sequences of changes in these configurations – became of paramount importance. In this sense the managerial tradition has brought about a tradition of topological representations, first in terms of hierarchical organigraphs (many of which resonate with a bureaucratic spirit), and later in the sense of more sophisticated organizational approaches including not only vertical but horizontal communication as well.[1] The latter in some cases led designers, managers and users of techno-organizational systems to adopt complex representations of network topologies as instruments for weighing up their action.

Of course management studies have a disadvantage in the sense that they are embedded in a non-reflexive modernization approach. They are too oriented towards certainties drawing on managerial philosophies. In this context it is not the unpredictable, unsuspected or unintended consequences of action that are regarded as the sources of risk, but the intended and the predictable. Managerial theories, even if they are infused with a social constructivist flavour, and even when they are following ideas about polycentric governance, always tend to be more architectural and less contingency or risk-oriented. They insist on building on the praise of the potency of innovators and leaders and on the operational standards managers try to impose on organizations. The idea that there are no risk-proof forms of managerial action is not their preferred source of inspiration. Such certainties are of course not the sole platforms of organizational action. Others prefer a focus on the connection between organizational design, management and risk perception. But ideas concerning the risk potential present in every kind of action were brought more intensely into the discussion after the 1980s, by theorists of reflexive modernization. Certainties were then suspected of causing unintended constraints and hazards, and not only of being positive movers of action. This changed the basis of the perception of the interplay between risk and certainty.[2] From this perspective the limits of the managerial tradition's usefulness become clear – as soon as we realize that risk perception and prospective management do not combine smoothly.

An additional challenge came from the escalated interconnection between external and internal threats. The economic environment – the volatility of the financial markets and competition – can be dangerous if not properly encountered. Recently counterparty risk has been added to the range of perils of complex inter-organizational environments (Hattori and Suda 2007; Kauko 2007; European Central Bank 2009). But locking the view exclusively on these menaces detracts from the potential of internal threats. For many bankers, and for a very long time, the internal environment was considered to be more tranquil, a domesticated domain where from time to time the appearance of deviant cases of fraudsters or incompetent employees caused damage that could be swiftly isolated and repaired (Mayer 1997). More fundamental issues of coordination were regarded as rather controllable operational matters. Internal organizational diversity and complex coupling between segregated domains of activity was not a reason for exceptional worry. However growing organizational complexity due to the diversity of products and services and to the multiplication of external roles in banks and in financial organizations, and the internal processes these were connected with, have created a sense of intertwining between internal and external threats. These came to be discussed under the term 'operational risk'. But again bankers, rating agencies and regulators declined from changing their approach to the risk objects, packaged under this new term. They refuted topological representations and preferred a reduction to new versions of accounting representations, in the belief that it would allow them to manage risks without bothering about any thorough understanding of the internal workings of their organizations.[3]

The stance of supervisory and regulatory authorities is not a negligible factor in the shaping of such managerial cultures and practices. This can easily be made apparent if we take a closer look at regulatory guidelines. According to the already mentioned report of the House of Commons Treasury Committee (2009), the Governor of the Bank of England, when he took up the issue of complex banks "*argued that the degree of interconnectedness between banks was a very good way of measuring the risks they posed to the system as a whole. ... [And] wanted to see capital requirements varying according to the interconnectedness of a bank*'. This led to the design of measures justified by the fact that 'highly complex, interconnected banks should face higher capital charges than simpler banks, because they impose a greater risk on the financial system as a whole'. The first problem inherent in this view is the insistence on risk originating in inter-organizational complexities, that is, on the external threats. From a transaction cost theory perspective there are many reasons to believe that the interconnectedness of risks distributed among various organizations with demarcated interest can produce stronger informational asymmetries than intra-organizational processes, and that in this sense priority should be given to counterparty risk. However there is no reason to believe that this should not apply also to intra-organizational complex interconnections between organizational and informational entities. The second and more detrimental problem with this approach is that it relies on the idea that these complexities should not be studied from a qualitative point of view (and thus through topological representations of the interconnections among agents), but only through quantitative variables. It is doubtful whether estimates of the pecuniary amount needed to repair eventual damage can give a conclusive evidence base for alternative organizational policies. However even this possibility doesn't seem to intrigue these auditors and regulators, or the managers trapped in the mentality of traditional accountants.[4]

For the overwhelming majority of bankers and regulators, 'operational risk' is a term under which all possible risks originating from suspected but not clearly visible negative organizational factors are bundled. But more important for understanding practices in banking and finance is to point out that everything which has to do with operational risk is sought to be correlated with short-term pecuniary costs. The estimate of operational risk exposure implies capital requirements in order to dispose of the resources needed to repair eventual damage, where the real meaning of damage is not clearly specified.[5] The fact that organizational issues have not been more thoroughly looked at is astonishing if we take into consideration the difficulty of measuring operational risk. What stands in the way of this kind of quantitative assessment is the difficulty of finding observable measures of operational risk exposure.[6] The problem has to do with how we conceptualize operational risk, without looking at organizational structures and processes the features of which could have been represented with diagrams, or perhaps even with structured narratives. It is obvious that the rating agencies and short-term investors in stocks and derivatives prefer to forget about eventual organizational complications. But for the rest of the economic agents, if processes related to operational risk could be better represented with topological schemes, it is not certain that they would continue to regard the invention of simple indicators, presumably measuring operational risk exposure, as a relevant exercise. For the management of operational risks, if solely hedged with capital without questioning technologies, leads to organizational systems and practices, which can under certain circumstances amplify operational failures.

Michael Power (2005) in his by now seminal paper on the reinvention of operational risk remarks that 'there is more than a slight suspicion that the invention of operational risk is an attempt to frame the unframeable, to assuage our deepest anxieties and fears about uncontrollable "rogue others", and to tame monsters which have been created and nurtured by the financial system itself'. The emphasis on the 'rogue others' is very well targeted here, as it refers to the unintelligible organizational other. But I think we should go one step further in trying to understand the implications of operational risk, and subsequent operational risk management. The point I want to make here is that in the case of operational risk, occurrences are one-sidedly ascribed to the users and not to the designers, and in this sense the user-organization is the main stage of generation of the potentials for eventual damaging occurrences. Although operational risk is a concept related to organizational procedures, we should bear in mind that organizations are social and often also socio-technical entities created by design, and that the assumptions of those who design, redesign and re-engineer can be of decisive importance. In the case of financial organizations, in the old days traditional accountants were the central figures designing operations and procedures. Later they lost part of their power to hybrid managers who had a feeling for techno-organizational matters. But in the 1990s, the real redesign and re-engineering of banks took place under the influence of the managerial culture of the era of securitization, which became a central feature of the financialization of many organizations both financial and nonfinancial (Watson 2009).

With the rising role of investment banking the most prominent managerial positions came gradually into the hands of financial engineers or managers who shaped their worldviews according to their understanding of what financial engineering was and how it should determine financial operations and markets (Derman 2004; MacKenzie 2006; Tett 2009; Triana 2009). These people had a far-reaching impact on organizational design philosophies and seriously underestimated the importance of the highly diverse internal social and institutional fabric of financial organizations (Partnoy 2003; Derman 2004; Lépinay 2007). However an emphasis on the direct or indirect designing roles of various holders of managerial positions should not necessarily lead to the inference that they are omnipotent. In spite of their hierarchical position and their high self-esteem, and the propagation of their reputed achievements, these actors are not the only decision makers. Decisions lean on other previously taken decisions; and such mutual dependencies stretch both upwards and downwards on the hierarchical ladder (Tsoukas 1996). Furthermore behind formal decisions there are a multitude of informal ones, which although they are less visible have a more significant impact on actions within all organizational echelons than bearers of business mythologies tend to realize. Both formal and informal decisions, either by powerful or weak organizational agents, create spaces within which there take place the definition and the accomplishment of tasks embedded in social networks of action.

Along these lines, the technologization of organizational processes can be crucial. Technological design is an exercise aiming towards moulding these systems of tasks into durable relationships. It is obvious that this requires durable procedures, reproducible knowledge bases and more or less stable configurations of both tangible and intangible artefacts. This is not an exclusively top-down process. In reality, in spite of limits set by power relations, many technological solutions emerge from or are modified by local knowledge and local tinkering. Blindness to such chains of events, as well as to the ways various stakeholders try to make visible through abstractions and techno-organizational mythologies the modalities of action they seek to induce, can be a major source of operational risks (Reason 1997). As we will see later in this chapter, a distorted view or limited techno-organizational visibility can result in the accumulation of sources of organizational accidents with severe consequences. The design of organizational technologies and their diagrammatic representations (for instance the ones that can be found in the white papers of powerful consultancies and are often uncritically adopted by managers) are very often reflections of these abstractions and mythologies aiming at the transformation of risk objects into objects of certainty. Unfortunately some of these rationalizations in the form of abstractions and mythologies obstruct the view of critical events influencing the operational underlay of finance.

Network topologies and abstract machines

Techno-organizational mythologies, and the representations of organizational realities these imply, are strong movers of organizational evolution. Diagrams in the form of network topologies or in the form of other kinds of models that managers or experts in banks can work with, are often the schematic translations of mythologies that shape mindsets. Those who induce action-by-design are also interested in the mapping of systems of rules onto technological systems, and thus in making arguments drawing on techno-organizational mythologies. This was, for example, the case with the 1990s trend of re-engineering banks. The idea was to connect all possible workflows across the organization and their technological backbones with the marketing and sales functions (Allen 1997: 135–71). The efforts related to re-engineering have created their own myths without which redesign and restructuring would have been impossible. The rate of failure of such projects was very high, mainly because of lack of top-management commitment, which can be understood as an inability of leading bankers to act the part of myth-makers and myth-disseminators. Leaving these roles to external consultants proved to be highly ineffective. In almost all cases this kind of externalization of symbolic resources turned out to be a major source of failure. But what made the whole situation treacherous was the target of changing the ways bankers and bank employees were seeing their organization. Through reorientating the entire range of functionalities towards marketing- and sales-dependence, project leaders and project managers were seeking to change the schematic representations of both the physical and the virtual geography of the interconnected activities of the banks. This meant also a pressure to realize possible diagrammatic representations of the techno-organizational systems of banks, which did not belong up to this point to the mental mappings of functionalities and processes prevailing among the staff of financial organizations (Allen 1997).

There are plenty of such examples from banks and other organizations, as well as from activities carried out by small groups or even by individuals, where the momentum created by mythologies related to design changed representational regimes. As the design theorist Adrian Forty points out, 'design alters the way people see commodities' (Forty 2000: 11); and thus alters the way people see systems. Forty draws on the structuralist view that the contradictions between beliefs and experiences are resolved by the invention of myths that shape reality itself. The accommodation within practices of artefacts and mental maps presupposes a modification of realities. This is not relevant only for material objects. It applies to both tangible and intangible objects of certainty such as hardware/software configurations. The mythological construction of the techno-organizational ground of banking and financial information systems (within limits set by structural constraints) can, thus, be the point of departure for understanding both the financial shaping of technologies and its reverse, namely the technological shaping of banking.

Not all organizational and technological domains are equally covered with mythologies. From some domains, stronger mythologies arise than from others; and many micro-fields of action are not articulate at all. This constitutes a major handicap for the knowing of socio-organizational and socio-technical systems. The opportunities for knowledge emerge to a great extent from the critique of preceding mythologies. If there are no mythological articulations of subordinate organizational entities, also the significance of disputes on organizational and technological issues related to organizational sub-units, or on the management of technological system components, tends to wane. In other words, access to certain less visible domains of knowledge-creation can be obstructed, if their mythologies are not perceived and elaborated by others in the organization. For example mythologies about banking technologies, about their inception and development and the innovations these may cause, exist in many cases but remain among small backstage groups with relatively low status within the organization. In a study on the introduction of computers and the evolution of the information systems of the National Bank of Greece, it could be shown that these various domains of mythological reconstruction of the role and evolution of technologies had a constitutive role. However this critical contribution to the overall efficiency of the operations of the bank was made in domains of techno-organizational action lying outside the horizon of the top management and of those entrusted with core banking activities (Kyrtsis 2008b). Furthermore the worlds of this kind of mythological reconstruction were highly fragmented among the various groups of informaticians or other specialists responsible for the adoption and development of technologies.

Of course, as everybody might suspect, one of the main and most powerful sources of mythologies related to the information systems of banks and other financial organizations are the vendor firms. Each segment of the technology market in which companies are producing hardware and software, or models for the financial sector, influences ways of seeing technologies. Their product management as well as their marketing strategies and tactics generate discourses that are then taken up by managers of the purchasing organization. The embeddedness of these discourses within the practices of various echelons and in socially differentiated sub-organizational units brings about dominant techno-organizational representations. Further, the system of both formal and informal meetings among managers and experts of various organizational echelons leads often to situations where bottom-up transmission of opinions can counterbalance top-down directed managerial directives. Academic discourses can also have a role in this respect. They can frame the cognitive background of both initial training and knowledge-management. Academic training can keep exerting a decisive influence despite the weight of consecutive waves of intra-organizational socialization and in-house training arising from business requirements. Academics also undertake consultancy roles (alone or as collaborators of established consultancies), and from this post they make use of the conceptual armoury they carry with them and try to sell to their organizational clients. Recourse to their research can give authority to opinions and a sense of reliability to products and services. Their wordings are often a critical ingredient for techno-organizational mythological constructions. Often these wordings constitute the functional elements of diagrammatic representations. Michael Porter's 'value chain' model, and the waterfall or SWOT models, often also applied to information systems development, are among the ones that can be named here.[7] A closer look at the ERP business can also offer us a plethora of examples in this direction.[8]

Wordings and diagrams, as means of representation, can be of high rhetorical significance in situations where the objective is to mobilize and train people for the accomplishment of specific goals. Yet their instrumental value rises as soon as both risk objects and objects of certainty are attributed an artefactual character. This can happen if, for instance, the belief prevails that the perception of organizational risks related to the efficiency of operations should be encountered with the standardization of procedures and their support with technologies. Schematic representations of the problems' definition, and of the scenarios of action that might lead to solutions, become crucial in this context. Through representations originating in mythological shaping and elaborations of realities we try to metamorphose the unfamiliar (due to strangeness or complexity) into something familiar.[9] Designers and cultivators of corporate cultures need to be, in one sense or another, craftsmen of familiarization. They cannot avoid searching for ways aiming to integrate ideas, in diagrams or in the use of diagrammatic representations as visual aids. One reason for this is that such visual aids enhance the messages emitted through metaphors and analogies.[10] Diagrammatic representations expand the effect of forms of propositional or textual agency, that is, of the performative role speech and texts can have in organizational settings.

Network topologies as representations of the information systems of banks or of other financial operations play a crucial role in this respect. 'Abstract machines', that is, standardized procedures for working with these diagrammatic representations, also make the diagrammatic representations more durable. Network topologies place objects and the interconnections among them on a non-linear two-dimensional space. Stocks of data, points of data entry, points of processing (physical or virtual), points of output (tangible or intangible) and flows of information are represented with drawings. But these drawings reproduce static images. Both dynamic equilibria and sets of principles of transformation require additional operational elements. These can be derived from abstract machines. The term 'abstract machine' and its usage are borrowed from the work of Giles Deleuze and Felix Guattari (1987: 141, 148). Despite their opaque language that is not up to the standards of analytical rigour, they offer a useful concept for the study of organizational technologies in banking and finance. Abstract machines are strong diagrammatic representations, closed semantic systems represented in drawings with high operational value. This strong aspect of diagrammatic representations makes us blind to any distinction between the artificial and the natural. The logic and the ontological framing of abstract machines define domains of transformation of risk objects into objects of certainty. Abstract machines represent realities as if they were manageable in mechanistic terms. They present the architectural interpretation of realities and downgrade their contingencies and fluidities. They make us see more structure than drift. The issues raised by these representations resemble the problems set by the act of drawing and using maps. A map can create the impression that it is possible to make all problems and adventures of travelling vanish.

Network topologies and abstract machines are instruments used for achieving visibility, from a perspective originating in techno-organizational myths and rarely in evidence-based theories. In large banks with complex information systems organizational visibility is very quickly reduced to technical visibility drawing on the relationship between network topologies and abstract machines. The social, economic and political visibility of the organizational and technological systems of banks is for obvious reasons not a priority. This facet causes too much anxiety and can in addition damage trust in the organization if perceived by external observers. Social and political aspects of organizations and information systems originate in incomplete or implicit contracts among organizational stakeholders and in unstable networks of cooperation, and thus in both rogue practices and unintended outcomes. Most occurrences stemming from these aspects of organizational dynamics are made visible more in moments of failure than in moments of undisrupted operation. The quest for certainty implies that they are preferably expelled into the realm of unwanted and invisible contingencies. Technically constructed certainties are considered to be more desirable. Hereby formalism – detaching the instrumentality of representations from their content – can be convenient. Patterns of representations drawing directly upon or inspired by accounting methods had this function, often detaching the technique from the content of operations. In the information and communication technology-intensive internal environments of banks, those who have reasons not to follow accounting patterns, tend to imagine structures and processes through diagrams of network topologies and through the abstract machines these imply.

Organizational technologies adopted or developed by banks can be conceived in this sense also as instruments for the interconnection of information stocks and information flows.[11] The objects that compose the technological landscapes in banks correspond to a great extent with such information stocks and flows among them. Complexities emerge from lists of objects and from interconnections between them, which have to be taken into consideration in any attempt to understand the information systems of banks.[12] Financial functionalities and other related operations are translated into functionalities of information and communication systems. Decisions on technological investment and innovation in banking also emerge out of such representations, both in cases of tactical reaction and in cases of strategic planning. For instance Elena Beccalli's categorization of the objectives of investment in technology and of the corresponding types of IT initiatives taken in banks (Beccalli 2007: 156) originates in these kinds of representations. She differentiates information system development efforts in banks into four areas of activity in which technological objects and their interconnections can be bundled: (1) improvements in quality through the management of information on customers (customer information management) and the automation of distribution channels; (2) business management and the rationalization of internal processes; (3) e-banking; (4) product innovation.

A different means of mapping information nexuses is through the topological representation of financial networks. Nagurney and Siokos (1997) propose to use network analytic representations in order to study entire financial systems consisting of multiple clusters of interacting economic agents. In this model financial networks are represented as configurations of objects: nodes; links and associated costs; supply and demand mechanisms for flows of information goods. The structure and evolution of these configurations are conceived as being driven by behaviour principles such as optimization or competitive equilibrium. Another assumption is that the places of decision making, which are bound to behaviour principles, are the nodes of the networks. Links represent choices for the push and pull of information and commodities. These lines connecting nodes can be viewed as directed channels with a quantitative attribute related to the volume of information and commodities moved from node to node. Decisions in the nodes can be related to various financial products and services or financial instruments. Links, as representations of choices, can be further characterized by the risk exposure of investment decisions that have triggered off the corresponding flows between nodes. The overall dynamics of the network can be represented by configurations of linkages among different individual or organizational agents and the portfolios they structure and manage. Such representations of network connections between organizationally differentiated parts can be more easily applied to complexes of activities external to the separate banks and financial organizations.[13] However they can be extremely useful for the understanding of the internal structure and organizational dynamics of banks. Of course all risks related to costs and to coordination are different in the case of internal processes, but this does not imply that input–output relationships among units within a bank are not subject to decentralized decisions and to the asymmetric information this internal decentralization may produce. Internal divisions and departments commission projects from each other, and despite the coordinative role and the power of a managerial core team, contracting (sometimes formal but more often informal) among the various units can be very tricky. Very often all these nexuses are reflected in the minds of those who have to take organizational decisions or in those who have to respond to directives. Sometimes even concrete diagrammatic representations of complex information systems can be indispensable for the creation of the appropriate mental maps.

Information systems divisions of banks especially tend to create such maps to allow them to keep track of functionalities, synergies and interoperabilities. This is not always an easy task. The difficulties explain why a specialized market for software based aids has been created. Many of the tools in this direction are integrated in software packages or in modules of ERPs. The problem these tools help to solve is that the lists of techno-organizational objects can be very long, especially in the cases of universal banks. However the length of these lists, and the operational implications of the functionality of each item on them, are only part of the concern here. Complexity can also grow from the recursive relationships between the internal and external environments of the banks. The various components of information systems are developed and then further evolve through drift in various settings. Environments of banking and financial technology, defined by economic, social, political and regulatory processes, can be of paramount significance. Innovations in financial products and services, which also imply innovations in organizational technologies, are a crucial factor. Further, information and communication technology products and services are developed and marketed by powerful vendors with their own strategies and commercial interests to promote.

The sender–receiver relations between these environments, which influence the technological decision making, can be depicted with topological schemes.[14] The complexity of these interactions is related also to the fact that the human resources izn each of these areas have their own way of prioritizing the constitution and use of information; and further, due to this, they tend to bracket out each others' views and stick to their own perspective. These partial views offer terms of abstraction, and most terms of abstraction are related to metaphors originating in familiar pieces of knowledge and emotional settings. In-depth research at the National Bank of Greece (Kyrtsis 2008b) or previous research in the

Scottish banks (Fincham et al. 1994) and consultancy experience from many other banks has shown that the main mechanism is delegation of knowledge and black-boxing, but without any recording or reporting of the various points of view. This process of black-boxing, already discussed by Donald MacKenzie in this volume with reference to derivatives operations, can be one of the main sources of representational regimes in banking and finance. Also auditors rely on a kind of black-boxing, by relying on check-listing and box-ticking. What do all these things mean for information system development and maintenance, as well as for the management of banks as techno-organizational systems? Technologists and organizers manage information profiled according to top-down bracketing of points of view. But there is a lot of information-profiling going on horizontally among departments and divisions that often does not appear in the dominant language adopted for talking about techno-organizational issues. One of the reasons for this is that this dominant language is overwhelmed by jargon disseminated by consultancies, by vendor companies, by interbank organizations like SWIFT or Euroclear, and sometimes by supervisory authorities and regulators.

The arrays of objects, and interconnections between them, challenge our intellectual capacities and can thus cause real managerial messes. The antidote may be decisions about conceptual framings that raise the potential to reduce complexity. Such framings always bear mythological dimensions, but this does not render them useless. Mythologies are compromises with realities and if this means that there is a part of the discourse that fits with facts, this part defines a perspective with practical value. In most cases we cannot start doing things without partial truths. This is always the formative part of courses of action, whatever the implications may be. The rest has to do with incremental corrections. Sometimes we have to substitute a techno-organizational mythology with another, but we always need one. Of course many would prefer to use the word 'theory', but this doesn't change much of the substance of the argument. Disputes over IT management philosophies have to a great extent to do with creating such perspectives. One such possible perspective is that proposed by Claudio Ciborra. He suggests that informational resources or sequences of processes that are directly supported or enabled by IT infrastructures could be better studied according to their *reach* and *scope* (Ciborra 2000: 17–18). Focusing on reach implies spotting and making lists of the activities or processes touched by the infrastructure. Focusing on scope implies spotting and making lists of the type and variety of applications kept running by the infrastructure. Scope in this sense has to do with full or partial automation, depending on the reliance of activities on the IT infrastructure, or on the non-automated informatization – more characteristic for pull than for push aspects of technology.[15] This means that there can be a direct or indirect but non-arbitrary correspondence between reach and scope. Detecting the sources of this non-arbitrariness can help us reveal the intentions and rationales of the agents who develop and manage systems. System integration and attempts to standardize system components and processes are crucial aspects of such activities. As Hanseth (2000: 57) points out, integration is strongly related to ideas about standardized interfaces of system components and the functionalities these represent. But standardization is for the most part not real but rather fictional, hypothetical, an 'as if' situation creating pressures for compliance that cannot always be realized.[16] Standardization – and this is a major issue for banking and finance – can spoil invaluable techno-organizational information.[17] The reason for this is that standardization, and especially if it is related to dogmatic quests for automation, relies on strong and often superficial opinions regarding the character of user groups and communities of practice. There are thus strong pressures on user groups and communities of practice to adopt views on the relationships between objects and actors in terms predetermined by the beliefs of innovators and designers (Akrich 1992; Kallinikos 2004b). They can, however, enact these pressures in unpredictable ways within varying limits of undulation between standardization and non-standardization (Monteiro 2000: 77; Ciborra 2002). Also network topologies and abstract machines undergo a translation that shifts both their meaning and their operational character. It can be that the staff and teams at various levels use the same words, but this does not necessarily mean that they understand the same things by them.

In those cases where we can detect such disparities we have to think hard about the implications of the design and use of technologies in organizational settings. For instance it wouldn't be wise to reduce without any further consideration the representations of the techno-organizational ground of banking and financial systems to software-based management aids or decision support systems, without bearing in mind the eventual exposure to model risk. Storing and representing the topological information and the plurality of facets of network functionalities on graphical user interfaces can imply model failures that can be a significant source of operational risk. System and network resources have their human side and, consequently, they comprise elements that can produce contingencies and hidden processes. It does not suffice to take into consideration only the physical, or further only those configurable information assets that can be represented by network topologies and abstract machines.

It is not the maps, but rather the communities of practice located in the maps and interpreting the maps from their ground perspective that drive the real life of the systems. The various socially differentiated groups create their own abstract machines and their own rhetoric. They can also, under certain circumstances, invent and cultivate their own distinct narratives. These narratives can dissolve and undermine the dominant abstractions imposed by higher-echelon managers or consultants. Relatively segregated communities of practice in banking and finance, in spite of communication between organizational sub-units, have unique experiences and cultivate their own expertise and craftsmanship originating in tacit knowing. It is this craftsmanship that saves these highly complexly structured financial organizations from collapse, despite the plethora of couplings and the frequent lack of managerial insights. Craftsmanship can reverse the delocalization of operational couplings and thus save systems through local action in the organizational sub-units and through the mobilization of local knowledge. This is of course not a panacea, but the only solution in situations in which top managers, top IT specialists and consultants are unable to create enough visibility or to invent and formulate in a persuasive manner the conceptual framing of techno-organizational action.

Manoeuvring through the techno-organizational fog: Maps and accidents

Not being able to see topologies of organizational diversity by departing from a reflexive use of network topologies and abstract machines can block the way to critical information. These kinds of conditions of limited ability to gain information will be called here 'techno-organizational fog'.[18] Techno-organizational fog is observer-dependent.[19] It arises as a problem from the intentions of observers who realize that there are shortages of information. Techno-organizational fog can thus hardly be discussed from an aesthetic or emotional perspective, as in the case of the romantic paintings or in literary descriptions. The term as introduced here refers to the hurdles in mapping out the characteristics of organizational risk objects. This implies that the relevance of its usage presupposes a perception of risk. From this perception arise the motives to look at the features of organizational and information systems; for example, by moving into the foreground problems of scope and reach of information infrastructures. For instance we may have difficulties in looking through the techno-organizational fog to see the configurations of inputs and outputs among functional entities. Or it may happen that we have difficulties in spotting operational inconsistencies within spatio-temporal configurations of functionalities. Lack of information, that is, lack of the news and raw data we are expecting to receive from various parts of the organizations, is a small problem compared to a lack of perspective and conceptual framing. The impasse is much harder if we don't know what we want to look at. The lists of things we are trying to figure out, the ontologies that these lists have the potential to bring about, and the systems of keywords and their conceptual content, can be the main source of our inability to create a picture. It is not primarily information overload that preoccupies us here. Absence of orientation is the problem: we do not know what the entities are that could mobilize our minds. The orientation towards such entities and the way we are seeking to achieve visibility, and then eventually to reduce complexity, either by perceiving or by assuming or presuming interconnections and interoperabilities between such entities, is the main cause of this sense of fogginess.[20]

Techno-organizational fog also hinders the understanding of processes dependent on organizational diversity and latent events. Organizational diversity and latent events have decisive cognitive implications. The kind of techno-organizational visibility discussed here is a problem depending on where we stand in a highly fragmented environment. Bracketing and fragmentation of perspectives can provoke emotions of unfamiliarity. In this way ontological risk is related to a sense of the existence of unfamiliar entities, as well a sense of unpredictable implications of the existence of such unfamiliar entities, that can be crucial for the shaping of mindsets. The perception of the unknown can lead among other things to pre-emptive strikes against complexity, that is, to attacks against imaginary objects even though the potential consequences of the existence of these objects will certainly remain undetected. This means acting before knowing, a stance peculiar to some version of the precautionary principle. As already mentioned, representations are a means of aiming at the familiarization of the unfamiliar. Being unable to cope with techno-organizational fogginess could mean being unable to find the means of representation, with the result that random decisions are made without first establishing visibility. And this problem of visibility can arise from not finding the way to provoke and empower the dispatch of messages from the less visible parts of the organization. In this sense, the perception of risk arising from the potential expressivity of less powerful agents can be an additional source of techno-organizational fog. Encountering difficulties in collecting the appropriate information and acting pre-emptively without having the means to weigh techno-organizational risks is not an unusual situation for those who have experience with the management of complex systems. In banks such problems often arise from the auditing function. This is the case especially with the auditors of information systems ('IS auditors') who enjoy greater autonomy in their job than accounting auditors, who are more closely monitored by top management and core bankers. IS auditors search for deviations from formal and dominant patterns in the use of key end-user or system and telecommunications applications. The difficulty they are facing is that they have to define the dominant patterns. But the problem they create is that they often trace system disruptions predominantly to intentional fraudulent actions of isolated users or to the anomic or erratic actions of whole groups (e.g. neglect of reporting etc.). They very rarely give thoughts to the implications of managerial or design and development activities that shape systems. (There are however efforts among those who follow more recent IS auditing philosophies to change this.) Problematic approaches to operational risk, overemphasizing the role of the rogue and more or less unknown other or of the unpredictable emergent structures and events due to anomic or erratic groups, have very much to do with particular aspects of auditing cultures.

One of the difficulties arising in the above landscape of complexities has to do with our tendency to overemphasize technical visibility. This can be justified as long as we can rely on automatisms and algorithms. In the rest of the cases, procedures and systems in banking and finance become visible through their crises and failures, and not through what is accepted as proper functioning. Trying to understand systems and procedures as things that never experience disruptions and collapses, however compatible with conventional ways of thinking this might be, does not correspond to real life experiences. Those with first-hand experience of technologically backed operations, if asked could tell quite different stories. The latter remark should not make us neglect technical visibility. It is true that the technocratic framing of views on techno-organizational processes stems from ideas about durability and systemic harmony. It is also important to bear in mind that systems always and in various senses fall short of perfect order, and this can lead us to search out ways of perceiving systems that overcome a narrow technical vision. Yet neglecting the technical visibility of systems facilitated by diagrammatic representations of network topologies and abstract machines, as many social constructionists driven by an excessive subjectivism would try to do, is not relevant. The fact that systems more often than not render visible through their social and political articulations, and this because of frequent failures and collapses (Stark 2009: 155–60), does justify the inference that formal technological representations should not be regarded as the only possible compasses of techno-organizational action. Consequently, if we want to manoeuvre through the organizational fog, we will need what are, from the technical point of view, rather formalized representations; but we will also need to uncover the source of inconsistencies, conflicts and contingencies.

In the case of financial systems, inconsistencies, conflicts and contingencies, which also destabilize representational regimes, arise from their hybridity. 'Hybridity' is a system-theoretic concept. It refers to the coexistence of interconnected continuous and discrete processes within the same system. This implies virtual multilevel and multi-pace spatio-temporal processes. Techno-organizational maps in the form of network topologies and methods of working with these, which constitute abstract machines, cannot cope easily in representational terms with the problem of hybridity. We would need too much mathematics. Diagrammatic and mathematical representations in this case could be suitable for research, but they would be totally impractical for managerial purposes. Handy system-representations with network topologies and abstract machines more easily depict the discrete aspects of the shaping and use of information. In other words, they can either help us understand configurations of discrete events in a moment of a hypothetical freeze of the system, or they can show us continuous flows and their ongoing but asynchronous impact on sequences of discrete events from the point of view of their structural features. But these structural features, too, can be made visible only through a hypothetical freeze of the system. The difference between the 'anytime' and the 'queuing' aspect of functions carried out at discrete time intervals cannot be simultaneously grasped by two-, or even three-dimensional diagrams. The logic of trading has to do with the 'anytime' aspect, whereas the logic of transactions related to all kinds of services and contracts with the clients, with maturities, clearing, settlement and custody are bound to discrete sequences of events. Both aspects of the dynamics of their recursive interrelationship cannot be simultaneously represented with diagrams.

Similar issues arise also from simpler problems. For instance there is a difference between the way online processes and batch processes in banking provoke information infrastructures. Deposit and withdrawing transactions are of immediate effect, whereas credit transactions, although they can be linked to continuous processes when leverage is traded, imply discrete sequences of subsequent events in order to get approved, and after this they are subject to a discrete protocol of actions and payments. There is also a difference in this respect between the way trading processes as opposed to contracting, clearing and settlement processes set systems in motion and exploit their network resources. Or there are neural-network-like processes in financial organizations and in financial networks that can be juxtaposed to fuzzy-logic based processes. It is also from this perspective that financial networks and financial organizations can be viewed as hybrid systems.[21] In this sense, engineering and re-engineering banks and other financial organizations or financial networks require a kind of hybrid engineering that interconnects discrete and continuous processes.[22] The representational problems encountered here set cognitive limits with operational implications because we cannot construct abstract machines that can work as reliable systemic compasses. This is one of the main reasons why the hybridity of financial networks and of financial organizations is an additional source of techno-organizational fogginess.

The representational problems arising from the technical and operational hybridity of information systems can be made worse if we set at the centre of discussion the internal social and political tensions of banks. Reliance on abstract machines in order to cope with fogginess can then collapse as a result of a different challenge. Shifts, drifts, postponement, diversion, and tinkering can be at least as important for the workings of the systems as formal plans for development, upgrading and maintenance. A great part of complexity stems from the improvisation of various actors, and this accelerates whenever we have a larger number of synapses of the organization in relation to its environment, through the multiplication of external roles of the staff distributed among various functions and echelons.

But most importantly, there are organizational accidents and these cannot be understood solely through the diagrammatic handling of topologies and geometries of information systems. Network topologies and abstract machines focus on space but remain blind to the places of the emergence of action. They create the illusions of maps. Seeing a map without seeing what agents are doing in the places on the map creates limited visibility and the fog remains. What we can see for instance from the organigraphs is the control dimension. What becomes visible in this way is the intention of control through demarcation and segregation of functional units and through the durable establishment of channels for the transmission of information and directives. Although organigraphs, or organigraph-like representations, hide many aspects of the reality of banking and finance, they are highly relevant for they are inscriptions of control philosophies, as is the case with every map (Lacoste 1976). Organigraphs are always useful in order to find the organizational addresses and thus create a bird's-eye view of the places and their interconnections.[23] But it is not enough to understand the geographies of systems solely in terms of space. We need also to understand how places are constituted and in addition we should understand what is going on in these places. Seeing things from the control perspective and not from the point of view of lived experience of actors located in organizational places, makes us blind to the origins of operational failures and operational risks. These failures and risks are not solely issues of abstract causalities and maps. All agents exposing their organizations to risk intentionally are constituted as subjects and articulate this subjectivity departing from experiences in localized and demarcated social networks. And those whose conduct damages their organization without having intentionally selected a risky or directly hazardous course of action comply with rules or implicit normative pressures. Understanding the places where this happens can be crucial. As David Stark points out (2009: 160), drawing on the work of Michel Callon, socio-technical networks are not connecting identities that exist prior to the dynamics of shifting configurations of interconnections among agents who are involved in action; especially when this action presupposes the mobilization of various techno-organizational resources. It is thus worthwhile to spot the places where ontological framing takes place; and to track the interconnections between these places behind the organizational boundaries.

Is this technological understanding of banks and financial networks enough? If we are interested in organizational accidents, looking only at the surface of network structures is definitely not sufficient. We should go one step further and try to understand the emergence of risks from the uncontrollable coupling of various operational domains. Operational risks can emerge from the deficient understanding of interrelations and from not knowing whom you can deal with, but they can in addition emerge from latent processes. Understanding these latent processes can be crucial for operational risk management in finance. In terms of technologies, this has to do with the more subtle aspects of information systems auditing. For instance in the Nick Leeson case, which led to the collapse of Barings, the IS auditors could have revealed the problems. But no steps were taken to verify the accounts or to make comparison with the trading records of clients (Reason 1997: 31). As James Reason (1997: 32) further points out, such checks are usually omitted not because of lack of segregation between front (trading) and back (settlement) offices, but rather because of a sense of priorities combined with a sense of time-criticality, that is, of having something more important and more pressing to deal with. This stance is very often encountered when we search for the sources of organizational accidents. These are in most cases not revealed until long after the negative occurrences. They remain latent and their manifestations, if at all, come very late to the surface (Reason 1997: 36). These latent conditions are also hidden in invisible or not discursively elaborated interconnections between operational units and system components, the operators of which are either unaware of the occurrences or for various reasons do not talk about them (Perrow 1999, 2007). The mechanisms by which this reliability is achieved can be opaque to those who operate and manage the system (Weick 1987). Weick's point is that safety is a 'dynamic non-event' that requires active knowledge-management. Network topologies and abstract machines if handled in a ritualistic manner create static non-events and this has consequences related to model risk and diminished reflexivity.[24] A reflexive use of network topologies and abstract machines is, then, the way to cope with techno-organizational fog. However in late neoliberalism this reflexive use of models, although it belongs to the culture of many traders (Beunza and Stark 2009), is not part of the techno-organizational culture for the most part imposed by regulatory approaches and the methods used by rating agencies to assess financial organizations. But things can be worse. In some instances managers and regulators are not interested in the problem of techno-organizational fogginess because they believe that techno-organizational risks can be hedged with capital that can be pumped up by diverting activities towards more intense trading in the financial markets or with opaque service oriented information system architectures.

Techno-organizational gestalts and the manageability of banks in late neoliberalism

The origins of the idea of Service Oriented Architecture (SOA) can be traced back to the first phases of the development of database systems in the late 1960s. David Gugerli, in Chapter 5 of this volume, referred to Edgar Codd's contribution to the development of databases as organizational technologies. Codd insisted that the use of large data banks must be made possible by external representations that have to differ from their internal representation and especially from the way data is organized in the machine. This approach has immensely enabled the development and the management of systems comprising a plethora of functionalities – corresponding to a number of services to customers, as well as services delivered between banks or between departments and divisions within a bank. The philosophy of database design, and especially of relational databases, led – in large service-oriented organizations – to what we call N-tier system architectures. N-tier architectures allow system designers to make database structures independent from the structural features of representations at the level of end-user interfaces.[25] These congenial solutions also have the advantage that they do not block the possibilities of mapping the one level onto the other. However, in spite of solutions that could be designed in this direction, the complexity of banks' information infrastructures remained a problem. Lack of transparency of the internal organization of databases and at the level of the organization of end-user interfaces, often due to the large number of applications at the system-software, and middleware and end-user levels, is always a source of acute problems of manageability.

SOA adoption projects, which multiplied in the first decade of the 2000s, have been very important in this respect. They introduced methods for bringing order to heterogeneous and messy systems. Their advantage was the possibility of finding short-term solutions corresponding to business objectives and to short-term needs for shaping and delivering services. Technically, this was possible through search and reconfiguration procedures, or through pattern recognition mechanisms enabling the retrieval of the relevant sets of information that could be made useful by the various teams responsible for products and services. But SOAs have been important also for an additional reason: every area of functionalities, especially in banks that have behind them at least three decades of computerization, relies on the successive layers of information system development that leave their traces behind. These remnants of the multifaceted history of systems, which sometimes include components assembled for the first time as early as in the late 1960s, compose a heterogeneous farm of technologies. It is not rare for IT specialists and operations managers to come upon an environment of objects corresponding to different generations of programming languages, of artefacts bringing to light almost forgotten technologies and old-fashioned philosophies of system configurations (Pan and Viña 2004). Data and software, originating in past and disconnected layers of the various phases of the history of the system, cannot easily be replaced by new components. Many system-modules, however obsolete, often programmed with Assembler or COBOL, must be kept in operation as long as they can run. They often continue to be of critical operational importance and thus have to be pulled into and made useful in configurations of software-modules at a later point in time. Rewriting applications, as was done in the late 1970s and 1980s when for performance reasons operating systems had to be changed, is impossible even for purely quantitative reasons. Systems at this stage encompassed a much smaller number of applications (also because of the smaller number of financial products and services, or because of smaller networks) and the younger age of the systems implied fewer layers and lower levels of heterogeneity. In systems with a longer, multifaceted history the viable solution is not replacement, but reusability by handling modularized application sets as data. This application agnostic approach enables switches between aggregation and disaggregation. It also enables the reconfiguration of modules that are considered to be useful in every specific situation. Capacity pressures also make necessary a change from push- to pull-technology approaches. SOAs deliver the platforms for solution in this direction.

As Baskerville et al. (2010) point out, it is very difficult to change and integrate the intractable legacy systems of banks without connecting and incorporating new functionalities in the existing IT environments. Closed architectures and silo-like segmentation of parts of the information infrastructure make things even more complicated. These observations lead Baskerville et al. to discuss, on the basis of case studies from banks, the importance of SOAs as prominent means of macro-managing information systems. As they remark, SOAs are built around the notion that the services will be mapped out onto business functions. SOAs make even obsolete applications reusable through their repackaging in new functionalities. The crux here is achieving business-process modelling combined with object-oriented design and the exploitation of distributed intelligence and network resources (Papazoglou and Georgakopoulos 2003). The interesting thing here is that the business processes in this context are not discursively elaborated from a business perspective, and the informational depositories and the mechanisms of their exploitation are not discursively elaborated from a technical perspective. What we get is a hybrid of business, organizational and technical language that does not really pay tribute to its origins, but reifies all its ingredients by creating a distinct level of perception.

These organizational solution-technologies have not appeared out of the blue. They are definitely a response to perceptions of complexity and to risks related to the unmanageability of large information systems. They are also the outcome of the interplay between a risk management culture and a regulatory culture leading to instruments of assessment and compliance. The originators of this culture can be named. They are the powerful investment banks and the rating agencies. Legislators have submitted to their pressure, not solely as a result of lobbying, but also for purely functional reasons. In a political-economic environment where not only leverage but also sovereign debt depend on speedy trading, evaluation of assets is crucial. This applies not only to financial instruments but also to organizations as well. In this environment it must be possible to swiftly correlate profiles of organizations with shareholder value, otherwise their leverage in disintermediated capital markets will be disadvantaged. This can apply also to their technological or information systems. From the moment information systems are considered as part of the operational underlay of shareholder value, there arises a need for an uncomplicated way to profile them without having to enter into extremely time-consuming procedures. Workflow analysis is a possible means of representation. This has been applied in cases where the aim was to combine ritualistic compliance with regulatory measures with the formalization and standardization of diagrammatic representations of techno-organizational processes. An example of this is the use of workflow techniques for representing the internal reporting and techno-organizational processes imposed upon banks and other financial organizations that are obliged to comply with the technical requirements of the Sarbanes-Oxley Act.[26] This combination of regulatory regimes with representational regimes is quintessential to an understanding of organizational technologies as a consequence of the transformation of financial markets. But in contrast these network-topology oriented approaches, configurations of business processes, as they appear and are handled with SOAs, offer significant advantages for those who want to make easy evaluations and quick decisions.

Management by covering complexities with systems of black boxes could deliver better results in cases where there is pressure for compliance with regulatory measures on the basis of external appearances and simplified ratings. This management of the interplay between risk perception and compliance with service oriented architectures can lead to a stronger intransparency than in the case of black boxes. The use of models for the valuation of assets can also, in certain cases, have this effect. In the case of 'black-boxing' we have contexts of macro-management that dictate the contexts of micro-management (see MacKenzie in this volume). What then prevails is a pressure to deliver results by reporting only on outputs and not on the internal workings of the black boxes, that define their content. It is important here to bear in mind that this implies a sense of difference between the objects of the context of macro-management and the objects of the content of micro-management. However, in the case of certain practices in finance, and in their techno-organizational translation, especially when SOAs or valuation and hedging models are used, we can observe a tendency towards not thinking about such differences. If the recursive relationships between context and content are transubstantiated into ontological frames that bracket out these encompassed relations between overarching context and underlying content, then we get gestalts.

Techno-organizational gestalts, such as contextual frames for the delivery of services and risk hedging that bracket out in this manner the perception of recursive relationships between context and content, are characteristic of the late phase of neoliberalism. Managers and regulators judge from external appearances. They avoid, more frequently than not, using correlates with underlying processes. They treat the appearances as if they were the real substance. This attitude originates to a great extent in economic theories of markets that abstract from processes of coordination, and in social-psychological mechanisms that shape the marketplaces. The idea permeating these theories – that there are no individual actors, but only aggregate actors' behaviours that make markets appear as configurations of functional entities – is transferred also to organizations. Organizations are viewed as having only external functional articulations and no internal social, political and technological life. Consequently it suffices to take these into consideration without bothering about whether the pertinent judgements are related to contextual parameters or, alternatively, to the content of action shaped at a lower systemic level. Appearances matter more and these give value to, or devalue, assets within markets – or give market-relevant ratings to organizations.

But what is a gestalt, really? If we want to be more precise we must get a bit more philosophical. The term originates in philosophical foundations of certain streams of early twentieth century psychology. Gestalts are wholes that render the elements they unify dependent upon existing in consort with the qualities that enable this unification. The perception is thus detached from the underlying elements, even if we sense their existence as a set of distinct units. Though we may sense that various elements have been combined or juxtaposed, in physical or virtual spatio-temporal settings, no perception of the various components can be differentiated from the perception of the whole. In metaphorical terms, we can say that there are situations in which our mind is prone to do a reverse-engineering of what could have been the application of our potential for analysing things through their decomposition. Applying this potential would mean fragmenting ontologies, whereas when we are overwhelmed by a gestalt we tend to defragment ontological spaces and unify them into one entity that gives us the ontological security we need for further cognitive operations. This defragmentation and unification of ontological spaces, then, defines also our sensory perception. Gestalts can redefine the perception of the qualities of underlying elements. But they can also reshape the wholes as they change the modalities of the abstraction of the parts. The intentional moment that leads to gestalt-based perception does not involve control of the parts, or counter-control of the whole from the perspective of the parts. Rather, it involves controlling the whole by exorcising its underlying qualities and by naming instead its aggregate qualities.[27] These aggregate qualities are then brought into connection with criteria and systems of evaluation. Gestalts have in this sense a high representational value that allows us to feel good with underlying complexities, and have no problems with evading these.[28]

SOAs create gestalt-like techno-organizational ontologies. But the same can be said, under certain conditions, of derivatives. Both SOAs and derivatives can be regarded as techno-organizational gestalts. Financial derivatives models can be techno-organizational gestalts in the sense that they can keep their operational value by hiding their underlying operations, such as those related to arbitrage. For many of those who accommodate a perception of these objects in their world of emotions, there can be no intentionality giving meaning to the differentiation between internal and external domains of qualities, as in the case of black-boxing. In the cases where agents view objects as black boxes, the sense of the difference between the external and the internal view does not vanish, despite the psychological repression of the anxieties that may be caused by the prospect of looking into the internal qualities. In the case of gestalt-oriented perception, even if we try to look at the separate constituent elements, these do not acquire ontological qualities that can be differentiated from those deriving from the contextual embeddedness of the whole. If we are trapped in a gestalt, going deeper into the black box will not change our perspective. If objects and mechanisms that could potentially alter our perspective come in our way, we tend to ignore them; we do not posses the ability to perceive them. We suffer from blindness even to the idea that there is something that can be unbundled. This does not apply to the way financial engineers and traders see derivatives; but there are other agents in the financial markets who take a gestalt approach to financial instruments. For instance we could say that investors who do not come into direct contact with traders, and perceive derivatives and the fluctuations of their market value from rating indexes, may suffer from this kind of gestalt-induced blindness to underlying processes. Regulators can suffer from the same condition if they reduce all possible qualities of organizations to the qualities of the profiles of their portfolios.[29]

Although the complexities and techno-organizational risks discussed in this and in the previous sections of this chapter all have to do with organizational articulations of neoliberalism, it does not hold that in all phases of neoliberalism we have had this orientation to external appearances and techno-organizational gestalts. These have not always constituted the main aspect of the shaping of the organizational technologies of banking and finance. Techno-organizational stances did not remain constant throughout the whole period defined by financial deregulation, the liberalization of the markets and the removal of geographical barriers as a result of globalization. Models of management and their techno-organizational side have undergone far-reaching changes since the late 1960s. In particular, the connection between techno-organizational philosophies and shareholder value of both financial and real-economy enterprises was radically redefined in the late 1990s when financialization of business models prevailed. Focus on organizational matters as a main aspect of shareholder value is an aspect of the first phase of the neoliberal era starting from the late 1970s. Ideas such as total quality management and anthropocentric management became a key aspect in the discussion on competitive parity and advantage. The main idea was that return on investment can primarily result from business models relying on the quest for the maximization of the quality of operations. This meant also that managers could best trade the products and services delivered by their enterprises by not neglecting activities aiming at the improvement of these enterprises' internal environments. Entrepreneurship was thus regarded as something different from financial speculation. This entrepreneurial attitude had a significant impact on the qualitative aspects of the business models of banks. From the moment markets were liberalized and a wide range of products and services could be offered to their customers, profitability and asset-liability accounting had to be related to organizational patterns. The techno-organizational development of banking and finance in this phase was a result of this perspective. Although this did not create top-management mentalities, it nevertheless created a set of competencies for middle and lower management and a wide range of corresponding consultancy activities and IT services.[30]

With the progress of financialization, attitudes to techno-organizational matters started shifting. In the total quality management (TQM) and business process reengineering (BPR) movement the quality of back offices and middle offices in combination with the quality of services at points of sale was supposed to constitute a strong factor influencing both competitive parity and competitive advantages. But the growing tendency to derive competitiveness form proprietary trading and multilayered leverage had made the approaches to techno-organizational matters increasingly dependent on the whims of the financial engineers and of the rating agencies. Consequently the deterioration of services to the banks' customers, whose portfolios were not significant enough for the management of bubble-dependent assets, was clearly felt by the wider public. The other consequence was that although after the late 1990s the techno-organizational complexity in the back offices of branch networks and delivery channels for financial products and services (such as ATMs, web banking, mobile banking, etc.) was not growing disproportionally to the growth of transactions in retail and personal banking, this was not the case with the back offices of trading rooms. Their operations implied among other things increasingly complex contracting, clearing, settlement and custody services. It is striking that handling this growing complexity with quality oriented operations management was not regarded as a key to competitiveness. Looking at the operational backstage was not considered a priority. As long as re-leveraging could go on and bubbles were continuing to grow, operational risk, which could potentially emerge from back-office operations, was predominantly perceived as related to extraordinary events. The problems with back-office complexity were not made very apparent in the dot.com bubble. Their devastating significance was revealed, as already discussed in the introduction, when the subprime bubble burst. These are important images for an understanding of the shifting landscapes of neoliberalism's techno-organizational complexity. They also pave the way for understanding the raison d'être of the techno-organizational gestalts peculiar to the late phase of neoliberalism.

Neoliberalism is usually discussed from its politico-economic or from its socio-economic side, and not from its techno-organizational side. David Harvey belongs to the few who have made an attempt to shed light on this point by putting emphasis on space–time compression as the main aspect of this link. According to Harvey (2005: 3–4), contractual relations in the marketplace aiming at the maximization of the reach and frequency of transactions threw into obscurity all other contractual dimensions of social and economic life. He connects this mechanism to the interest of key players in neoliberal political-economic settings in information and communication technologies. Technologies are according to this line of argumentation indispensable for guiding especially short-term decisions, supplanting long-term aspects of social and economic life, in the global marketplace. Space–time frames of economic processes change through this. But as we have seen from the previous chapters this is only one possible facets of the connection between neoliberalism and technologies. As we have seen technologies are not solely directly instrumental. They can be a constituent element of mindsets and organizational practices leading to the ideational or actual transformation of risk objects into objects of certainty. In this sense they do not have only instrumental value, but can be the basis for the conceptual framing of financialized operations. They can also shape the way of seeing and handling business models. This was certainly so of the techno-organizational facets of the later phase of neoliberalism, in the radical transformation of business models as a consequence of financialization.

The main aspect of neoliberal financialization on which we want to focus here is the downgrading of operating profits with parallel excessive emphasis upon the non-operating profit of enterprises. Revenues from consecutively re-traded leverage cover the commodity- or service-oriented organization of business activities. This conceptual approach has been adopted by various kinds of enterprises. Famous manufacturers like General Electric have been partly transformed into asset-management companies. In the case of banks, asset management and proprietary trading overshadowed utility banking destined for providing for the liquidity of the real economy. These references may sound strongly economistic, compared to the previous discussion of organizational issues. However these processes, beyond the devastating consequences we have experienced with the burst of the financial bubbles, also had societal and micro-social consequences that 'trickled up' to the systemic level. In this sense micro-processes resulted in macro-crises. The sociological significance of this can be found in Sennett's work on changing attitudes to work and management. The extension of this would be to discuss the contribution of the corrosion of the character of work – and, further, of the corrosion of the social dynamics of organizational sub-units – to the exposure to techno-organizational risks. What we do not realize is that late neoliberalism is a period in which the crisis is intensified because of the combination of financial bubbles with organizational bubbles that occurs in the world of finance; that is, because of growing organizational complexities surrounded by techno-organizational fog. Like financial bubbles, which can burst because of unfulfilled expectations for potential liquidity, organizational bubbles can burst because of the vanishing trust in their manageability. And just as financial bubbles can be kept inflated with further leverage, techno-organizational bubbles can be kept blown up by having managers and regulators who are not preoccupied with their potential techno-organizational risks or by believing that they possess the means for their radical mitigation. Techno-organizational gestalts are one of the main cultural expressions of this. In this context abstract machines are set up as constructs that can be disconnected from network topologies. Network topologies in their turn are set up as if they could be detached from physical or virtual places (i.e. from dense fields of social-network interactions), breeding organizational accidents. If we are interested in organizational accidents, looking only at the surface of network structures – or, even worse, seeing complex techno-organizational processes from a gestalt perspective – can be a main source of problems of manageability. Hedging complexities with gestalts, as in the case of SOAs or in the case of valuation-model-based organizational solution technologies, does not seem to be a viable perspective for a post-credit crunch world of financial intermediation. Bringing back techno-organizational worth (as was the vision of many organizational theories) will definitely significantly more controllable those risks to which the organizational bases of our economies are exposed., As Charles Perrow argues in his recent studies on organizational vulnerabilities (Perrow 2007), this is probably almost impossible without breaking huge structures into smaller and less tightly coupled ones. Challenges related to the limits of intellectual capacities, personal integrity and stamina of those who take the responsibility of managing banks can be of decisive importance. But representational regimes matter as well. Neoliberalism has brought about representational regimes that dramatically reduce the manageability of corporations, and especially of banks, as techno-organizational entities.

This issue of techno-organizational worth is related to more fundamental issues of political theory that might be usefully taken into consideration in discussing the impact of financial markets on organizational technologies. To paraphrase Alan Wolfe's reference to John Locke (Wolfe 2009: 3), organizations cope best with the fulfilment of their aims, and the avoidance of the risks that can put these in jeopardy, when no top management can take away the worth of communities of practice, or when none of these communities of practice can overshadow others that make a significant contribution to the core competencies of the organization. These technological systems are uncontrollable without local reflexivity and subsequent local expressivity. Somebody has to tell the stories in order to make them known. The shrinking of organizational discourses of bankers into a grand financial narrative of proprietary trading, with the purpose of enabling action adapted to the originate-to-distribute model of credit intermediation, is not the appropriate way to avoid techno-organizational collapse. What makes these systems, of which bankers have made themselves the leaders, unmanageable is that it gets increasingly difficult to know how backward- and forward-linkages of information are formed. It seems also that very few bankers can imagine how decisions and tasks in financial organizations can be put under a contractual umbrella of polycentric articulation serving as the compass for risk perception and risk management. In this sense it is the organizational anti-liberalism of late-neoliberal banks and financial organizations, operating at a pace dictated by derivatives trading, which creates the risks that bearers of managerial and technological roles have to cope with.

Notes

1. Problems of representations with organigraphs have been discussed by Mintzberg and Van der Heyden (1999). Questions related to the representation of organizational processes and information infrastructures open a wide field that can mobilize a variety of theoretical resources. Research on 'genres' is one of the possible directions of congenial inquiry (see as a relevant source of inspiration the contributions in Coe et al. 2002). Configurations of semantic resources that can help actors to cope with the signals and the information emerging in situations defined by techno-organizational parameters can draw our attention to other neighbouring areas of research, which can be made useful for understanding techno-organizational dynamics – such as social network analysis, semantic network analysis and analysis of narrative networks (Burt 1992; Kollock 1994; Kumbasar et al. 1994; Ahuja and Carley 1998; Wellman 2001; Viégas and Donath 2004; Castilla 2005; Wineman et al. 2009).
2. For the sociological background of this theoretical turn see Beck 1992 and Luhmann 1993. For the organizational dimensions see contributions in Hutter and Power 2005; also Reason 1997; Sparrow 2008.
3. Worries about this stance have triggered a discussion on countermeasures, as well as on the possible refinement of regulatory interventions, which takes into consideration the internal processes defining the features of financial infrastructures. For an approach developed by the research staff of the Bank of England, which puts issues of governance in the foreground, see Allen et al. 2006.
4. Koch's views on operational risk are typical of this approach (1995: 108): 'There are many causes of earnings variability in a bank's operating policies. Some banks are relatively inefficient in controlling direct costs and employee processing errors. Banks must also absorb losses due to employee and customer theft. Operating risk refers to the possibility that operating expenses might vary significantly from what is expected, producing a decline in net income and firm value. A bank's operating risk is thus closely related to its burden, number of divisions or subsidiaries, and number of employees.

Because operating performance depends on the technology a bank uses, the success in controlling this risk depends on whether a bank's system of delivering products and services is efficient and functional. Most banks have in-house support systems that provide check-clearing and cash settlement services. Other banks farm these services out to third-party vendors such as IBM and EDS'. And further (Koch 1995: 122): 'Operational risk refers to the cost efficiency of the bank's activities. The measures indicated represents expense control or productivity. Typical ratios focus on total assets per employee or total personnel expense per employee. There is no meaningful way to estimate the likelihood of fraud or other contingencies from published data'. Or in Hempel et al. (1994: 88): 'Operational risk, sometimes called burden risk, is the ability of the bank to deliver its financial services in a profitable manner. Both the ability to deliver services and the ability to control the overhead associated with such delivery are important elements'.

5. According to the Basel Committee on Banking Supervision (2004: 144), operational risk is the risk of loss resulting from 'inadequate or failed internal processes, people and systems or from external events [including] legal risk'. In this sense, as Tarullo (2008: 28) points out, 'the current notion of operational risk includes everything from the physical disruption of bank's operations by natural or human agents to a massive liability judgement entered against the bank'. Although this concept refers in a vague manner to organizational issues, its translation into the language of organizational theorists and into the language of those designing and implementing operations and information infrastructures remains unaccomplished. The same problem face also the ones who seek to control information infrastructures with efficient techno-organizational forensics.
6. On the inherent difficulties of attempts to match potential harm from operational risk exposure with capital adequacy, see Chernobai and Yildirim 2008.
7. In many situations in organizations persuasion depends on the presentation of diagrams or the dissemination of methods based on diagrams the staff can effectively work with. The application of instructional design to facilitate the dissemination of knowledge and skills, or to raise operational efficiency, is not rare in organizational settings. Although inscription devices have been more thoroughly studied, especially in ethnomethodologically inspired laboratory studies, expression devices in the form of diagrams that can be used for rhetorical purposes by managers are not a central topic in the studies of processes of information system development, management and organizational design. Most studies are concentrated in the field of *sensu stricto* technological design and engineering (Henderson 1998). Of course 'genre studies' can offer useful conceptual frameworks, but even these do not really help us to go to the heart of the problem. For the cognitive dimensions see Larkin and Simon 1987. For the link between instructional design and diagrammatic rhetoric see Branch 1996.
8. The connection between academic or quasi-academic expertise and the ERP business has been studied from various perspectives by Pollock and Williams (2009: 50). As they characteristically remark, 'the organizational software packages follow a complex trajectory, shaped by their history and the strategy of a range of players – suppliers, organizational users, consultants and, increasingly, industry analysts'. On ERPs, see also Kallinikos

2004a. A more fragmented world of connections between expertise and techno-organizational dynamics appears in the material included in the empirical research by Fincham et al. (1994), conducted at a time when pressures for standardization and dependence on external IT providers seemed to be less acute. On the dependence of internal technological developments in organizations on external and standardized expertise, see D'Adderio 2004. Also Darr and Talmud 2003; Håkanson 2007. On the role of the consultancies as knowledge producers: Werr and Stjernberg 2003; Pozzebon et al. 2006.

9. The work of Serge Moscovici on social representations can be used as the basis for this discussion (Moscovici 2001). Science, and especially post-Galilean or post-Cartesian science, tries to make the familiar unfamiliar in order to make it operational through a symbolic language (mathematical or quasi-mathematical). However technological representations make the scientific representations the instrument of re-familiarization, by allowing us to work with these, and this is also the importance of diagrammatic representations and the metaphors these mobilize. These processes of re-familiarization are, however, socially differentiated in organizations because of the segregation of bearers of local or tacit knowledge.
10. For the connection between metaphors and textual agency as the basis for the creation of representations see Cooren 2004. Cooren focuses on propositional representations that can be of crucial importance for managerial and generally for organizational processes, but his analysis may also be used as a basis for finding the homologies to diagrammatic representations. On the relationship between propositional and diagrammatic representations: Stenning 2002. See also Katz et al. 1998.
11. Information stocks are reservoirs of promises, whereas through information flows the resources for the fulfilment of these promises are connected. Financial engineering focuses on one of the two main kinds of information stocks, namely financial instruments as dynamic information stocks, and thus does not pay attention to the other, which comprises databases that always depend on search engines and thus institute the main problem of information infrastructure. Searching, finding, reporting, authorizing, formulating policies and customizing policies, are however critical aspects of banking without which data and information stocks (and, for that matter, dynamic information stocks) lose their meaning as parts of transactions.
12. Although these stocks and flows are mostly made technologically visible, there are situations of breakdown that shift the view to social and perhaps also micro-political aspects. Modes of use of the instruments for representating information stocks and flows can bring about a similar situation, as in the case of reflexive uses of models and instruments. See Stark 2009, also Beunza and Stark 2009. To the extent that these processes are regarded as depending on social constructivism, the limits are set by the internalization of external representations that make organizational sub-units dependent upon ideational factors stemming from the wider context in which they are embedded (see Kallinikos 2004b).
13. Others have used neural networks for such representations, but most of these are applied to inter-organizational rather than intra-organizational

networks. For an example of the use of neural networks-based representations for the analysis of financial processes: McNelis 2005.

14. Compare with Hitt et al. (1999). They discuss technological decision making in banking and finance.
15. The distinction between push and pull technologies corresponds to the difference with the difference between push and pull operations. Push operations require knowledge of the addresses of destinations of goods or packages of information, whereas pull operations require the creation of patterns of search, and then the exploitation of depositories. This presupposes the creation of depositories in advance through push operations that send to the right place the elements that will constitute stocks. Push operations can be more easily automated and embedded in server functionalities aiming at the automatic or quasi-automatic distribution of information. Pull technologies, because they depend on pattern definition and then on pattern recognition, require higher levels of reflexivity and thus a higher level of discourse robustness of information systems. Pull technologies are the main driver of informatization as opposed to automation in the sense of Zuboff 1998.
16. The idea of hypothetical contracts can be traced back to the Kantian discussion of the regulative employment of the ideas of pure reason. The idea was then revisited in Hans Vaihinger's and also in Charles Sanders Peirce's work. On the application of related ideas about regulation and risk management, see Power 2007: 183–203.
17. The problem of standardization has been discussed in connection to legal formalism and proceduralism and its implications for the creation of dysfunctional conditions (Bardach and Kagan 2002). But in a more recent literature it has been related also to whistle-blowing as a typically organizational problem. As Andrew Lo has set out in his testimony before the US House of Representatives, obstructing whistle-blowing (especially when it comes from risk managers) can have devastating effects for financial organizations (Lo 2008). On whistle-blowing and organizational processes, see also De Maria 2008. These ideas can also be applied to technological whistle-blowing and techno-organizational expressivity in organizations or inter-organizational networks with complex information systems.
18. This organizational problem has already been discussed as a problem of configuring resources and information in battles, in Clausewitz's theory of war, in an astonishingly provocative way for the organizational analysts of today. He is trying to explain that in the fog of the battle, it is very difficult to control the configuration of units and their interaction with the units of the enemy. We can use metaphors and analogies stemming from these ideas, despite the differences, due mainly to the fact that 'battles' within techno-organizational systems with the aim of creating advantages from blowing asymmetric information are, to a great extent, virtual, multi front and take place in shifting configurations of micro-fields of action.
19. On this see the highly relevant discussion in Haridimos Tsoukas' book on complex knowledge (2005). See also Gareth Morgan's *Images of Organization* (1997).
20. This is also a problem for a special category of technologists who are appointed to control networks and who are closer to social network

dynamics: these are the telecommunication specialists of banks. Their work is related to techno-organizational fog in a different sense. Their role has not been discussed much and is not quite visible to either the insiders or the outsiders who try to understand banks. If the work of these specialists combines with the work of relational database specialists, and especially when it happens that they are oriented towards thinking in terms of open system architectures, then their work gets very interesting. However in the case of telecommunication specialists the problem is that they want to combine local with global durabilities – they seek to reduce entropy both at the nodes and at the level of the graph. And of course they want to maintain the lines of communication, whereas the content of the signals is the work of other specialists focusing on end-user applications. Technology becomes socially visible when there are problems at the intersection of telecommunications and end-user applications. And this can happen, not only because of technology failures but also because of reflexivity in the process of using technology or because of pressures from the external environments of demarcated groups that use technologies. Solutions, which are then needed, cannot be found through standard operating procedures or manuals. All the involved specialists must negotiate with user groups, but also under the pressure of hierarchies, 'standard setters' and providers or under the pressure of consultancy companies. National telecommunications networks can play a significant role here, and the politics involved at various levels are extremely interesting. This also means that these technological processes become visible not only from a social point of view but also from a political one (i.e. from the point of view of organizational politics but also of government policies related to the politics of telecommunications providers).

21. In reality they are three-tier hybrid systems. The first two tiers have to do with the differentiation between front- and back-office operations. The third tier has to do with design, development, monitoring (infrastructure management) and maintenance operations. In general it has to do with the differentiation between the world of users as contrasted with the world of 'engineers' (operation and/or development engineers) – between the ones who navigate the vehicles, and the ones who deal with the engines through which information is being restructured and used as a fuel for the manipulation and/or navigation in financial markets. We have a constant but shifting contradiction between discrete shaping and continuous enacting. Neural networks and fuzzy sets can be instruments of representation of these aspects of information systems. Neural networks require a set of pre-defined patterns that enable the adaptability of parts of the system. Fuzzy systems, the components of which can be described as fuzzy sets, do not require patterns but rules for the processes of potential generation of patterns. The interconnection between the two aspects causes difficulties in describing fuzzy neural networks that combine fuzziness of the approximation of 'images' with neural network techniques. There is vast literature on these issues. For a useful example see Zadeh (1994), also various more recent publications in the journal *Fuzzy Sets and Systems*.
22. This is a problem regulators are facing, which can be realized if we look at the workflows as methods of organizational auditing that have been introduced by

the Sarbanes-Oxley Act in the US and for all companies listed on the New York Stock Exchange, and which have become significant for operational risk assessment procedures.

23. For social-geographical origins of this idea and of its metaphorical use in the case of techno-organizational processes, see Agnew 2005.
24. James Reason cites the Dutch psychologists Willem Albert Wagenaar and Jop Groeneweg, who have explained: 'Accidents appear to be the result of highly complex coincidences that could rarely be foreseen by the people involved. The unpredictability is caused by the large amount of information and by the spread of information over the participants. ... Accidents do not occur because people gamble and lose, they occur because people do not believe that the accident that is about to occur is at all possible'. See Reason 1997: 39.
25. For the application of N-tier architectures in the financial services industry, see Dobbin 1999.
26. The mapping of processes onto workflows as required by the Sarbanes-Oxley Act has led to a new market for software-based tools. This has created a new category of technological gestalts that play a role in the financial world, like similar technological gestalts for the management of the compliance with Basel II regulations, with the International Accounting Standards, or with anti-money laundering procedures imposed by supervisory authorities.
27. For a presentation of the idea of 'gestalt' and of its origins in philosophy and psychology see Peterman 2007 and Smith 1996: 243–84. For an application of the concept of gestalt to software engineering, see Lemon et al. 2005.
28. ERPs and MISs have played a very important role here. They had to do with the visualization of organizations, but mainly with profitability and risk exposure. SAP for instance has developed products and services for the IASs, for Basel II and for AML (anti-money laundering). ERPs, if they are installed to meet regulatory requirements, can be viewed as techno-organizational instruments of late neoliberal re-regulation. Data warehousing and data-mining through pattern recognition is another interesting aspect of gestalt-like techno-organizational solutions.
29. Techno-organizational governance without techno-organizational forensics, as seen in the case of techno-organizational gestalts, creates short-term financial value and downgrades long-term organizational worth and capacities to manage operational risks. From the perspective of the constructors and managers of financial techno-organizational gestalts, fogginess – as discussed in this section – is a problem of the intensity of shading. The more they cannot see through, the more they transpose risks elsewhere, to virtual places where they can be managed with the use of accounting representations (McSweeney 2009). Often this is an outstanding way to make financial innovation succeed. Financial innovation aiming at enhanced leverage can be equally important to financial innovations aiming at evading regulatory pressure (Partnoy 2003).
30. This had a much greater impact on European than on US Banks. The latter were divided between commercial and investment banking officially until 1999, when the Glass-Steagall Act was officially abolished. This caused a segregation of various business streams in banking and thus created leaner organizational structures than in the case of mostly continental European models of universal banking.

Bibliography

Agnew, J. (2005), 'Space: Place', in P. Cloke and R. Johnston (eds), *Spaces of Geographical Thought*, London: Sage: 81–96.

Ahuja, M. K. and Carley, K. M. (1998), 'Network Structure in Virtual Organizations', *Journal of Computer-Mediated Communication*, 3(4), http://jcmc.indiana.edu/vol3/issue4/ahuja.html.

Akrich, M. (1992), 'The De-Scription of Technological Objects', in W. E. Bijker and J. Law (eds), *Shaping Technology/Building Society – Studies in Sociotechnical Change*, Cambridge, MA: The MIT Press: 205–24.

Allen, H., Christodoulou, G. and Millard, S. (2006), 'Financial Infrastructure and Corporate Governance', *Bank of England, Working Paper*, No.316.

Allen, P. H. (1997), *Reengineering the Bank*, New York: McGraw-Hill.

Bardach, E. and Kagan, R. A. (2002), *Going By The Book*, New Brunswick, NJ: Transaction Publishers.

Balling, M., Lierman, F. and Mullineux, A. (eds), *Technology and Finance. Challenges for Financial Markets, Business Strategies and Policy Makers*, London and New York: Routledge.

Basel Committee on Banking Supervision (2004), *Implementation of Basel II: Practical Considerations*, Bank of International Settlements, Basel.

Baskerville, R. L., Cavallari, M., Hjort-Madsen, K., Pries-Heje, J., Sorrentino, M and Virili, F. (2010), 'The Strategic Value of SOA: A Comparative Case Study in the Banking Sector', *International Journal of Information Technology and Management*, 9(1): 30–53.

Beccalli, E. (2007), *IT and European Bank Performance*, Basingstoke: Palgrave Macmillan.

Bech, M. L. and Atalay, E. (2008), 'The Topology of the Federal Funds Market', *European Central Bank, Working Paper Series*, No. 986.

Becher, C., Millard, S. and Soramäki, K. (2008), 'The Network Topology of CHAPS Sterling', *Bank of England, Working Paper*, No. 355.

Beck, U. (1992), *Risk Society – Towards a New Modernity*, London: Sage.

Beckert, J. (2009), 'The Social Order of Markets', *Theory & Society*, 38: 245–69.

Beunza, D. and Garud, R. (2007), 'Calculators, Lemmings or Frame-Makers? The Intermediary Role of Securities Analysts', in M. Callon, Y. Millo and F. Muniesa (eds): 13–39.

Beunza, D. and Stark, D. (2005), 'How to Recognize Opportunities: Heterarchical Search in a Trading Room', in K. Knorr Cetina A. and Preda (eds): 84–101.

Beunza, D. and Stark, D. (2008), 'Tools of the Trade: The Socio-Technology of Arbitrage in a Wall Street Trading Room', T. in Pinch and R. Swedberg (eds): 253–90.

Beunza, D. and Stark, D. (2009), 'Looking Out, Locking In: Financial Models and the Social Dynamics of Arbitrage Disasters', Available at SSRN, http://ssrn.com/abstract=1285054.

Branch, R. M. (1996), 'Perceptions of Instructional Design Process Models', Selected Readings form the Annual Conference of the International Visual Literacy Association, Cheyenne, Wyoming, October 1996, Retrieved on 30 January 2010 from http://www.eric.ed.gov/ERICDocs/data/ericdocs2sql/content_storage_01/0000019b/80/16/b0/db.pdf.

Boss, M., Elsinger, H., Summer, M. and Thurner, S. (2004), 'Network Topology of the Interbank Market', *Quantitative Finance*, Vol. 4, No. 6: 677–84.

Boss, M., Krenn, G., Metz, V., Puhr, C. and Schmitz, S. W. (2008), 'Systemically Important Accounts, Network Topology and Contagion in ARTIS', *Österreichische National bank, Financial Stability Report* 15.
Burt, R. S. (1992), *Structural Holes: The Social Structure of Competition*, Cambridge, MA: Harvard University Press.
Callon, M., Millo, Y. and Muniesa, F. (eds) (2007), *Market Devices*, Oxford: Blackwell.
Castilla, E. J. (2005), 'Social Networks and Employee Performance in a Call Center', *American Journal of Sociology*, 110(5): 1243–83.
Checkland, P. and Holwell, S. (1998), *Information, Systems and Information Systems: Making Sense of the Field*, Chichester: John Wiley & Sons.
Chernobai, A. and Yildirim, Y. (2008), 'The Dynamics of Operational Loss Clustering', *Journal of Banking & Finance*, 32: 2655–66.
Ciborra, C., Braa, K., Cordella, A., Dahlbom, B., Failla, A., Hanseth, O., Hespø, V., Ljungberg, J., Monteiro, E. and Simon, K. A. (2000), *From Control to Drift: The Dynamics of Corporate Information Infrastructures*, Oxford: Oxford University Press.
Ciborra, C. (2000), 'A Critical Review of the Literature on the Management of Corporate Information Infrastructure', in C. Ciborra, K. Braa, A. Cordella, B. Dahlbom, A. Failla, O. Hanseth, V. Hespø, J. Ljungberg, E. Monteiro and K. A. Simon: 15–40.
Ciborra, C. (2002), *The Labyrinth of Information: Challenging the Wisdom of Systems*, Oxford: Oxford University Press.
Clark, G. L. and Thrift, N. (2005), 'The Return of Bureaucracy: Managing Dispersed Knowledge in Global Finance', in K. Knorr Cetina and A. Preda (eds): 229–49.
Clausewitz, C. von (1991 [1832]), *Vom Kriege*, Berlin: Ullstein.
Coe, R., Lingard, L. and Teslenko, T. (eds) (2002), *The Rhetoric and Ideology of Genre*, Cresskill, NJ: Hampton Press.
Cooren, F. (2004), 'Textual Agency: How Texts Do Things in Organizational Settings', *Organization*, 11(3): 373–93.
D'Adderio, L. (2004), *Inside the Virtual Product: How Organizations Create Knowledge through Software*, Cheltenham: Edward Elgar.
Darr, A. and Talmud, L. (2003), 'The Structure of Knowledge and Seller-Buyer Networks in Markets for Emergent Technologies', *Organization Studies*, 24(3): 443–61.
Davis, G. and Robbins, G. (2005), 'Nothing but Net? Networks and Status in Corporate Governance', in K. Knorr Cetina and A. Preda (eds): 290–311.
Davis, L. N. (2001), 'R&D Investments, Information and Strategy', *Technology Analysis & Strategic Management*, 13(3): 325–42.
Day, J. (2007), 'Strangers on the Train: The Relationship of the IT Department with the Rest of the Business', *Information Technology and People*, 20(1): 6–31.
Dechow, N. and Mouritsen, J. (2005), 'Enterprise Resource Planning Systems, Management Control and the Quest for Integration', *Accounting, Organizations and Society*, 30: 691–733.
Deleuze, G. and Guattari, F. (1987), *A Thousand Plateaus: Capitalism and Schizophrenia*, Minneapolis, MN and London: University of Minnesota Press.
De Maria, W. (2008), 'Whistleblowers and Organizational Protesters – Crossing Imaginary Borders', *Current Sociology*, 56(6): 865–83.
De Masi, G. (2009), 'Empirical Analysis of the Architecture of the Interbank Market and Credit Market Using Network Theory', in A. K. Naimzada, S. Stefani, A. Torriero (eds), *Networks, Topology and Dynamics*, Berlin and Heidelberg: Springer: 241–56.

Derman, E. (2004), *My Life as a Quant: Reflections on Physics and Finance*, Hoboken, NJ: John Wiley & Sons.
Dobbin, G. (1999), 'Distributed Solutions in N-Tier Design in the Financial Services Industry', in J. Keyes (ed.): 3.1–3.9.
Dodd, R. (2002), 'The Structure of OTC Derivatives Markets', *The Financier*, 9: 1–4.
Drucker, P. F. (1972 [1946]), *Concept of the Corporation*, New York: New American Library.
Drucker, P. F. (1954), *The Practice of Management*, New York: Harper & Row.
Drucker, P. F. (1993), *The Ecological Vision: Reflections on the American Condition*, Piscataway, NJ: Transaction Publishers.
Economist, The (2009), 'Managing Banks: It Wasn't Me', 10 October.
Egusquiza, I. F. and Sastre de Miguel, T. (2003), 'The Effects of Technology on the Costs and Risks of Spanish Banks', in M. Balling, F. Lierman and A. Mullineux (eds): 68–88.
European Central Bank (2009), *Credit Default Swaps and Counterparty Risk*, Frankfurt a.M.: ECB Publications.
Fincham, R., Fleck, J., Procter, R., Scarbrough, H., Tierney, M. and Williams, R. (1994), *Expertise and Innovation: Information Technology Strategies in the Financial Services Sector*, Oxford: Clarendon Press.
Forty, A. (2000), *Objects of Desire: Design and Society Since 1750*, London: Thames & Hudson.
Frey, B. S., Benz, M. and Stutzer, A. (2004), 'Introducing Procedural Utility: Not Only What, But Also How Matters', *Journal of Institutional and Theoretical Economics*, 160: 377–401.
Fujiwara, Y., Aoyama, H., Ikeda, Y., Iyetomi, H. and Souma, W. (2009), 'Structure and Temporal Change of the Credit Network between Banks and Large Firms in Japan', *Economics e-journal*, Vol. 3, 2009–7, 16 March 2009, http://www.economics-ejournal.org/economics/journalarticles/2009–7.
Gai, P., Kapadia, S., Millard, S. and Perez, A. (2008), 'Financial Innovation, Macroeconomic Stability and Systemic Crises', *Bank of England, Working Paper*, No. 340.
Galbiati, M. and Soramäki, K. (2008), 'An Agent-Based Model of Payment Systems', *Bank of England, Working Paper*, No. 352.
Gandy, A. (2000), *Banking Strategies and Beyond 2000*, Chicago, IL; London; New Delhi: Glenlake.
Gray, P. H. (2001), 'The Impact of Knowledge Repositories on Power and Control in the Workplace', *Information Technology and People*, 14(4): 368–84.
Grover, V., Cheon, M. J. and Teng, J. T. C. (1996), 'The Effect of Service Quality and Partnership on the Outsourcing of Information Systems Functions', *Journal of Management Information Systems*, 12(4): 89–116.
Gu, Q. and Lago, P. (2009), 'Exploring Service-Oriented System Engineering Challenges: A Systematic Literature Review', *Service Oriented Computing and Applications*, 3: 171–88.
Guillén, M. F. (1994), *Models of Management: Work, Authority and Organization in Comparative Perspective*, Chicago, IL and London: The University of Chicago Pres.
Hagedoom, J. and Duysters, G. (2002), 'Learning in Dynamic Inter-Firm Networks: The Efficacy of Multiple Contacts', *Organization Studies*, 23(4): 525–48.
Håkanson, L. (2007), 'Creating Knowledge: The Power and Logic of Articulation', *Industrial and Corporate Change*, 16(1): 51–88.

Hanseth, O. (2000), 'The Economics of Standards', in C. Ciborra, K. Braa, A. Cordella, B. Dahlbom, A. Failla, O. Hanseth, V. Hespø, J. Ljungberg, E. Monteiro and K. A. Simon: 56–70.

Harvey, D. (2005), *A Brief History of Neoliberalism*, Oxford: Oxford University Press.

Hattori, M. and Suda, Y. (2007), 'Developments in a Cross-Border Bank Exposure "Network"', *Bank of Japan Working Paper Series*, No. 07–E–21.

Hempel, G. H., Simonson, D. G. and Coleman, A. B. (1994 and 2009), *Bank Management – Texts and Cases*, New York: John Wiley & Sons.

Henderson, K. (1998), *On Line and On Paper: Visual Representations, Visual Culture, and Computer Graphics in Design Engineering*, Cambridge, MA: The MIT Press.

Hirschheim, R., Klein, H. K. and Lyytinen, K. (1995), *Information Systems Development and Data Modelling: Conceptual and Psychological Foundations*, Cambridge: Cambridge University Press.

Hirschheim, R., Klein, H. K. and Lyytinen, K. (1996), 'Exploring the Intellectual Structure of Information Systems Development: A Social Action Theoretic Analysis', *Accounting, Management and Information Technologies*, 6(1/2): 1–64.

Hitt, L., Frei, F. X. and Harker, P. T. (1999), 'How Financial Firms Decide on Technology', *Brookings-Wharton Papers on Financial Services 1999*: 93–136.

Holmstrom, J. and Stalder, F. (2001), 'Drifting Technologies and Multi-Purpose Metworks: The Case of the Swedish Cashcard', *Information and Organization*, 11: 187–206.

Horvitz, P. M. and White, L. J. (2000), 'The Challenge of New Electronic Technologies in Banking: Private Strategies and Public Policies', in P. T. Harker and S. A. Zenios (eds), *Performance of Financial Institutions: Efficiency, Innovation, Regulation*, Cambridge: Cambridge University Press: 367–87.

House of Commons Treasury Committee (2009), *Banking Crisis: Regulation and Supervision*, Fourteenth Report of Session 2008–9, July 2009.

Howcroft, B. (2003), 'Consumer Behaviour and the Usage and Adoption of Remote and Direct Banking in the United Kingdom', in Balling, F. Lierman and A. Mullineux (eds): 89–111.

Howcroft, D. and Wilson, M. (2003), 'Paradoxes of Participatory Practices: The Janus Role of the Systems Developer', *Information and Organization*, 13: 1–24.

Hutter, B. and Power, M. (eds) (2005), *Organizational Encounters with Risk*, Cambridge: Cambridge University Press.

Iori, G., De Masi, G., Precup, O. V., Gabbi, G. and Caldarelli, G. (2007), 'A Network Analysis of the Italian Overnight Money Market', *Journal of Economic Dynamics & Control*, 32(1): 259–78.

Jackson, J. P. and Manning, M. J. (2007), 'Comparing the Pre-Settlement Risk Implications of Alternative Clearing Arrangements', *Bank of England, Working Paper*, No. 321.

Jarzabkowski, P. (2004), 'Strategy as Practice: Recursiveness, Adaptation, and Practices-In-Use', *Organization Studies*, 25(4): 529–60.

Kallinikos, J. (2004a), 'Deconstructing Information Packages: Organizational and Behavioural Implication of ERP Systems', *Information Technology and People*, 17(1): 8–30.

Kallinikos, J. (2004b), 'Farewell to Constructivism: Technology and Context-Embedded Action', in C. Avgerou, C. Ciborra and F. Land (eds), *The Social Study of Information and Communication Technology*, Oxford: Oxford University Press: 140–61.

Kallinikos, J. (2006), *The Consequences of Information: Institutional Implications of Technological Change*, Cheltenham: Edward Elgar.

Kalthoff, H. (2005), 'Practices of Calculation: Economic Representations and Risk Management', *Theory, Culture & Society*, 22(2): 69–97.

Karatani, K. (1995), *Architecture as Metaphor*, Cambridge, MA: The MIT Press.

Katz, A. N., Cacciari, C., Gibbs, R. W. and Turner, M. (1998), *Figurative Language and Thought*, New York, Oxford: Oxford University Press.

Kauko, K. (2007), 'Interlinking Securities Settlement Systems: A Strategic Commitment?', *Journal of Banking & Finance*, 31: 2962–77.

Kellogg, K. C., Orlikowski, W. J. and Yates, J. (2003), 'Enacting New Ways of Organizing: Exploring the Activities and Consequences of Post-Industrial Work', *MIT Sloan School of Management, Working Paper*, No. 4321–3.

Keyes, J. (ed.) (1999), *Handbook of Technology in Financial Services*, Boca Raton, FL: Auerbach.

Kim, H., Iijima, J. and Ho, S. (2005), 'A Framework for Analysis of Systems Failure in Information Systems Integration', *IEMS*, Vol. 4(2): 207–17.

Knorr Cetina, K. (2005), 'How are Global Markets Global? The Architecture of a Flow World', in K. Knorr Cetina and A. Preda (eds): 38–61.

Knorr Cetina K. and Bruegger, U. (2002), 'Inhabiting Technology: The Global Lifeform of Financial Markets', *Current Sociology*, 50(3): 389–405.

Knorr Cetina, K. and Grimpe, B. (2008), 'Global Financial Technologies: Scoping Systems That Raise the World', in T. Pinch and R. Swedberg (eds): 161–89.

Knorr Cetina, K. and Preda, A. (eds) (2005), *The Sociology of Financial Markets*, Oxford: Oxford University Press.

Knorr Cetina, K. and Preda, A. (2007), 'The Temporalization of Financial Markets: From Network to Flow', *Theory, Culture & Society* 2007, 24(7–8): 116–38.

Koch, T. W. (1995 and 2009), *Bank Management*, Fort Worth, TX: The Dryden Press.

Kollock, P. (1994), 'The Emergence of Exchange Structures: An Experimental Study of Uncertainty, Commitment, and Trust', *American Journal of Sociology*, 100(2): 313–45.

Kolodinsky, J., Hogarth, J. M. and Shue, J. F. (2000), 'Bricks or Clicks? Consumers' Adoption of Electronic Banking Technologies', *Consumer Interests Annual*, 46: 180–4.

Köppl. T. V. and Monnet, C. (2007), 'Guess What: It's the Settlements! Vertical Integration as a Barrier to Efficient Exchange Consolidation', *Journal of Banking & Finance*, 31: 3013–33.

Kumbasar, E., Rommey, A. K. and Batchelder, W. H. (1994), 'Systematic Biases in Social Perception', *American Journal of Sociology*, 100(2): 477–505.

Kyrtsis, A-. A. (2005), 'Context-Aware Uses of Information Technologies and Technophobia', in G. Kouzelis, M. Pournari, M. Stöppler and V. Tselfes (eds), *Knowledge in the New Technologies*, Frankfurt a.M.: Lang: 71–88.

Kyrtsis, A-. A. (2008a), 'Software Design Processes: A Note on Micro-Sociological Perspectives', in A. Bammé, G. Getzinger and B. Wieser (eds), *Yearbook 2007 of the Institute of Advanced Studies on Science, Technology and Society*, München-Wien: Profil Verlag: 193–223.

Kyrtsis, A-. A. (2008b), *National Bank of Greece – Technology and Organization 1950–2000*, Publications of the Historical Archives of the National Bank of Greece, Athens (In Greek).

Lacoste, Y. (1976), *La Géographie, ça Sert, d'abord, à Faire la Guerre*, Paris: Maspero.

Larkin, J. H. and Simon, H. A. (1987), 'Why a Diagram is (Sometimes) Worth Ten Thousand Words', *Cognitive Science*, 11: 65–99.
Lemon, K., Allen, E. B., Carver, J. and Bradshaw, G. (2005), 'Gestalt Principles Applied To Software Engineering Diagrams: An Initial Study', 5th ACM-IEEE International Symposium on Empirical Software Engineering – Vol II: Short Papers and Posters: 48–50.
Lethbridge, T. C., Elliott Sim, S. and Singer, J. (2005), 'Studying Software Engineers: Data Collection Techniques for Software Field Studies', *Empirical Software Engineering*, 10: 311–41.
Lépinay, V-. A. (2007), 'Parasitic Formulae: The Case of Capital Guarantee Products', in M. Callon, Y. Millo and F. Muniesa (eds): 261–83.
Lin, Z., Zhao, X., Ismail, K. M. and Carley, K. M. (2006), 'Organizational Design and Restructuring in Response to Crises: Lessons from Computational Modeling and Real-World Cases', *Organization Science*, 17(5): 598–618.
Linstead, S. and Thanem, T. (2007), 'Multiplicity, Virtuality and Organization: The Contribution of Gilles Deleuze', *Organization Studies*, 28(10): 1483–501.
Llewellyn, D. T. (2003), 'Technology and the New Economics of Banking: A UK Perspective', in M. Balling, F. Lierman and A. Mullineux (eds): 51–67.
Lo, A. W. (2008), 'Hedge Funds, Systemic Risk, and the Financial Crisis of 2007–2008', Written Testimony of Andrew W. Lo – Prepared for the US House of Representatives Committee on Oversight and Government Reform, 13 November 2008, Hearing on Hedge Funds.
Luhmann, N. (1993), *Risk – A Sociological Theory*, New Brunswick, NJ: Transaction Publishers.
Luneborg, J. L. and Nielsen, J. F. (2003), 'Customer-Focused Technology and Performance in Small and Large Banks', *European Management Journal*, Vol. 21(2): 258–69.
McGrath, K. (2006), 'Affection Not Affliction: The Role of Emotions in Information Systems and Organizational Change', *Information and Organization*, 16: 277–303.
MacKenzie, A. (2005), 'The Performativity of Code: Software and Cultures of Circulation', *Theory, Culture and Society*, 22(1): 71–92.
MacKenzie, D. (2005), 'How the Superportfolio Emerges: Long-Term Capital Management and the Sociology of Arbitrage', in K. Knorr Cetina and A. Preda (eds): 62–83.
MacKenzie, D. (2006), *An Engine, Not a Camera: How Financial Models Shape Markets*, Cambridge, MA: The MIT Press.
Matthews, C. and Tripe, D. (2004), 'Bank Computing in a Changing Economic Environment: The IBIS Project in New Zealand', *Accounting, Business & Financial History*, 14(3): 301–15.
Mayer, M. (1997), *The Bankers – The Next Generation*, New York: Truman Talley Books.
McMahon, M., Sterne, G. and Thompson, J. (2005), 'The Role of ICT in the Global Investment Cycle', *Bank of England, Working Paper*, No. 257.
McNelis, P. D. (2005), *Neural Networks in Finance: Gaining Predictive Edge in the Market*, Burlington, MA: Academic Press.
McSweeney, B. (2009), 'The Roles of Financial Asset Market Failure Denial and the Economic Crisis: Reflections on Accounting and Financial Theories and Practices', *Accounting, Organizations & Society*, 34(6/7): 835–48.

Merrouche, O. and Nier, E. (2009), 'Payment Systems, Inside Money and Financial Intermediation', *Bank of England, Working Paper*, No. 371.

Merrouche, O. and Schanz, J. (2009), 'Banks' Intraday Liquidity Management During Operational Outages: Theory and Evidence from the UK Payment System', *Bank of England, Working Paper*, No. 370.

Metcalfe, M. (2002), 'Argumentative Systems for IS Design', *Information Technology & People*, 15(1): 60–73.

Millo, Y. (2007), 'Making Things Deliverable: The Origins of Index-Based Derivatives', in M. Callon, Y. Millo and F. Muniesa (eds): 215–40.

Milne, A. (2007), 'The Industrial Organization of Post-Trade Clearing and Settlement', *Journal of Banking & Finance*, 31: 2945–61.

Mintzberg, H. and Van der Heyden, L. (1999), 'Organigraphs: Drawing How Companies Really Work', *Harvard Business Review*, September–October: 87–94.

Monteiro, E. (2000), 'Actor-Network Theory and Information Infrastructure', in C. Ciborra, K. Braa, A. Cordella, B. Dahlbom, A. Failla, O. Hanseth, V. Hespø, J. Ljungberg, E. Monteiro and K. A. Simon: 71–83.

Morgan, G. (1997), *Images of Organization*, Thousand Oaks, CA; London; New Delhi: Sage.

Morgan, G. and Sturdy, A. (2000), *Beyond Organisational Change: Structure, Discourse and Power in the UK Financial Services*. London: Macmillan.

Morton, S. C., Dainty, A. R. J., Burns, N. D., Brookes, N. J. and Backhouse, C. J. (2006), 'Managing Relationships to Improve Performance: A Case Study in the Global Aerospace Industry', *International Journal of Production Research*, 44(16): 3227–41.

Moscovici, S. (2001), *Social Representations – Explorations in Social Psychology*, New York: New York University Press.

Muniesa, F. (2008), 'Trading-Room Telephones and the Identification of Counterparts', in T. Pinch and R. Swedberg (eds): 291–313.

Nagurney, A. and Siokos, S. (1997), *Financial Networks: Statics and Dynamics*, Berlin: Springer.

Nagurney, A. and Ke, K. (2003), 'Financial Networks with Electronic Transactions: Modeling, Analysis and Computations', *Quantitative Finance*, 3: 71–87.

Nagurney, A. and Qiang, Q. (2008), 'A Network Efficiency Measure with Applicatito Critical Infrastructure Networks', *Journal of Global Optimization*, 40(1–3): 261–75.

Narula, R. (2001), 'Choosing Between Internal and Non-internal R&D Activities: Some Technological and Economic Factors', *Technology Analysis & Strategic Management*, 13(3): 365–87.

Nicolaou, A. I. (1999), 'Social Control in Information Systems Development', *Information Technology and People*, 12(2): 130–47.

Nier, E., Yang, J., Yorulmazer, T. and Alentorn, A. (2008), 'Network Models and Financial Stability', *Bank of England, Working Paper*, No. 346.

Orlikowski, W. J. and Barley, S. R. (2001), 'Technology and Institutions: What CanResearch on Information Technology and Research on Organizations Learn from Each Other?', *MIS Quarterly*, 25(2): 145–65.

Pan, A. and Viña, Á. (2004), 'An Alternative Architecture for Financial Data Integration', *Communications of the ACM*, 47(5): 37–40.

Papazoglou, M. P. and Georgakopoulos, D. (2003), 'Service-Oriented Computing', *Communications of the ACM*, 46(10): 25–8.

Partnoy, F. (2003), *Infectious Greed – How Deceit and Greed Corrupted the Financial Markets*, New York: Holt.
Perrow, C. (1999), *Normal Accidents: Living With High-Risk Technologies*, Princeton, NJ: Princeton University Press.
Perrow, C. (2007), *The Next Catastrophe – Reducing Our Vulnerabilities to Natural, Industrial, and Terrorist Disasters*, Princeton, NJ and Oxford: Princeton University Press.
Peterman, B. (2007), *The Gestalt Theory and the Problem of Configuration*, London: Koteliansky Press.
Peters, S. C. A., Heng, M. S. H. and Vet, R. (2002), 'Formation of the Information Systems Strategy in a Global Financial Services Company', *Information and Organization*, 12: 19–38.
Pinch, T. and Swedberg, R. (2008), *Living in a Material World: Economic Sociology Meets Science and Technology Studies*, Cambridge, MA: The MIT Press.
Pollock, N. and Williams, R. (2007), 'Technology Choice and its Performance: Towards a Sociology of Software Package Procurement', *Information and Organization*, 17: 131–61.
Pollock, N. and Williams, R. (2009), *Software and Organisations: The Biography of the Enterprise-Wide System or How SAP Conquered the World*, London and New York: Routledge.
Pollock, N., Williams, R. and Procter, R. (2003), 'Fitting Standard Software Packages to Non-standard Organizations: The "Biography" of an Enterprise-Wide System', *Technology Analysis & Strategic Management*, 15(3): 317–32.
Poon, M. (2007), 'Scorecards as Devices for Consumer Credit: The Case of Fair, Isaac & Company Incorporated', in M Callon, Y. Millo and F. Muniesa (eds): 284–306.
Power, M. (2005a), 'The Invention of Operational Risk', *Review of International Political Economy*, 12(4): 577–99.
Power, M. (2005b), 'Enterprise Risk Management and the Organization of Uncertainty in Financial Institutions', in K. Knorr Cetina and A. Preda (eds): 250–68.
Power, M. (2007), *Organized Uncertainty: Designing a World of Risk Management*, Oxford, Oxford University Press.
Pozzebon, M., Titah, R. and Pinsonneault, A. (2006), 'Combining Social Shaping Oftechnology and Communicative Action Theory for Understanding Rhetorical Closure in IT', *Information Technology & People*, 19(3): 244–71.
Preda, A. (2007), 'Where Do Analysts Come From? The Case of Financial Chartism', in M. Callon, Y. Millo and F. Muniesa (eds): 40–64.
Preda, A. (2008), 'Technology, Agency, and Financial Price Data', in T. Pinch and R. Swedberg (eds): 217–252.
Reason, J. (1997), *Managing the Risks of Organizational Accidents*, Aldershot: Ashgate.
Rescher, N. (2005), *Cognitive Harmony: The Role of Systemic Harmony in the Constitution of Knowledge*, Pittsburgh, PA: University of Pittsburgh Press.
Sassen, S. (2005), 'The Embeddedness of Electronic Markets: The Case of Global Capital Markets', in K. Knorr Cetina and A. Preda (eds): 17–37.
Saunders, C., Gebelt, M. and Hu, Q. (1997), 'Achieving Success in Information Systems Outsourcing', *California Management Review*, 39(2): 63–79.
Scott, S. V. (2000), 'IT-Enabled Credit Risk Modernisation: A Revolution Under the Cloak of Normality', *Accounting, Management and Information Technology*, 10: 221–55.

Schwarz, G. M. (2002), 'Organizational Hierarchy Adaptation and Information Technology', *Information and Organization*, 12: 153–82.

Sennett, R. (1998), *The Corrosion of Character*, New York and London: W. W. Norton.

Sennett, R. (2006), *The Culture of the New Capitalism*, New Haven, CT and London: Yale University Press.

Seyman, M. R. (ed.) (1998), *Managing the New Bank Technology: An Executive Blueprint for the Future*, Chicago, IL: Glenlake.

Sinclair, T. (2005), *The New Masters of Capital: American Bond Rating Agencies and the Politics of Creditworthiness*, Ithaca, NY and London: Cornell University Press.

Smith, B. (1996), *Austrian Philosophy: The Legacy of Franz Brentano*, Chicago, IL: Open Court Publishing Company.

Soramäki, K., Bech, M. L., Arnold, J., Glass, R. J. and Beyeler, W. E. (2006), 'The Topology of Interbank Payment Flows', *Federal Reserve Bank of New York Staff Reports*, No. 243.

Sparrow, M. K. (2008), *The Character of Harms: Operational Challenges in Control*, Cambridge: Cambridge University Press.

Spencer, P. D. (2003), 'Market Structure, Innovation and the Development of Digital Money', in M. Balling, F. Lierman and A. Mullineux (eds): 302–13.

Stark, D. (2009), *The Sense of Dissonance: Accounts of Worth in Economic Life*, Princeton, NJ and Oxford: Princeton University Press.

Stenning, K. (2002), *Seeing Reason: Image and Language in Learning to Think*, Oxford: Oxford University Press.

Swanson, E. B. and Ramiller, N. C. (1997), 'The Organizing Vision in Information Systems Innovation', *Organization Science*, 8(5): 458–74.

Sylla, R. and Wright, R. E. (2004), 'Networks and History's Generalizations: Comparing the Financial Systems of Germany, Japan, Great Britain, and the United States of America', *Business and Economic History On-Line*, 2, http://www.thebhc.org/BEH/04/syllaandwright.pdf.

Tapking, J. and Yang, J. (2004), 'Horizontal and Vertical Integration in Securities Trading and Settlement', *Bank of England, Working Papers*, No. 245.

Tarullo, D. K. (2008), *Banking on Basel: The Future of International Financial Regulation*, Washington, DC: Peterson Institute of International Economics.

Tett, G. (2009), *Fool's Gold*, New York: Free Press.

Thurner, S., Hanel, R. and Pichler, S. (2003), 'Risk Trading, Network Topology and Banking Regulation', *Quantitative Finance*, 3(4): 306–19.

Triana, P. (2009), *Lecturing Birds on Flying – Can Mathematical Theories Destroy the Financial Markets?* Hoboken, NJ: John Wiley & Sons.

Tsoukas, H. (1996), 'The Firm as a Distributed Knowledge System: A Constructionist Approach', *Strategic Management Journal*, 17: 11–25.

Tsoukas, H. (2005), *Complex Knowledge – Studies in Organizational Epistemology*, Oxford: Oxford University Press.

Urry, J. (2000), *Sociology Beyond Societies: Mobilities for the Twenty-First Century*, London and New York: Routledge.

Urry, J. (2003), *Global Complexity*, Cambridge: Polity.

Van Lelyveld, I. and Donker, M. (2003), 'Technology and the (Re)location of Financial Activity: A European Perspective', in M. Balling, F. Lierman and A. Mullineux (eds): 131–61.

Viégas, F. B. and Donath, J. (2004), 'Social Network Visualization: Can We Go Beyond the Graph?' *Computer Supported Cooperative Work*, 4: 6–10.
Von Peter, G. (2007), 'International Banking Centres: A Network Perspective', *BIS Quarterly Review*, December 2007: 33–45.
Watson, M. (2009), 'Investigating the Potentially Contradictory Microfoundations of Financialization', *Economy and Society*, 38(2): 255–77.
Watson, T. J. (1995), 'Rhetoric, Discourse, and Argument in Organizational Sense Making: A Reflexive Tale', *Organizational Studies*, 16(5): 805–21.
Weick, K. E. (1987), 'Organizational Culture as a Source of High Reliability', *California Management Review*, 24: 112–27.
Wellman, B. (2001), 'Computer Networks as Social Networks', *Computer and Science*, 293: 2031–4.
Werr, A. and Stjernberg, T. (2003), 'Exploring Management Consulting Firms as Knowledge Systems', *Organization Studies*, 24(6): 881–908.
White, H. C. (2002), *Markets from Networks. Socioeconomic Models of Production*, Princeton, NJ and Oxford: Princeton University Press.
White, H. C. (2008), *Identity and Control: How Social Formations Emerge*, Princeton, NJ and Oxford: Princeton University Press.
Willison, M. (2004), 'Real-Time Gross Settlement and Hybrid Payment Systems: A Comparison', *Bank of England, Working Paper*, No. 252.
Wineman, J. D., Kabo, F. W. and Davis, G. F. (2009), 'Spatial and Social Networks in Organizational Innovation', *Environment and Behavior*, 41(3): 427–42.
Wolfe, A. (2009), *The Future of Liberalism*, New York: Alfred A. Knopf.
Wong, W. L. P. and Radcliffe, D. F. (2000), 'The Tacit Nature of Design Knowledge', *Technology Analysis & Strategic Management*, 12(4): 493–512.
Zadeh, L. A. (1994), 'Fuzzy Logic, Neural Networks, and Soft Computing', *Communications of the ACM*, 37(3): 77–84.
Zuboff, S. (1998), *In the Age of the Smart Machine: The Future of Work and Power*, New York: Basic Books.

Author and Name Index

Subject Index